The Impossible Takes Longer

THE IMPOSSIBLE TAKES LONGER

The Memoirs of

VERA WEIZMANN

Wife of Israel's First President

as told to

DAVID TUTAEV

Difficult things take a long time,
the impossible takes a little longer

CHAIM WEIZMANN

Harper & Row, Publishers

New York and Evanston

FIRST U.S. EDITION

LIBRARY OF CONGRESS CATALOG CARD NUMBER: 67-22510

CONTENTS

LIST OF ILLUSTRATIONS

The following are grouped in a separate section after page 148:

FOREWORD

VERA WEIZMANN died early on the morning of September 24 1966, having seen and approved the text of this book as it is now published. As her collaborator in these Memoirs, first in London and then in Israel, I came to appreciate her qualities of character, her exacting civilized standards, and her independence of spirit. She was indeed the first 'First Lady' of Israel, and her passing severs the link with the heroic past in which her husband Chaim Weizmann, Israel's first President, played such a remarkable part. Scientist, humanist, statesman and prophet, this builder of Israel was its outstanding diplomat and, as he himself has stated, was greatly aided in his work by his wife's help and counsel. For Vera Weizmann was a person in her own right, strong in her views, her likes and dislikes, and ready to spring to the defence of her opinions.

There will be much in these Memoirs which both the general and specialist reader will find controversial and challengeable, especially in Vera Weizmann's assessment of events and personalities. But she herself repeatedly told me that she had no intention of recounting the Zionist struggle, nor of writing a diplomatic document: she was anxious to set down impressions, drawn from a remarkable well of memory—in itself a feat for a woman well over eighty—of her life with Chaim Weizmann, with all its pains, disappointments and triumphs.

It would not have been seemly for me as her collaborator to steer her into the calmer waters of recollection, nor to abate her passion for what she thought to be right and wrong. Once she had taken the plunge, she would swim unaided to the farthest shores of memory. In all her actions Vera Weizmann was adventurous, courageous, and even enchanting, and on ome occasions, infuriating.

Now she belongs to history, a tribunal before which she would not have flinched.

★

Mrs. Weizmann would have liked to express her thanks to all those who participated in the preparation of this book: to Mrs. Flora Solomon who helped to initiate this endeavour, and to Mrs. Ethel Hayman who worked so indefatigably and generously in the revision of the manuscript: to Mr. Boris Guriel, formerly curator of the Weizmann Archives, to Mr. Julian Meltzer, on whom we relied greatly, as well as to Mr. Leonard Stein who facilitated our work. Mr. Josef Fraenkel also gave us useful help at the proof-reading stage. We are also indebted to Mr. B. W. Goodman for his help in organizational matters, and to Mr. J. de Samogyi and his staff for the accurate and speedy preparation of the manuscript.

D. T.

The Impossible Takes Longer

I

A Day in November

I FIRST met Chaim Weizmann at the Jewish Club in the Grande
Rue, Geneva, in the late autumn of 1900, probably some time in
November. November has always been a fateful month for me:
my husband and I shared a common birthday in November, he being
seven years older than I; my younger son Michael was born in November. And by some peculiar coincidence the Balfour Declaration and
the Bolshevik Revolution in Russia occurred within six days of each
other in November 1917. Perhaps it is due to my innate Russian
superstitiousness—but I have always anticipated some event of
great emotional or political significance with each passing November. . . .

I do not know what had impelled me to go to the Jewish Club
instead of the more popular Russian Club towards which the majority
of Russian-speaking students, most of them Jewish, gravitated: it may
have been 'fate' or the attraction of the substantial luncheon which the
Jewish Club offered at sixty centimes, a consideration which I, a first-
year medical student with a healthy appetite and little money, found
irresistible despite the somewhat dull, stodgy menu.

I was sitting with a group of young fellow-students at a well-
scrubbed deal table eating my meal, when a tall, impressive
man, with a fine, imposing head which was almost bald despite his
comparative youth—he was only twenty-seven at this time—walked
in and, standing with one foot on a chair, began to talk to someone. He
was pale, dedicated, very frail yet serene, with a faintly ironic gleam in
his eyes, mingled with deep and affecting sadness, and he seemed to carry
all the burdens of the Jewish world.

I was not to know that Chaim Weizmann had only recently returned
from the Fourth Zionist Congress in London which he had attended
as a delegate from Pinsk. There he had battled, as he was to do on so

many occasions, with official reports which exaggerated the rapid expansion of the Zionist cause in Russia. But at the same time he had welcomed the truly historic decision to set up the Jewish National Fund, designed to purchase land in Palestine 'as the inalienable property of the Jewish people',[1]*which Herzl, the great father figure of Zionism supported. Chaim found the attention paid to this fund was 'completely overshadowed' by talk of charters and negotiations. He returned to Geneva very despondent.

I was sufficiently struck by his appearance, his aura of destiny and dedication, to turn to one of my neighbours and enquire who he was. 'Oh, he's just a Jewish intellectual', my companion murmured.

I do not remember whether Chaim Weizmann noticed me on this occasion. Some time later he met the beautiful Miss Halevskaya, one of my friends from Rostov, to whom he paid court for some months before she upset him by flirting with every student of her acquaintance. Certainly on this occasion Chaim Weizmann and I did no more than exchange a passing greeting; yet I knew at that moment that this man would change my life and outlook to a profound, even disturbing extent.

Some weeks passed before Chaim Weizmann and I met again, this time in a pupil-teacher relationship. Most of the students from Russia knew no French, nor was chemistry part of the curriculum in Russian secondary schools, and they could not, therefore, follow lectures at the university. Chaim Weizmann generously volunteered to coach a group of students in the Jewish Club: whereupon a large number of students from the Russian Club flocked to the Jewish Club. His own impression of the studious, nineteen-year-old girl who listened with such rapt attention to his brilliant and succinct discourse was that Vera Chatzman [my maiden name] was of a particularly quiet and retiring nature, inclined to be pensive, almost sad—so that she was set apart even among her companions. 'I used to call her affectionately *princesse lointaine*'.[2]

The distance between us was accentuated not only by his greater intellectual maturity—Chaim was born mature!—and fierce dedication to Zionism, of which I had barely a smattering, but also to the differences between our respective backgrounds. These differences created something of a challenge which widened the scope of my own inquisitive nature and eventually led me to embrace with profound concern the cause closest to his heart: the well-being and development of the Jewish people and their rightful homeland.

* Superior numbers refer to Notes, p. 291.

Chaim was born in the small township of Motol in the Pale of Settlement in the marshland of western Russia. This enclave had been set aside since the days of Catherine the Great for a Jewish population, by this time of some five millions, which lived among an illiterate Russian peasantry and a haughty Polish nobility. Chaim Weizmann grew up one of a family of twelve. His father, a timber-merchant, often found it difficult to make ends meet. Yet such was the general poverty in the Pale of Settlement that his modest occupation of tree-felling and marketing was regarded as a 'capitalist' enterprise by his less fortunate neighbours.

He was a man of a serious and unbending disposition: I recall Chaim's telling me that on one occasion when his father returned home to Motol for one of the greater Jewish festivals, his wife, usually gentle and easy-going, upbraided him for being late. Chaim's father replied gently, 'Instead of rejoicing that I have returned, would you have preferred me to be dead?'

Despite the almost annual increase in her family, my future mother-in-law seemed to suffer no particular hardship from childbirth: she continued to have children after her eldest daughter Maria Lubin had had a child. This eldest daughter had, in fact, acted from the age of seven as 'mother' to the other children, and for this had sacrificed a promising career. She was most intelligent, and a fine Hebrew scholar.

My own recollection of my future mother-in-law is that she was very charming and alert, interested in everything. She demanded nothing, but expected everything! When she settled in Palestine with her eldest son Feivel, they became our responsibility. She died in her eightieth year shortly before the outbreak of the Second World War. All but two of Chaim's brothers and sisters received a university education. One of his sisters, Guita Dunia, created a well-known school of music in Haifa, which has had more than a thousand pupils.

The greatest impression left on my husband's earliest days was made by his grandfather, the patriarch of the family. Chaim lived with him from the age of five until he was eight. His grandfather, a tender and loving man, used to get up at six o'clock each morning to light the samovar, after which he would regale his young charge with Biblical stories. When he died in 1882, Chaim went into the garden and wept bitterly. When asked why he cried, he answered, 'My grandpa hurts me!'

Such fragmentary tales of my husband's early life I have drawn from the deep well of memory; but in his autobiography *Trial and Error* he has already himself described his earliest childhood in his own way, and I must return to my own antecedents and earliest recollections if I am to set our lives into some perspective.

My own background was altogether different from Chaim's. I was born on 27 November 1881 in the flourishing town of Rostov, in the hard-riding, prosperous Cossack Territory of the Don, in what had been one of the proudest and richest outposts of the Russian Empire since the early eighteenth century. My good-looking, six-foot-six father, who originated from Vilna 'where the best Jews come from', had, like so many other Jewish children, been abducted very young and forcibly recruited into the Czar's army, in which he served for some twenty-five years. He very rarely spoke of his military experiences, but I know that he took part in the Crimean War. I told my British-born grandson about this when he was eight years old, and he said gloomily, 'But, Granny, he fought on the wrong side!' I think my grandson still feels that.

My father's military service, however, earned him a number of special privileges, among them the right to live outside the restrictive Pale of Settlement. In the fulness of time, he came with his wife and some of her relatives to raise his own family of seven children at Rostov-on-Don, where he established himself as a wholesale clothes dealer and a fairly prosperous member of the 'guild merchant' class. Beyond this, I know little of our family background. We Jews are strange people: we remember Moses, King David, and Solomon, but we know little of our own ancestry beyond our parents and occasionally our grandparents. My mother, for example, who came from Voronezh in central Russia, knew almost nothing about her family past. She had married at the age of fifteen, as was the custom of the time, a man twenty-five years her senior, and brought her mother (our granny) and her divorced sister (our aunt) to live in Rostov. Our granny was about the same age as my father, and they used to carry on long political arguments. She attended to most of the domestic affairs of the house, and went out shopping every morning with the *dvornik*, our yardman. She was an inveterate old grumbler, and my youngest sister Rachel and I, who shared a room with her, did not like her. We were, therefore, delighted when our cat disappeared one day, to be discovered later sitting sedately in Granny's best Victorian bonnet of lace in which she had given birth to five healthy kittens.

My earliest recollection goes back to the marriage of my eldest sister.

4

I was four at the time, she seventeen. I can hardly remember her at home. Only after she had married, and came to lunch every Saturday with her husband, did I wonder, 'Who is that lovely lady?' She was a magnificent-looking young woman. I remember very little about her —but I can recall her French governess because I was so impressed by her beautiful shantung coat, with four large shiny mother-of-pearl buttons, and her large hat.

Another event which stands out in my memory is my first train ride with my father. As a dealer in ladies' clothes, my father went on a yearly trip to Moscow to bring back the latest fashions. On one occasion I was allowed to accompany him. I remember staring out of the carriage window at a field of browsing cows, animals I had never before seen as I had been brought up in a big city. 'What are those?' I asked, breathlessly. 'They are wolves', said my father with complete solemnity.

But, setting aside for a moment such anecdotes from my earliest childhood, I must confess that I was very little aware of our Jewish background. My father had managed, somewhat miraculously, to preserve his Jewish identity despite the indoctrination he received in the Czar's army from Christian officers; but we were far from being an Orthodox Jewish family. My father did head one of the two local synagogues, which he attended on all High Holy-days; in our house we kept the Day of Atonement, all the festivals—Passover, New Year, Succoth, and so on, and a Rabbi came to give Hebrew lessons and to teach prayers to my two brothers; but the five girls received no religious instruction. My own knowledge therefore did not stretch much further than that Jews went to synagogue and Christians went to church. Of Palestine I knew next to nothing: I had heard that the respected Menachem Mendel Ussishkin of Ekaterinoslav [Dniepropetrovsk] had urged Jews to make their way to the Promised Land of their fore-fathers; and there was a lithograph hanging on the wall in our dining-room—as, indeed, it must have hung in the homes of many Jewish families—of the 'good Jew' Sir Moses Montefiore who had been to Damascus to refute the gross forgeries in which Jews were accused of using sacrificial Christian blood at Passover in their unleavened bread. Such at that time was my knowledge of Zionism and the 'Jewish problem'. Many years later, when I had imbibed an extensive acquaintance with Zionism from my husband, I remember once singing one of Lermontov's famous poems to my father, who by this time was old and ailing:

Tell me, o branch from Palestine:
Where did you grow, in what fair place?
Where did your lovely blossoms shine,
What hill or valley did they grace?*

It probably brought to my father long-forgotten vestiges of his childhood, for he wept quietly.

The contrast of temperament between my mother and my father could not have been more marked. Whereas he was warm and affectionate, she seemed distant and reserved. She was tiny and very good-looking, always preoccupied to see that we had the best possible education; but she was too busy to caress us or show us any outward signs of the affection which my father lavished upon us, and upon her sister's children who grew up in our house.

It was not until I became the mother of my first son that I appreciated mother's preoccupation with our education and future professions, which was deeper than any outward show of affection.

Mother was a capable organizer: she was always re-arranging the house or having it remodelled, so much so that my father used to call her 'our architect'. Later, after I married, she had another floor built on to our house. This 'flat' became a source of indispensable income when my father fell ill and had used up his financial reserves.

Our house, as I recall it, was fairly spacious, built in a neo-Colonial style, reminiscent of houses I saw later when I visited America. There was a large dining-room, my parents' bedroom, a bedroom which I shared with my youngest sister when my two elder sisters were studying in Moscow and Warsaw, a double drawing-room, and the annexe where my two brothers and my sister Rachel and I lived when we were young. But we had no garden, and we spent most of the warm summer days in our lovely courtyard with its few flowering trees, long wooden table and benches, and a tall lantern. On this table a samovar was constantly on the boil from four o'clock in the afternoon, to provide tea for anyone who happened to drop in, as is the habit in Russia. In summer this table was always crowded with callers who spent long hours arguing about such vital issues of the day as the Dreyfus Affair, on which my parents held strong views. They staunchly upheld the hapless French officer's innocence in the face of contrary opinions, and the arguments were often acrimonious.

My earliest years were attended by the presence of wet nurses. My

* Trans: Jacov Hornstein.

mother, who had nursed her first five children, could not nurse the last two. My youngest sister Rachel and I were therefore, as was the practice of the day, mothered by wet nurses, women who had had illegitimate children. Rachel's wet nurse was a pleasant, good-natured woman, mine was highly intelligent and somewhat explosive. The main contention between these two women was to decide which of their two charges was the prettier, my sister or I. Whenever we were taken out walking, strangers would stop us in the street and press flowers into our hands, a form of attention which flattered and delighted these good women. Later when, already a student, I was on holiday, my wet nurse came to wash my hair which grew thick and long, and needed frequent attention. Whenever she wished to annoy me, my sister called my nurse 'a witch on three legs', an insult I found very bitter, and I cried for hours. I was very attached to my wet nurse.

My sister Rachel, with whom I shared a bedroom, did not resemble me in appearance, character, behaviour: indeed, each of the children in our family was strikingly different and individual. I was meticulously tidy, but Rachel had the appalling habit of throwing her hairbrushes all over the dressing-table, upsetting my carefully arranged toilet articles. She was also a tomboy and regularly got into scrapes. On one occasion when she was unaccountably not guilty, but had been punished, my father exclaimed, in exasperation, 'Never mind, it will do for the next time!'

I myself had an inordinate fear of punishment, due more than anything else to my sense of dignity. I recall that on one occasion when, at the dinner table, I had the temerity to call one of my father's employees 'a fool', I was promptly ordered out of the room and told to stand in a corner. And stand there I did, long after the period of punishment was over. I not only went without my evening meal, but also went fast asleep, slumped in the corner. This show of character prompted my mother to exclaim to father, 'Can't you leave that child alone?'

At the age of five I was sent to a French kindergarten, a fashionable place of instruction designed to give children an early mastery of that elegant language. Two years later my sister Rachel joined me. We were forbidden to utter a single word in Russian on pain of losing our luncheon baskets, the contents of which, if we disobeyed, were distributed to the school's boarders by the headmistress. But the distribution of our luncheon baskets achieved two objects at one stroke: the boarders received a free lunch at our expense, and we were taught a salutary lesson which we were in no hurry to have repeated!

I was nine when I went to the Marinskaya Imperial Gymnasium. I was not over-fond of that school. We received only a modicum of instruction there since the teachers spent most of the time reading to us from books, something we could have well done for ourselves. I was a good pupil, however, and took great care not to be punished. Tidiness, punctuality, and order were my cardinal virtues, and I received top marks in every subject with the exception of gymnastics and handwork such as sewing. Our gymnastics mistress—we suspected she was a gipsy—knew little about the science of physiculture: all she did was to bellow an incessant stream of 'one, two and three' at us. And our sewing teacher was so old-fashioned that she did nothing except show us how to make the sort of camisole that may have been decorative on my great-grandmother but was not calculated to interest a new fashion-conscious generation. We were also taught to knit uninspiring, drab-looking socks and undervests. As a result of the poor marks I received in these two subjects I was not given the coveted gold medal awarded to pupils, who, like myself in other subjects, had consistently high marks. Much later in life I was to find relaxation in embroidery and petit-point.

My first aspiration towards a medical career began when, at the age of five, I was given an illustrated book in which a 'sick doll' was attended by a doctor. I felt so sorry for that sick doll that I determined to devote myself to medicine. My mother followed the educational development of her children very closely, and insisted not only on our instruction in foreign languages, but that we should all have some grounding in music. I was sent to the Rostov Conservatoire of Music, and reached a high degree of proficiency; but by the time I was fourteen my mother insisted that I should choose unequivocally either medicine or music. I chose medicine, and my musical career came to an abrupt end. I was more fortunate perhaps than my second sister Sophia (Sonia), who had tried to persuade my parents to allow her to take a course in medicine. As it was not considered quite 'nice' for a young lady to study medicine, she was sent off to Warsaw to study dentistry. By the time I grew up, medicine had just become acceptable for a girl.

With the exception of my eldest sister, who married at seventeen, all my other brothers and sisters, like most of Chaim's, went to a university. My third sister Anna completed her course at the Moscow Conservatoire, but refused to appear at public concerts because of her excessive shyness and stage fright. Instead, she gave private lessons. My two brothers became engineers: for my second brother Michael this was something of an accomplishment since he had to sit for the same examination in five successive years. He was the unfortunate victim of the 'quota' system which discriminated against Jewish students in Russian universities. In Rostov, the population of some one hundred and fifty thousand comprised a mixture of Russians, Greeks, Jews, and Armenians; of the total, the Jewish minority made up about a tenth. The intake of Jewish students into the university was therefore limited to ten per cent. The marking of Jewish students' examination papers was deliberately stricter, and my second brother was consistently failed by just one mark! Happily, my father was acquainted with a friendly Hetman, or Cossack headman, in Novocherkask, the capital of the Voisko-Donskovo region, who used his influence to steer my brother at last through this pernicious quota system.

Yet despite quotas and restrictions, Rostov was remarkably free from the wilder and more vulgar Jew-baiting and anti-Semitism which prevailed in other parts of Russia. The Russian and Jewish intelligentsia—doctors, lawyers, and other men of professional standing—lived in reasonable amity with each other. This may explain my lack of awareness of the 'Jewish problem' at this stage of my development. I also had an innate feeling of being Russian, which has never entirely left me. There may also be another reason. We were all very great readers in my family. We read everything we could lay our hands on from Tolstoy to Dostoyevsky, including the great treasures of Russian poetry: like all Russians, I knew most of the works of Pushkin by heart, and I doted on Nekrassov and Lermontov. We even read Oscar Wilde in Russian, although I must admit we did not always understand what we were reading.

On one occasion, we managed to get hold of some 'illegal literature', a book about the life of Gershunin, a famous revolutionary who managed to escape from Siberia to America. Our parents confiscated this book; but when Rachel and I peeped into their bedroom late at night, we found them poring over it by the light of an oil lamp. In the morning, we made a joke about their interest in the book. They did not know what to say, or where to look! They kept the book hidden beneath their mattress.

My mother constantly reproached us for reading too much and for not giving her enough help in the house; but we were never able to discover what help she needed, since we always had two maids—a cook and a housemaid—and a yardman. To salve her conscience and mine, I was given all the mending to do for our large family; I proved fairly adept at this, and soon became a champion sock-mender. Another thing my mother objected to was our teaching the illiterate staff to read and write, for this naturally took them away from their daily duties.

I was growing up by this time, but all forms of recreation were strictly forbidden. For some reason, even going to the theatre was prohibited. It was always work, work, work. . . . I myself took a great interest in the children who attended a local Jewish school and helped them through their examinations. I even gave my lovely and treasured collection of butterflies to this school.

As I grew older, I grew prettier and the boys soon began to run after me. But I was so serious-minded that I never accepted more than one admirer at a time. Stupidly enough, my parents objected even to the mild and innocent flirtation which consisted in little more than permitting my current beau to escort me to and from school.

One charming Jewish lad, Benjamin Hossudovsky (Yomah, for short) was devoted to me for five years: I was thirteen when this began and Yomah was fifteen. Yomah belonged to a very religious Orthodox family and I soon developed a special attachment to his synagogue. I loved the lad and the choir! Then one day, after a visit with Yomah and one of my sisters to the local 'Photokino' (cinema), we discovered that we had forgotten our latchkey. Our parents were waiting for my sister and me on the landing. A dreadful scene ensued as we submitted to their cross-examination. On another occasion, after we had visited a 'Traktir' (a Georgian wine-cellar), where we listened to some spirited singing and ate delicious 'shashlik' (kebab), we return-ed home to tell our parents about this innocent escapade. There was an almighty row. My mother took away our best shoes and clothes, and refused for some time to allow us to wear them. I retaliated for this gross injustice by refusing to speak to her for several days: she knew only too well how fond I was of new and attractive clothes. Not that I always got them, for Rachel and I often had to wear clothes handed down by older sisters.

Even more than this, I disliked mother's insistence on dressing Rachel and me alike, although we were quite different both in char-acter and in appearance. Rachel was very pretty, with the loveliest rosy cheeks, but I was always pale. I envied her her rosy cheeks, but to spite myself I used to rub the whiting off the walls and use it to 'powder' my cheeks and make myself even paler! My natural pallor made my parents think I was very frail, so they missed no opportunity of sending me away for the summer holidays. One day I was sent to join my beautiful eldest sister at Liman near Odessa. Here I met two dashing young brothers, one of whom came in the morning to propose to me and the other followed in the afternoon with a similar offer. It was like a scene from Gogol! But I rejected both of them, since I did not care for either, nor did I intend to marry at eighteen. My mind was set on higher things. Now that I had left school I began to study Latin for the entrance examinations for medicine. Then I found that I should have to enter a foreign university since no single Russian university offered any places for women. My Latin teacher was a young student who was a convinced Marxist, and between lessons and attempts at indoctrination, he declared his undying love for me. I understood little of Marxism; but I took an instant dislike to him because of his dogmatism, dryness of character, and complete detachment.

My feelings for Yomah also had changed: I had outgrown him emotionally and intellectually. He was a law student in Kharkov by now, and one day he turned up at our house, complaining bitterly that I had stopped writing to him and threatening to kill himself. Six years later he married and was divorced in the space of six months. When much later I took my elder son Benjamin to Rostov, Yomah visited us and became very attached to his namesake, my first-born.

By the time I was eighteen my parents reluctantly agreed to let me go to Geneva to study medicine. I chose Geneva because I was afraid to go to a large capital city like Paris. The parting with my family at the station was strained and artificial, as such partings are apt to be. 'Keep well. . . . Don't forget us. . . . Write. . . .' We said all the usual things as the train slowly drew out of the station. I departed with two school-girl friends. We all burst into tears! We cried and then began to laugh and to cry again. Our childhood was behind us, with all its troubles and problems, its pains and half-formed resolutions. A new life was opening before us, and each of us, in our different ways, tried to imagine what a strange and wonderful experience that was going to be.

2

Geneva 1900-1906: the Education
of a Zionist

WE reached Geneva at midnight—after a journey lasting three full days and nights—exhausted, hungry, full of excitement and of apprehension. My two companions and I took an inexpensive room with three beds in the Hotel de la Poste near the station. Our first thought was to picnic on the ample provisions we had brought with us, rather than to spend our slender resources on a meal in a restaurant.

After opening a couple of tins of sardines, which we ate with great relish, we hurled the empty containers out of the window, listening to the resounding tinkle they made as they struck the pavement! We were being very daring and were, at the same time, not a little frightened. It was a most uncivilized form of behaviour, of which none of us would have been guilty at home; but it somehow relieved our pent-up feelings, already homesick and uncertain of the future as we were in this unfamiliar European city, far away from our friends and families.

We were also short of money. Just how poverty-stricken we were can be judged from the fact that I was considered something of a 'capitalist' by poorer students because my eldest sister was sending me a monthly allowance which amounted to about three pounds ten. But I was able to temper this impression of 'wealth' by sharing my allowance with one of my less fortunate companions who had only two pounds a month, or less. Our diet was restricted, and consisted mainly of bread and sausage—especially towards the end of each month when our allowances had nearly run out!—supplemented now and again by inexpensive meals at the Jewish Club where I first met Chaim Weizmann in the autumn of 1900.

Our early meetings were infrequent. There was to begin with a difference in age of seven years; and there were other barriers: Chaim was already a *Privat-Dozent* (an unpaid assistant lecturer), while I was only a first-year medical student. Chaim was also much absorbed by his Zionist activities, of which I had little or no understanding. Zionism was, and for some time remained, as he so pertinently stated, more or less a 'closed book' to me. Yet Chaim was patient and gentle; he allowed me, without undue interference or prompting, time to find my own level of understanding, to make my own mistakes and, above all, to formulate my own views and prejudices. But I was a willing and serious student, and we were gradually drawn together.

In the warm summer days that followed the first spring of our acquaintance, we began to meet in the Café Landolt, talking and arguing for hours over a glass of weak 'Russian' tea. (I might add that I have not drunk better tea at Claridges!) At this time Chaim was receiving royalties from a dye process which he and Professor Pictet had developed, and this had enabled Chaim to finish his academic studies.

Chaim and I shared a passion for music—his favourite composers at this time were Tchaikovsky, Beethoven, and Chopin—but only twice in our three-year-long friendship in Geneva did we find the time—and the means—to go to concerts. And if memory serves, we went once to the theatre, after queueing for hours, to see Sarah Bernhardt. Chaim had developed a strong liking for the theatre while he was a student in Berlin: he told me that he had learnt German by following the text of the plays of Goethe and Schiller as they were being performed on the stage.

But the stuff of drama was being played outside the confines of the theatre, in the numerous student societies which dominated extramural activities in Geneva. Names later to become famous in the annals of Zionism and the Russian Social Democratic movement—soon to be split into Bolsheviks and Mensheviks—were beginning to make their mark. There were such divergent personalities as Plekhanov, the 'father' of socialism, Lenin, Trotsky, Martov and numerous other refugees who had made their temporary home in Geneva, whence, 'beyond the reach of Cossack knouts', as Chaim said sardonically in a letter to me, 30 January 1905, they waged 'war' against the Czarist government. The competition for politically-unattached Jewish young people was unremitting and bitter. Jewish Bundists (socialists) and Zionists like Chaim, Berthold Feivel, Martin Buber, Zvi Aberson, Schmarya Levin, Leo Motzkin, and Kohan-Bernstein (to mention but a few of the young men who had associated themselves with the 'Democratic Faction' formed at the Fifth Zionist Congress in 1901) strove to win over as many 'souls' as possible. At the same time, the well-organized fugitive Russian Social Democratic contingent, headed by Plekhanov and Lenin, resented this 'interference'. They did their best to recruit us to their movement, knowing that we youngsters would ultimately return to Russia where we could continue their underground work.

Passions ran extremely high. On one occasion, after Chaim's eloquence had moved some seventeen Jewish students to make common cause with Zionism, Plekhanov approached him angrily, demanding what business Weizmann had to take these young people away from *his* group. Chaim's immediate reply was, 'Monsieur Plekhanov, you are not the Czar!' It may be that the hostility to Zionism felt by the future leaders of the Bolshevik Revolution dated from these early conflicts: it has certainly led to much misrepresentation of the purpose and aims of Zionism, which, after more than half a century, is not ended.

The internal conflicts within the Zionist movement were no less fierce. The division between the 'Western' and 'Eastern' wings of the movement was due in part to geographical accident, but there were deep historical and emotional cross-currents which could not be easily bridged. The centuries' long oppression of the Jewish population in Poland and Russia had created among the Jews of those countries a special kind of resistance and a special longing for their ancestral home that was not easily comprehensible to Western Jewry, living as it did in surroundings that, despite anti-Semitic overtones, were comparatively stable.

It is not my purpose to revive these ancient battles or to pass judgement on individuals or on their cherished beliefs. Time has done its destructive and constructive work on their reputations. Within the narrower compass of my own memories and experience are more than twelve hundred letters written to me by Chaim[3], which may throw light not only on our own personalities but also on famous scenes of bygone days. Perhaps even more important, these letters describe most poignantly the inner struggle and the dilemmas which beset Chaim in this formative period. His earliest letter to me, dated 3 June 1901, contains this revealing sentence: 'It looks as if one's private life must not interfere with the execution of one's duty'. This was an ever-recurring theme in his letters, the expression of a single-mindedness which cost him, and those who loved him most, very dear.

But in the first year or so of our acquaintanceship, we barely touched on anything as serious as our 'private life', or our future together. It was not until 1902 that we began to discuss the possibility of marriage which we both knew would have to be postponed for some time. Just how long, neither of us anticipated.

There were many reasons for this postponement. In the first place my father was far from well and his economic position had deteriorated. Moreover, my mother was in no position to help us. I myself was absolutely determined to complete my medical studies and return to Russia to practise. Chaim, too, had not achieved even a modicum of economic independence since he felt he had to help his family. At the same time, a savage tug-of-war between his scientific inclinations and Zionism raged inside of him. His conscience, he has declared, forbade him to devote more than a part of his time—usually the smaller—to his personal ambitions. Later these two polarities were to coalesce and become 'supplementary aspects of a single purpose', but meantime the seeming division of his impulses gave him much suffering.

Chaim often begged me not to allow him to become a *Luftmensch* (an expressive German word which may be literally translated as 'a man of air'), a Flying Dutchman who flits from one interest to the other, and succeeds in neither—the fate of many talented 'professional' Zionists who abandoned their careers in midstream. He had, indeed, already begun to consult me in almost everything except those things of which he knew beforehand I would not approve—these, of course, remained dead secret! But such 'secrets', which contained the core of some dilemma, invariably came into the open, as the early correspondence between us in the summer of 1902 showed only too clearly. I had returned to Rostov for a brief reunion with my family and had just gone through a crisis of my own: I had come face to face, for the first time, with a crude example of anti-Semitism which had baffled as much as it had annoyed me.

I told Chaim of this incident, which occurred in the train taking me from Vienna to Volochiansk on the Russian frontier, in a letter dated 5 July 1902 (New Style). An elderly Jew had entered my compartment, and was immediately subjected to taunts and insults by other passengers because of his origin. I expressed my outrage to Chaim, telling him, somewhat naïvely, that I could not have imagined that anti-Semitism prevailed in Austria in the same virulent form as in Russia. I went on

I approached the old Jew and asked him to sit next to me. The other travellers, shocked at my taking his side, began pulling his hair. I then exchanged seats with him. It was then that these people realized that only a Jewess could behave like that. One of them grabbed me by the arm, calling me a 'Yid'. I went to look for the guard: if I had known German I should have tried to find a station master. The guard told the rowdies to stop; but I could see that he would have behaved in much the same way if he had been in their position. It is terrible, Chaimchik. . . .

I do not recall whether Chaim made any comment on this incident which had moved me so profoundly. He had witnessed even grosser insults in the Pale of Settlement; he may even have thought that my 'platonic' Zionism had received a salutary jolt. Three weeks later, there came a bolt from the blue which was to disturb me even more. In a letter of 30 July 1902 which I received a week later, Chaim told me of his plan to open an office in Geneva for a Hebrew University. So far so good: the University project was his cherished dream. But he added that he was faced with this insoluble dilemma: if he did open such an office:

it will be unthinkable for me to work at chemistry at the same time. I need not explain to you. . . . You know very well what chemistry, what the laboratory, with its joys and sorrows, means to me. But you also know the University project is even dearer to me. Chemistry is my own private affair— the work in which I find rest and relaxation from my public activities. Setting aside all material considerations, I should like to put the problem to you from a purely moral angle: it is a difficult, a horribly difficult alternative. But I do not want to hide this dilemma from you. I am putting it before you, naked and unadorned, as I see it myself. Our lives are inextricably bound together, and it is for you to have the last word. I shall wait impatiently for your reply. . . .

To soften the impact, another letter, written on 6 August, arrived at the same time: it assured me that he would rent a room next to mine where we could work together. 'Can you imagine what a wonderful, warm, full life it is going to be? I am quite dizzy from joy—I'm sorry we can't start straight away'.

Two days later, Chaim elaborated on the theme:

You complain that your Zionism is platonic: it was so while you were only a novice. But we shall draw you into the work—that is why I am trying to get you interested, why there is not an idea you have not been told about. Now it will be different: we shall work together, and enjoy it together. You will never know how much I rely on your opinions—how I cherish them. I believe this is a flower that will bear good fruit—the fruit will be a new generation which will follow up our work—good and really Jewish.

I wrote an answer that did not mince matters. My letter, I think, astonished Chaim, but I think it also pleased him. He had asked for my frank opinion, without perhaps realizing how frank a young woman of twenty-two could be:

My dear Chaim,

I received your letter of 30 July only today, although later letters arrived yesterday. Yes, Chaim, the alternative is difficult, and that is why it is not only desirable but absolutely necessary for us to meet to talk it over. What can I say, what can I tell you at present? I never wanted our relationship to influence your work for the cause, and I would never have agreed to become your wife if I thought that I should stand between you and the cause and take you away from Zionism. You know very well how sympathetic I am to it; but think of your health. I cannot look back on last year without shuddering —the smallest upset made disastrous inroads on your health. This is my main and almost total reason why I cannot give you a simple answer—although I have every right to give a frank opinion. Have pity on me, Chaim. . . . If only you knew how every minute of our happiness is poisoned by the thought of the poor state of your health.

Chaim, it is your duty to weigh things up, bearing in mind the heavy responsibility which lies on you and the gravity of the task which you have undertaken. Remember, you are alone in Geneva. There is no point in discussing those who helped you last year. As for me, I am prepared to help you in every possible way, but I have no illusions as to how valuable my help could be to you, and thus the full burden falls on you and on you alone. As for the secretaries you intend to employ, these are only secretaries, whereas you need people.

I really don't know how to answer you. On the one hand, I have no right to take you away from the cause, and on the other I have no right to advocate a course of action which might affect your health. I beg you to reconsider the whole problem once more, Chaim. Think of yourself, your physical capacities, and then a little, only a little, of me.

Then I came to the real crux of the problem: the moral and material issue which lay at the heart of the dilemma. I told Chaim that I could not understand how he could divide one from the other and went on:

By giving up chemistry, you would deprive yourself of a means of subsistence, without which unfortunately one cannot survive. Surely you do not intend to take Jewish money? You could never reconcile yourself to that. And once you give up chemistry, you'll find it difficult to return to it later. The whole matter is so involved that I can't even discuss it. My one wish is that you never give up chemistry. Kohan-Bernstein wore himself out in the Jewish cause, only for people to say, 'He's getting paid for it!' I think you could arrange things differently. Toldy [Berthold Feivel] and other more or less active people could stay in the Geneva bureau: then you could all share the work and it would not fall exclusively on you, my dear, and then you could also continue with your chemical research.

Please think things over and answer immediately. I shall await your reply with impatience. I shall need a great deal of patience for my punishment began today: I received your photographs, but no letter from you. . . .

Chaim had sent me from Leysin some photographs of himself and his friends, but he was either too busy, or perhaps he felt that he had overwhelmed me with sufficient letters, and he did not enclose a note.

I think my long missive of 6 August made its impact on Chaim. In his answer, written on 10 August, he told me not to worry too much about his health, and quoted a famous saying uttered by one of the greatest of Jewish sages, the Rabbi Hillel, a man esteemed for his modesty and meekness, whom Renan for some reason called 'the first Christian'. 'This most modest of men said quite immodestly', wrote Chaim, ' "if I am not there, who will be there? If I am there, all will be there".' Hard work, Chaim assured me, never killed anyone; but he did promise to cut down the lengthy itinerary which he planned to make throughout the length and breadth of Russia that same autumn to report on the condition of Zionism in the Czar's domains. He made no mention of the Geneva office for the projected Hebrew University, or of giving up his chemical research.

In order to avoid misunderstanding, I must emphasize that I was in no way opposed to the *vision* of the Hebrew University: it was a dream which took exactly a quarter of a century to come to fruition, after the First World War and the Balfour Declaration. All I did was to insist that Chaim should never become the paid servant of Zionism. The funds which Chaim, together with others, raised for various Zionist causes, were never frittered away on 'personal expenses'.

It was during Chaim's extensive tour of Russia whilst he was busy writing a report on Russian Zionism (which he later presented to Herzl) that he first met my family in Rostov. My mother's reaction on greeting him was fairly typical. 'Poor Verotchka', she lamented, 'she's so young and beautiful—and he's so old!' But my sisters and other relations were captivated by him, and so, indeed, was my mother later. Chaim himself was delighted. 'I shall never forget how you received me and arranged everything for me in Rostov. I was always afraid that I should be a stranger in your family, but I return feeling quite different.' (Letter of 2 October 1902.)

It was about this time that tentative approaches were made to Zionist leaders by Lord Lansdowne, the British Secretary of State for Foreign Affairs, suggesting that a large tract of land might be set aside somewhere for Jewish immigration. In fact, the only practical proposal made by the British Government was for free immigration into Uganda, similar to the arrangement for Jewish immigration into Argentina. The nearest settlement to the land offered was a hundred miles away. No protection was offered or suggested, and the only positive offer was local autonomy.

This offer led to the famous crisis over 'Uganda', as this project came to be known. I do not intend to re-trace this familiar ground nor re-echo the reverberations and arguments which raged over the whole plan; but my friend Sir Isaiah Berlin characterized this offer with his usual perspicacity when he said that it was 'the first time that Jews had been recognized as a national entity by a great sovereign state'.

Chaim, who was irrevocably opposed to the whole Uganda project, wrote to me from Paris (5 October 1905) that '. . . the best Zionists in Paris are against Africa—even Nordau is wavering'. But I hardly understood what all the fuss was about. Palestine still seemed so remote, so firmly secure within the Ottoman Empire. This grip could hardly be relaxed through cajolery, offers of economic advantage from Jewish immigration, or diplomatic pressure, as Herzl and some of his followers fondly believed. Herzl, it will be recalled, had not only made approaches to Kaiser Wilhelm but had negotiated with the reactionary Russian Minister of the Interior, von Plehve, in order to persuade him to use his influence on that most reactionary Turk, the Sultan Abdul Hamid, to get him to open the gates of Palestine to the Jews. In Chaim's opinion, 'lack of realism could go no further'.

The differences between Herzl and Chaim came to a head over the Uganda issue at the Sixth Zionist Congress held in Basle in the summer of 1903, but they had been simmering for a long time. Herzl was older than my husband; he may also have had a premonition of death (he had barely another year to live) and been anxious to take some effective steps that would bring his dreams to swift realization. Chaim, in contrast, with the pragmatism and patience of a scientist, believed that diplomatic and political work should go hand in hand with immigration and settlement. Despite his regard and affection for Herzl, Chaim never hesitated to tell him when he believed he was on the wrong path. Chaim's attitude to the Uganda project was best described in a speech he made at a students' meeting which followed the Sixth Congress:

What we want is not some kind of underhand colonization, as our opponents argue. All we say is that five thousand settlers without a charter are better than a charter without any settlers. The charter can be secured when we are in Palestine.

Zionism is not simply an answer to present distress: for us it is a complete world outlook which encompasses all the values of our lives. If you deprive me of Zionism, my life is not worth living. But for the distress of the present there is no remedy. We must tell people this.

The Jewish people are sitting on a volcano, and this position will continue until an appalling disaster occurs. . . . Then ultimately the solution to the Jewish question will be found. This unique solution is that of national Zionism: the revival of Israel in its historic land!

I myself was never introduced to Herzl. The great man, a patriarchal figure with a large beard, was constantly surrounded by a body of admirers. As Chaim and I were not officially engaged, I sat in the gallery with other young students and followed the proceedings with rapt attention. Someone nudged Chaim and pointed to me, asking who 'that attractive young woman' was!

It was towards the end of the Congress that Herzl introduced the controversial motion on Uganda, and, as a compromise, suggested that Congress should vote only on the issue whether to send an investigation commission to East Africa to report back to the next Congress.

The motion electrified the delegates. It divided them almost in half, and cut deeply across family loyalties. Chaim's father and younger brother Shmuel, who were both delegates, were pro-Uganda, something which very much grieved Chaim; but the majority of Russian Zionists, for instance Schmarya Levin, Victor Jacobson, and Kohan-Bernstein, were firmly among the 'antis'. Even more astonishing, the delegates from Kishinev, the Bessarabian town which had only recently witnessed one of the ugliest anti-Semitic pogroms in Russia, voted against the proposal. The refusal of these delegates to contemplate the Uganda 'lifeline' so impressed Herzl that he exclaimed in the lobbies afterwards, 'These people have a rope around their necks, and still they refuse!'[4]

An even more dramatic moment occurred when Aberson's young wife ran on to the platform and tore down the large map of Uganda which had been hung behind the dais.

When the final vote was taken, although 295 delegates voted in favour of the Uganda project, 175 voted against, and something like one hundred delegates abstained. It was a still-born 'victory', and the

Seventh Congress held in 1905 rejected Uganda out of hand and brought some measure of renewed unity into the ranks of Zionism.

In October of 1903 Chaim went to London to rally British Zionists against Uganda, and possibly to make some tentative arrangements for his residence in England. His first enthusiasm for London seemed boundless. On 9 October he wrote,

> I am very glad I came to London . . . very glad indeed. I feel well and have succeeded in working and resting here. . . . I have been paying calls— was in Whitechapel and went to the synagogue there. When I finish my work I shall spend a whole day in the British Museum, especially *in the Colonial Section*. . . .

Was this, I wonder, to gather some first hand ammunition to hurl at the 'Ugandists', or had he a prophetic vision of British Mandated Palestine so many years away? The next day, 10 October, Chaim wrote,

> If help ever comes to us, it will come from England, which I have no doubt would help us with Palestine.

This obsessive idea that England would somehow fulfil the dream of Jewry had been with him since he had written in September 1885, as a schoolboy of eleven, to his Hebrew teacher in Motol:

> . . . Let us carry our banner to Zion and return to the original mother upon whose knees we were reared. For why should we expect mercy from the Kings of Europe, expect that they should, in pity, give us a resting place? In vain! All have decided that the Jew is doomed to death; but England, nevertheless, will have mercy on us. . . .

But to return to his letter of 10 October. He went on,

> I have also been trying to arrange my personal affairs. I have talked with Gaster[5] and Gordon[6] about my desire to move to London, and they both promised to look round for something. . . .

Chaim had also made a few purchases for me, not without some Herculean labour! He informed me,

> . . . I have obtained the collars you asked for with great difficulty. It seems they have gone out of fashion here. And the English simply cannot understand a man buying women's dress accessories—the salesgirls were all laughing at me—'What a funny man!'. . . .

All the same, I got my 'unfashionable' collars.

In the summer of the following year, Chaim made one of the most momentous decisions of his life: he decided to settle in England. The effect of this decision on both our lives—and on the course of Zionism —cannot be exaggerated. He has spoken of his reasons for coming to Britain, his need for work and study away from the daily turmoil of Zionist politics; but our separation brought us no pleasure. From Paris he wrote on 8 July 1904,

> You can imagine how sad I am to be so far away from you. There are so many obstacles which still separate us from a life together. I have one consolation: we are Jews, and to us falls a different fate from that of other peoples. We are a Chosen People—chosen for suffering. I feel my attitude towards the world at large is turning ascetic—and I fear it! Our personal future gives me no fears at all: I am sure everything will be satisfactorily settled.

That settlement was still two years away. Meanwhile, from New-haven he wrote in a buoyant mood,

> . . . Just arrived on English soil: managed very well at the Customs. I am the complete 'gentleman' now! In an hour and a half I shall be in London. For some reason I feel better here. The crossing was perfect.

My own arrival in Rostov, where I had again gone to spend the summer with my parents, was far from perfect. A telegram awaited me announcing the death of Herzl. It shook me profoundly, and I knew how it would grieve Chaim. Whatever their differences, the loss of 'the father figure' of Zionism was particularly tragic at that time. Chaim wrote, 'A great disaster has occurred and I feel that a heavy load has fallen on my shoulders'. He asked me to put a black band on the sleeve of my coat, saying, 'We have all done this. . . .'. I wrote to Chaim at once, on 6 and 12 July, describing the pathetic attempts made by the Jews in Rostov to commemorate the passing of this truly remarkable figure. In the letter of the 12th I said:

> I have just received your letter from Paris which was full of despair and sorrow. How I would love to be near my boy at this moment. You know, Chaimchik, I was somewhat prepared for Herzl's death, as I had already been told in Berlin how poorly he was. I learnt about his death from telegrams, on the exact day of my arrival. My first day at home began terribly sadly . . . with the news of Herzl's death, my grandmother's death, and the prospect that my father was living out his last days. . . .
>
> As for the general state of Jewish affairs —it is best not to speak about it. Everything is dead and lifeless. If only you could have seen how, thanks to Eisenstadt, whose courage is not his greatest virtue, they marked the occasion

of the death of this great man. Eisenstadt went to ask for permission for a
memorial service, which was granted, though all speeches were banned. But
as a Rabbi he could easily have said at least a few words. The synagogue was
to have been draped in black, but our Rabbi was afraid to do even that. The
[memorial] service without words was extremely lifeless. There were huge
crowds—the whole of Rostov was present. But it would have been better to
have nothing rather than this. I was hurt for Herzl and for all Jews. I am sure
that in no other town was this event commemorated in so humiliating a way
as here.

Chaimchik, my dear friend, I am sorry Herzl died so young, at such a
critical moment for all of us. But why all this despair and hopelessness? Herzl's
death is the loss of a great man, but it will not destroy the work which has been
begun. . . .

Herzl's death produced a hiatus not only in Zionist affairs but also
in Chaim's physical and spiritual well-being. It was a period of gesta-
tion during which Chaim began to formulate some of the scientific
experiments and discoveries that made him famous later. His hopes
ran alternately high and low. Beset as he was by financial difficulties,
prejudice, and the aching inertia he found in the ranks of British and
Continental Zionists, he pursued his primary goal, holding to his belief
that London would somehow become 'a great Zionist centre'.

Dr. Gaster had managed to arrange a meeting for him with Lord
Eustace Percy at the Foreign Office, 'perhaps tomorrow', Chaim wrote
to me on 20 July 1904. The significance of this meeting lay in the fact
that this was Chaim's first contact with a leading British statesman (the
first of many hundreds of meetings he was to have with British statesmen and politicians before the Balfour Declaration was issued). Lord
Eustace, who was a sensitive and deeply religious man, could not bring
himself to believe that the Jews would voluntarily give up their
historic and religious claims to Palestine. He also saw Sir Clement
Lloyd Hill, chief of the African Department of the Foreign Office.
Sir Clement's pithy description to Chaim of his attitude to the Uganda
project was, 'If I were a Jew, I would not give a halfpenny for this
proposition!'

After the interview, Chaim went into an adjoining office and wrote
all the details of this talk to me on Foreign Office headed letter paper.
He asked Lord Eustace to confirm the minutes of the interview. Chaim
told me to keep it a dead secret until he got this confirmation. A little
later Chaim wrote to me that Lord Eustace had confirmed the whole
conversation, but Sir Clement had asked Chaim to omit one

sentence: his remark that if he had been a Jew, he would not have accepted the Uganda proposition.

Strangely enough, Chaim's opponents denied that Chaim had ever had this conversation with Lord Eustace Percy. Chaim's letter written on Foreign Office paper is filed in the Weizmann Archives in Rehovoth! It provided the basis for the lengthy memorandum which he later circulated among the anti-Uganda faction in Russia. This memorandum, as he himself wrote later, 'contributed not a little to the final defeat of the Uganda proposal' at the Seventh Congress in 1905.

The letters Chaim wrote to me from Manchester were, however, distinctly gloomy. He was in great financial straits: apart from the money he had saved from his dye patent, he received some ten pounds a month from Shrirow, a Baku oil prospector, for a process he was developing. Professor William Perkin, the head of the department of Chemistry of Victoria University, Manchester, to whom Chaim had brought letters of introduction, had spoken vaguely, before leaving for his summer holidays, of some paid appointment. Perkin had, however, offered to let a basement laboratory to Chaim for a fee of six pounds, an offer Chaim accepted, little as he could afford it. He said nothing to me about the dinginess and grime of that archaic laboratory where, he claimed, he developed 'housemaid's knee' scrubbing the dirt-laden tables and chemical apparatus. But Perkin 'seems a decent fellow', he wrote on 5 August. 'The laboratory—the main University laboratory—here is considered to be the best in England'.

Two days later, he wrote, 'In London every day brought something new, but here daily life is monotonous and my letters will be less lively'. He had taken on himself the rôle of

a self-appointed diplomat to the British Government on behalf of Russian Zionists. But the trouble is they don't give me even the money for the stamps! I have to write my fingers to the bone—long letters and Civil Service reports. . . .

He was extremely anxious that I should come over to join him, but warned me that 'the régime here is very strict—none of our Geneva nonchalance! From five p.m., I shall always be free—but no sooner'. As it turned out, this was a highly optimistic assessment of his 'free time'. He also made enquiries on my behalf at London University, where I had contemplated finishing my medical studies, but found that I could not be admitted simply to the finals. After months of protracted negotiation and muddle, I decided to complete my medical studies in Geneva.

On 24 August, Chaim wrote to me from Berne shortly after the end of the Seventh Zionist Congress which had seen the defeat of the Uganda motion. The confusion in Zionist ranks, he said, had been exaggerated by Herzl's death: 'the Berlin people hate the Russian Jews'. They even pointed to the respected and venerated figure of Menachem Ussishkin, leader of Russian Zionists, as 'the "murderer" of Herzl'. Chaim made a prophecy:

> We are entering a difficult transition period, when every living thought will be killed by ghosts. Herzl had made great mistakes, but he had the outlook of an eagle and was a great force. These small people, continuing Herzl's tactics, do such stupid things that I am frightened. The whole time we discussed *wie machen?*—how are things to be done? But nobody seemed to think of *was machen?*—what's to be done? . . .

This was a period of gradually increasing depression for Chaim which could not be dispelled by hopes and anticipations. Professor Perkin had told Chaim he was pleased with his work and that 'by Christmas I shall be a fellow with a salary of £50 a year!' (letter from Manchester, 1 October 1904). But Christmas passed and nothing had materialized. I paid a brief visit to Chaim in Manchester, and he came to Geneva to see me. 'I must confess that the moment the train pulled out of Geneva my heart sank, and it took me some time to control myself', he said in a subsequent letter. But then something occurred which lifted his spirits considerably.

In a letter of 24 January 1905, he wrote,

> . . . Tonight, I am going to a meeting at which Balfour, the Prime Minister, will speak. Perhaps I shall succeed in having a word with him—though I doubt it.

On the 28th, however, he told me,

> . . . I went yesterday to Balfour's meeting and talked to him about Zionism: not for long, only five minutes, but he promised me that when I was in London he would give me a chance to talk to him at greater length and in more detail.

The introduction to Balfour had been arranged by Chaim's friend Charles Dreyfus, chairman of the Manchester Zionist Society. That exchange between the British and the nascent Zionist statesmen has passed into the annals of Zionist literature and may be familiar to many readers—as familiar as the frequently mentioned second meeting, which took place in January 1906.[7]

Blanche Dugdale, Balfour's niece, who became a passionate adherent of the Zionist cause and a much-loved friend of ours, described this meeting between her famous uncle and Chaim Weizmann in her biography of her uncle.[8] It took place in the ornate, pillared Queen's Hotel in Piccadilly, Manchester—subsequently mistaken by some authors for Piccadilly, London—during one of Balfour's pre-election tours. Only a quarter of an hour had been allocated in advance for this meeting, but it stretched into a full hour and a quarter.

I shall repeat only one phrase of Chaim's from the memorable dialogue (Chaim, it seems, did most of the talking)—a phrase which is firmly impressed on my memory. When Balfour asked Chaim why some Zionists were so bitterly opposed to the Uganda idea, Chaim said that if Moses had come to the Sixth Zionist Congress as it was adopting the resolution in favour of sending a commission to Uganda 'he would surely have broken the tablets again'.

I may be forgiven for digressing if I remark here on the striking parallel between Chaim and Moses: like Moses, Chaim Weizmann led the children of Israel through the wilderness before they again reached the Promised Land. Like Moses, Chaim had insisted that the Jewish people should be both spiritually and materially prepared to fulfil their destiny, and like him, Chaim too was often tempted to break the tablets of the Law.

The meetings with Balfour in 1905 and 1906 were the forerunners of future meetings during the First World War, which eventually led to the famous Declaration that bears Balfour's name. In the beginning, as Chaim wrote in his autobiography, Balfour had 'only the most naïve and rudimentary notion of the movement'. Later Balfour, one of the most perceptive of British statesmen, came very close to understanding the Zionist cause. Chaim, too, learnt much from Balfour, whom he had captivated with his charm and dedication. The meetings on those rainy January afternoons were a prelude to new and exciting possibilities opening before Chaim Weizmann.

On 30 January 1905, a few days after his first meeting with Balfour, Chaim wrote to me about a world-shaking event in our Russian homeland: the first abortive Russian Revolution which had shaken the Czarist régime without destroying it, and without bringing relief to the suffering Jewish masses of the country.

The Russian affair has ended. The Czarist régime has temporarily drowned the Revolution in a river of blood. But I think this is only a momentary truce. I can imagine how excited they will all be in Geneva—how the heroes will sit in Carouge and in all their accustomed haunts where Cossack whips can't reach them. . . .

The horrors which had happened, Chaim said in another letter, 'will not allow the Russian people to go to sleep again'. He had little sympathy with 'the heroes' in Geneva who were planning their own revolutionary blood-baths; indeed, Chaim Weizmann showed a consistent hatred of violence, and this led to much misunderstanding later.

He also had plenty of troubles of his own: the ten pounds a month he had been receiving from Shrirow dried up; but through his friend Charles Dreyfus he had found employment as a chemist at the Clayton Aniline Works in Manchester. His total income, however, did not amount to more than three pounds a week. We had discussed the possibility of my coming to live in Manchester, but on 14 February he wrote to me that 'the financial aspect of your coming here is another worry; but I hope everything will be all right'. Later the same month, after I had told him that I was thinking of postponing my final medical examinations for a year, he described this idea as 'monstrous'. Rumours as to the reasons for the delay in our marriage also infuriated him. He wrote on 20 April,

. . . I can't understand who can be so interested in us as to busy himself with speculations about our separation—or our marriage! It seems to me that no one has any reason to do so; but obviously some eye is watching us attentively. I hope his observation blinds him!

These rumours and speculations were hurtful to me too. Talk had even reached me that Chaim was contemplating marriage with someone else! He tried to put my mind at rest. On 6 June he wrote,

Of course you understand that the whole story about the wedding was not serious? I have written to Mother that we shall get married (of course I meant *you*—nobody else in sight!) as soon as you have taken your finals, and I would love the wedding to take place in Motol. But, my God, everything still looks infinitely remote and I can hardly believe in it myself. But it will happen. I only wish it may happen soon!

In a later letter that same month (23 June), he spoke of going to Palestine

when we have passed through all our schooling here. In three or four years I shall get a Professorship and you will be a good doctor. We shall have a great influence in Palestine, and there I shall start to build up the University. . . .

On 22 July Chaim wrote to tell me that he had been appointed chief assistant in the department of chemistry at Victoria University of Manchester, and was to receive the princely salary of £120 per annum, adding 'and I shan't have much more work to do'.

Chaim no longer saw life in England through such rose-coloured spectacles:

> I can't say that I regret having come to England—it would be ridiculous to suggest that. I knew when I came what I was coming to: I knew what awaited me; and in the end everything has turned out better than I anticipated. Yet in many respects I am disappointed. . . .

This is from a letter dated 23 June 1905. On the following 8 August he wrote,

> The materialism here is dreadful, pitiless. To occupy oneself here with anything not directly connected with earning one's bread, it is necessary to be either very rich or very talented. It is not only in Zionism that there is moral poverty: even in the English themselves there is a lack of the intellectual plenty to be found in either Germany or France. The British Labour Movement, with its one and a half adherents, has produced neither a Jaurès nor a Bebel. The country is ruled by an oligarchy of the hereditary nobility. . . . The chief educational establishments, Oxford and Cambridge, with admirable institutions and talents, contain the same mass of obsolete scholastic forms. For our people here it is very hard to fit in, and particularly so for me. Of course, I hope that in times to come we may create something here. Meanwhile I must arm myself with patience. . . .

Yet while Chaim armed himself with patience, and as his love and understanding of England grew, he became more and more convinced that he had done the right thing in choosing England as our domicile. 'If England should fail either politically or economically, it would be the end of the world', he once said to me.

The extracts I have quoted from the voluminous correspondence we conducted in those early years provide an insight into the formative years of our relationship. They show Chaim's hopes and disillusionments, as well as the driving force behind all his actions. As I have already noted, in his earlier letter to me Chaim had written, 'It looks as if one's private life must not interfere with the execution of one's duty'.

In the summer of 1906 nothing seemed to stand between him and me: I had passed my medical finals and he had achieved a small measure of recognition in his own scientific field. He had also fought a good fight at Zionist Congresses. We were married at Zoppot, near Danzig, in August that year. Only members of Chaim's family were present, the journey from Rostov being too long and expensive for my family. Earlier that summer I had sent Chaim all the documents necessary for a civil marriage in Germany, but on my arrival I found that one document, not previously asked for, was missing. We had to be satisfied with a Jewish marriage ceremony—not held to be legal in Europe without a civil marriage as well. On our arrival in England, we went through a civil marriage: but a little later a Rabbi in Manchester said that according to Jewish marriage law it was not legal for the civil ceremony to be performed after the Jewish ceremony. So we were married for the third time! Perhaps the three ceremonies made our marriage all the more solid!

We stayed with his family for two days in Zoppot, which I found tiresome, and then went to Cologne, where Chaim attended meetings of the Zionist Actions Committee. As Chaim has recorded,

> I remember coming home—to the hotel, that is—at five o'clock one morning, with a great bouquet of flowers and a basket of peaches as a peace offering. It wasn't necessary, but it made me feel a little better. Such was our honeymoon.[9]

We then took third-class tickets and went on a steamer up the Rhine. When we got to England, we made our way to Manchester. I was greatly puzzled by the large 'Bovril' signs I noticed at every station, and I asked Chaim why every station in Britain was called 'Bovril'.

At Manchester we were met by many of my husband's friends, among them Harry Sacher, who was then working on the *Manchester Guardian*, and who subsequently became one of Chaim's trusted advisers. As we had spent our last penny on sandwiches which we had bought on the train, we had to borrow a half-crown from Harry to pay our cab fare to our lodging. Harry Sacher still teases me by reminding me that we never returned that half-crown.

3

'Let There Be Light . . .': Manchester
1906-1913

SOME of my most difficult and most depressing years were spent in Manchester. They were dark days indeed, both spiritually and physically. Even as I recall them now, their gloom is bound to pervade my narrative. But I shall try to set them down without regret or self-pity. Like so many other things in life, they had to be survived. They were, after all, a prelude to happier and fuller days to come, a time of struggle in which to grow stronger, a testing period from which both Chaim and I emerged as fuller, rounder personalities. The hammer of time did not break us: it brought us closer.

Chaim had taken furnished rooms in a depressing lodging-house at Rusholme and it was to this destination that Harry Sacher's half-crown took us. It proved to be a semi-detached house, in front of which was a cab rank with numerous taxis from which came an unholy racket at all times of the day and night. Chaim's bachelor establishment consisted of three modest rooms: a drawing-cum-dining-room, dominated by a long table and six chairs, with two easy chairs by an unlit fireplace; a bedroom—cold as charity; and a smaller room in which we spent our free time reading, writing, and talking: we found the drawing-room too uninviting for such friendly pastimes!

Our landlady turned out to be a very good-natured person, tall, thin, and full of rectitude. I could not make out why she wore curling pins for the whole week, taking them out only on Sundays. In my naïveté I concluded that this was an English custom. I myself was blessed with naturally curly hair and could not understand why anyone had to bother with curling pins. But the good lady had other faults which I could not forgive so easily. She was supposed to look after the house, and do the cooking and cleaning, but she seemed to spend most of the time reading detective stories. She was also inclined to be untidy and rather messy, so that one of my first actions on arrival was to buy a couple of dusters and, after locking our doors—so as not to hurt our landlady's feelings—give all the rooms a thorough dusting.

I cannot say that I took a liking to this place: on the contrary, I hated it from the very beginning; but I did not divulge this secret to my husband. He had enough troubles of his own. As an overworked assistant lecturer, he had an income, at this time, of barely three hundred and fifty pounds a year, a quarter of which went to help his two sisters who were studying medicine in Zurich. Indeed, throughout his life he was always conscious of the need of his family for help—a sense of obligation I have already mentioned. So intense was his feeling of family devotion that I used later to tease him, saying that I felt as if I had married his family, and not him alone!

In addition, I was desperately cold and lonely. My knowledge of English was nil and I did not know a soul. The sun, which came out only a few times a year, looked like a big penny vaporized in a fog on those November days of 1906. I tried to brighten things up as best I could. To defeat the freezing cold and damp, I bought a little oil heater which I placed in the bedroom since I could not bear to dress or undress in its clammy atmosphere. Chaim was away nearly every week-end, making speeches to Zionist circles up and down the country, and it was then that I felt most alone, a foreigner in a strange city without friends or command of the language. I spent many days in tears which I did my best to hide from Chaim. But I did try to improve my English by reading the *Manchester Guardian* every day—with the aid of an Anglo-French dictionary, the only one I had. Unfortunately, most of my husband's friends spoke German, even in my presence, so I had to force myself to study German also—a language in which I was not very proficient.

Rising early, Chaim went to the University and returned for a short break for lunch. He came back from his week-end trips late at night. I used to light the stove in the bedroom and he would find his supper on a table in front of the cosy red warmth.

It was not always so devastatingly sad, perhaps. But Chaim was over-working himself dreadfully, and I feared for his health. He spent his evenings preparing lectures—he was now giving not only advanced lectures but lecturing on the fundamentals of biochemistry; and in his free time he was conducting research in his laboratory.

My only recreation at this time was when, after supper, I accompanied him to his laboratory to see the results of his experiments. On occasions, we would take a bus to Cheetham Hill, a Jewish district, corresponding to Whitechapel in London, where my husband would deliver a lecture on Zionism. Afterwards we would go to a printing house where an old man and his daughter would talk to Chaim in Yiddish, a language I did not understand. I would sit in silence, sniffing the smell of print, waiting for us to go home.

But these first days of abysmal loneliness soon passed. I found that people in the University were more than kind to me. Most of the wives of the professors and lecturers were more than twice my age. But they treated me as an equal, with great charm and hospitality, although some of the habits and customs of 'polite' society puzzled me greatly. For example, in those days, a lady had an 'At Home' once a week. Although I never had such an 'At Home', the wives called on me, leaving three visiting cards: two from their husbands and one from themselves. I suspected that all this was sacrosanct—a part of the British Constitution! By the end of a year, I had a whole library of visiting cards.

But these 'At Homes' had their own particular charm, with their innumerable cups of tea, toast, and cakes. One or two of the professors' wives made brave attempts to speak French with me—but with such peculiar accents that I could hardly follow them.

Two of my earliest acquaintances were Professor Perkin and his wife. Professor Perkin in the early stages of Chaim's Manchester career showed him much kindness and encouragement, holding out the possibility that Chaim might succeed to his professorship on his retirement. Perkin was a first-class chemist and an accomplished pianist. We were frequently invited to their house for his private concerts. He also had a hot-house in which he grew prize-winning blooms that he would show off. He was a tall, solid-looking man, with glasses, who laughed frequently and loudly.

But it is to Mrs. Perkin that I was indebted for my first lessons in English. I, in my turn, offered to instruct her in German, in which I had become fairly fluent. Mrs. Perkin was a large, rather splendid Englishwoman, with all the manners and prejudices of half a century ago. I remember that I upset her unwittingly one day. I remarked that someone had been 'sacked' from his job. Mrs. Perkin's face immediately clouded over: she looked at me as if she had seen a ghost! 'Never, never, never use that word!' she exclaimed.

I was certain that I had said something obscene! When I went home I burst into tears. I told Chaim of my lapse, but he laughed, assuring me that the word 'sacked' was far from obscene, it was merely slang. I thereupon implored him never to use slang in my presence, because I wanted to acquire a command of perfect English.

There was another friendship which brought me much joy and, occasionally, a touch of amusement. I had become friendly with the attractive and intelligent Mrs. Schuster, later Lady Schuster. We had taken to each other at once. We were fortunately able to converse in French. One day Mrs. Schuster said she would be happy if I would bring my husband to tea with them. While we were there, I could see she was fascinated by Chaim. When we were leaving she drew me aside and whispered, 'But, my dear, your husband also is a personality!' I never forgot this remark: in our long friendship together, which lasted to the day of her death, I frequently teased her about it.

There were many other pleasant interludes which helped to diminish my feeling of loneliness in Manchester, a city for which I gradually began to feel some affection. It was after all my first 'home' in England. There were occasional visits to Miss Horniman's Repertory Theatre, where many of the plays performed subsequently found their way to London. There was also the celebrated Hallé Orchestra, under its conductor Richter, a pupil of Wagner's. The tickets were sometimes beyond our means; but friends who subscribed to these magnificent concerts would let us have their tickets when they were unable to go. Chaim was often sorry that he himself could not play a musical instrument, but he sang in a pleasant baritone. These moments of relaxation, however, were few and far between. Chaim was still away lecturing most week-ends, and I often spent forty-eight hours on my own. After one of his absences, longer than usual, I said to him on his return, 'Next time—if there is an after-life—I shall marry a peasant! We'll stay close to the soil, grow trees and flowers!' Feeling a little guilty, Chaim answered, 'And then you'd be bored!' Probably I should be.

Chaim's exertions both in the University and in his Zionist work were beginning to tell on his health. He began coughing up blood. My alarm and anxiety knew no limits. I borrowed fifty pounds from the bank and sent him to the south of France for a month. As salaries at the University were paid three times a year, at the end of term and not in advance, I was always in debt after a month or so. While my husband was away, I went to collect his pay-envelope, and placed it in a deep pocket of my skirt. On the way back, in the bus, a woman struck up a conversation with me. We both alighted at the same bus-stop. On reaching my home, I felt in my pocket for my keys and, to my horror, discovered that the pay envelope with one hundred pounds had disappeared! I could not pay my bills, let alone pay for the provisions for the next term. I kept this incident from my husband by borrowing the missing hundred pounds from a great personal friend, who shortly afterwards left Manchester. I did not see this friend for some years, but was happy to be able to repay this long-standing debt when he came back to the city.

Even on vacations, Chaim was far from idle. By 1906-1907, Chaim had exhausted his interest in the dye-process which he had developed with Professor Pictet, and the income from the patents for this process had dried up. 'We must now try to imitate nature', he explained to me, 'and attempt to produce rubber. Why should I do all the work? Let nature and bacteria work for me and produce synthetic rubber!' And so he went to Berne to study biological fermentation processes under Professor Burri.

Chaim would put starch into a test tube, together with the bacteria—'bugs' he, like most chemists, called them; during the fermentation process, the microbes would eat away the starch, changing the remnants in the absorption process into acetone and buthyl alcohol. As Chaim could see no use for the acetone, he threw it away, retaining the buthyl alcohol, which he converted by various chemical means into synthetic rubber.

Such 'reversals' are not unusual in chemistry. Acetone was an essential solvent used by the British Navy and indispensable in the First World War; while synthetic rubber became the vital product of the Second World War after the Japanese conquered Malaya. These early chemical experiments of his not only had unexpected results on the fortunes of the two wars, but also brought Chaim closer to those nebulous 'Corridors of Power' about which we hear so much.

Meanwhile, shortly before the birth of my elder son Benjy in the summer of 1907, we were able to move into a home of our own. We rented a charming 'doll's house', as I called it, at 57 Birchfields Road, for the surprisingly low sum of thirty-three pounds a year. But even this proved too much for our income and we could not afford to furnish it! Chaim therefore took on the marking of examination papers, at half-a-crown a paper. He used to work with Benjy on his knee: no easy task, for Benjy was a difficult baby who cried a great deal. But Chaim wanted to give me some rest, since I often did not have a proper night's sleep for days on end. We managed to furnish our 'doll's house' comfortably, if modestly, on Chaim's extra earnings from this arduous work.

My own sense of 'economy' was far from strong, although it improved with time. I also knew very little about housekeeping. We hired a maid, a girl of seventeen, to help me with the running of the house. In her very first week, the maid came to me saying, 'Madam, the butcher is at the door . . .'—'All right', I replied, 'order some meat'.— 'But *what* meat, Madam?' she asked. I didn't know! My answer was, 'just meat'.

Like most well-brought-up Russian girls of that time, I had never been allowed inside a kitchen for fear I should learn bad language! Hence my ignorance. But next day I bought a cookery book and began to study the culinary art. The maid had enough to do with the washing, cleaning, and other work of the house, and I became quite an expert cook, so much so that my present cook in Israel tells me, when she is in a particularly good mood, that she learnt how to cook from me, a tribute I hardly deserve since lack of practice has made me forget all I knew.

Three weeks after Benjamin was born, my husband's parents came to stay with us. My mother-in-law was particularly shocked because of the absence of a sideboard in our dining-room, and because I had only one good suit, so that I always changed into an old frock when I was in the house. I have disliked sideboards ever since. I never would have one.

Chaim left for the Eighth Zionist Congress at The Hague in 1907 at which he made his celebrated speech on 'synthetic Zionism', stressing the need for a synthesis between political action and practical work. My sister, Rachel Blumenfeld, and her sister-in-law came to stay with me to keep me company while Chaim was away at The Hague and on the lengthy trip—his first—to Palestine that followed.

It was before The Hague Congress that Chaim had been approached by a wealthy Viennese industrialist named Kremenetzky, once a member of Herzl's 'royal entourage', who said to him, 'Weizmann, you talk too much. Why don't you go to Palestine to see what industrial developments are possible there?' 'But I can't afford it', was my husband's reply. 'I will finance your trip', was Kremenetzky's generous response.

Chaim's first trip to Palestine occupied more than a month. He travelled by donkey, by camel, and on foot—there were no cars in

Palestine at this time—and he wrote some remarkable letters to me. I should like to quote one particular sentence: 'Palestine is a wonderful country: much has been accomplished here already [this was wishful thinking on his part, as he admitted later]. If we don't get Palestine for our State, it will be entirely our own fault'.

When he returned home, I said to him, 'Forget you are a Zionist and tell me what was so wonderful about Palestine'.

'It was magnificent', he answered.

'But what was magnificent?' I insisted.

'The air', he replied. 'It is difficult to understand without experiencing it. The air is crystal pure, so pure that you can look back over three thousand years of history'. This remark of Chaim's has often been repeated: it contains its own particular truth.

When Benjy was two years of age, I grew homesick for my family in Russia. I begged Chaim to let me take Benjy with me on the long and arduous journey to Rostov. Chaim, not unnaturally, was reluctant to let us go. Benjy had developed into a talkative, highly original and intelligent child, very attached to his father. Perhaps Chaim also had some lurking suspicion about my capacities as a young mother. Although I was a trained doctor, my sense of mothercraft was far from perfect. When Benjy was born, I hardly knew how to hold him! And I had prepared no layette because I did not know what clothes babies wore.

But in the summer of 1909 Benjy and I set out for Rostov. And what a journey it was! We travelled third class for three days and nights, on hard wooden seats, which I softened with a wool blanket. I had decided to go through Vienna rather than Berlin because I so much disliked all the *verboten* signs which festooned German carriages. I had another terror to contend with—the bane of all travellers in Russian trains: the bed-bugs which attached themselves to my long hair. On my arrival home my old nurse washed and combed my tresses, and that settled this problem. But there were other, more serious troubles on the horizon. While I was on holiday in the Caucasus, we received a telegram telling us that Michael, the younger of my two brothers, who was engaged in building a bridge over the Volga at Astrakhan, had suddenly been taken seriously ill. My mother, my sister Anna, and I travelled to Astrakhan, although Anna, who was very delicate, had been told not to undertake the journey. Since my brother, who was suffering from typhoid fever, showed marked improvement on our arrival, Anna was sent back home to the Caucasus. But then my brother suffered a relapse and died in our arms; he was only thirty-two. My mother and I, two strangers in a predominantly Persian city, had to make all the funeral arrangements. We returned home heartbroken by our loss. My mother did not say a word; but grief, together with a bad heart, brought on her own early death. She died two or three years later on the day of my brother's death. He, the younger of her sons, had been her favourite.

During the few weeks I was in Astrakhan, I left Benjy with my family. They knew no English and he could speak no Russian, but when I returned I found him lisping 'Heb . . . Heb . . .' No one could understand what he was trying to say. In the end I realized that he was trying to say *hleb*, the Russian word for bread. Benjy, it seems, was hungry. On our return to Manchester he developed measles. Thus ended my 'holiday' in Russia. . . .

Despite all the hard work Chaim put in at the University, our economic situation showed little improvement. We still had only about three hundred and fifty pounds a year on which to maintain our small household, fifty pounds of which I set aside for the books Chaim needed. His own tastes were expensive and he had little monetary sense. I soon realized that we needed two salaries to keep going; so early in 1911 I told Chaim I wanted to sit for an English medical degree. 'But who will look after us?' was Chaim's first reaction. 'For a change, you'll have to look after yourself!' I answered.

I think Chaim was very surprised by my attitude. I had always been very compliant and had tried to fall in with his wishes. But it was impossible for him to go on working at the University, taking extra work at the Clayton factory, and at the same time conduct his extensive correspondence and exhaust himself with lecture tours. Something had to be done to take the pressure off him and enable him to enjoy an occasional break from his labours. 'When I get my medical qualifications in England, you'll be able to have lots of holidays!' I argued, and I think it was this prospect of increased 'working holidays' during which he could develop his experiments that finally won him over.

Because of the medical degree I had obtained in Geneva, I was required to take only the last two years of the medical curriculum at Manchester. I engaged a nurse to look after Benjy, and set out on my new course. It was no easy task. I worked from nine to six every day, with a further period of home study in the evenings. So the three of us set out each morning: my husband to his scientific work, Benjy to school, and I to attend lectures and to work in the hospital.

I took my finals in 1913. But I had only just completed the written examinations in medicine and surgery when Benjy fell sick on the eve of my orals. I nursed him throughout the night, and the next day when I discovered that Benjy was suffering from a particularly virulent attack of 'flu, I asked my examiner, Professor Murray, to see me and the child. I told him that I had decided to forgo the oral examinations. But Professor Murray replied that I had done so well in my written examinations that it would be 'criminal' not to take the orals. Failure to do this would mean I should have to take the whole examination again in a year's time. I took Professor Murray's advice and passed all my examinations with flying colours and was rewarded with a medical degree and a medal. But by this time Benjy had developed a serious inflammation of the middle ear. He was so ill that I had to have the assistance of a medical nurse to attend to him. Benjy hated that nurse and proved to be a difficult patient.

After taking my degree, I went with Benjy for three months to the south of France. The change of climate and surroundings soon restored him to health. It was at this time that Chaim wrote me one of his most delightful letters which I shall quote in full:

My dear little Verotchka,

Thank you very much for your dear and frequent letters. They always bring me a little sunshine and a little of the fresh air of the Côte d'Azur. The Mediterranean always seems to me dear and attractive—perhaps subconsciously—because it washes the coast of Palestine.

My child, you are mistaken in thinking I shall become estranged from you and Benjy because of our long separation. I couldn't live without either of you. You sometimes think, Verotchka, that I love you less than you love me. Perhaps I love you differently. This love is unshakable and unbreakable.

If, as you say, I at times seem to indulge in flirtations, it does not in any way damage my love for you which stands in the centre of my consciousness and existence. And in any event, these interests have dropped out of my life. I suffered in the past and have now forgotten it, and I hope you will think nothing about it. Don't blame me, my darling.

I don't know why I started to write on this theme. But never mind.

You must appreciate the beauty of Cannes, remembering that here there is storm, drizzle, and snow. It's so good that Benjy has begun to improve. But you don't say a word about your own health.

In the laboratory the work goes on well and at home all is in order. Fräulein is very efficient and accurate. Of course I give her very little work. To prove my domestic authority, I told her to clean and polish the taps in the bathroom!

Write, darling, more about yourself.

In Cannes, the days must pass quickly. Have you been to Grasse and Metchnikov's milk laboratory?

You have the right to have a flirtation with anybody, except that I forbid you to do so with a grand duke kicking his heels in Cannes!

By the way, my friend Balfour is now in Cannes, playing golf. As a joke, tell him I'm not pleased with him.

I kiss you and embrace you—you and the child—many, many times.

Yours lovingly, Chaim.

When I returned to Manchester I had a different 'patient' on my hands. Chaim was in a very depressed state of mind which I was unable to relieve. The professorship he had hoped to succeed to on Professor Perkin's retirement went to Professor Lapworth, Perkin's brother-in-law, an *inorganic* chemist.

At about the same time, Chaim received a pressing invitation from the Actions Committee in Berlin to uproot himself from Manchester and join the committee as a paid Zionist official. Disappointed and frustrated over his lost professorship, Chaim was tempted to accept. But for perhaps the first time in my married life I was adamant and flatly refused to go to Germany. Apart from my fear that everything was *verboten* in Germany, I was not prepared to take my medical degree for the *third* time after having completed my examinations successfully in Manchester! But, far worse, I could not contemplate the idea that Chaim should give up his beloved science to become a paid Zionist civil servant. 'Our road to Palestine will never go through Berlin', I said firmly.

Chaim did not speak to me for three weeks!

Looking back, I dread to think what would have happened to us all, with the advent of Hitler, if we had gone to Germany. Who would have had the intuition, courage, persuasive power and charm to convince Balfour, Churchill, Lloyd George, Smuts and so many others of the need for the Balfour Declaration, without which, after so many struggles and disappointments, trials and errors, and such despair, the Jewish State would never have been proclaimed in 1948? I recall that Nehemiah, Ben-Gurion's A.D.C., once said to me, 'If it had not been for the War of Liberation, we should never have got the State'. My reply was, 'If it had not been for the Balfour Declaration, there would never have been a War of Liberation, because the number of Jews in Palestine up to the Declaration was negligible'. Nehemiah became thoughtful.

But in 1913, such thoughts were far from my mind. Shortly after I passed my finals, I was offered a three-weeks' *locum tenens* in the sadder slums of Manchester—a temporary appointment during which I was in charge of seven clinics for expectant mothers and for babies up to a year old. On the salary I received for my three weeks' work, I was able to go with my husband to the Zionist Congress held in Vienna in 1913. It was in Vienna, incidentally, that I witnessed my first anti-Jewish demonstration, in 1925, most of the participants in which, strangely enough, were women.

After a tiring Congress in which my husband took a prominent part, Harry Sacher, who had become a close friend of both of us, Mrs. Schuster's daughter Nora, Chaim and I went on a fortnight's walking tour in the Austrian and Italian alps. We stayed in alpine huts, some of which contained only a bed, a wash-stand, and a chair, and we thoroughly enjoyed ourselves. We returned tired but exhilarated to Lugano. After our primitive life in the alpine huts, the excessive luxury and comfort of our hotel were too much for us, and we decided to return home.

Immediately on our arrival, I received a letter from the Manchester clinic for expectant mothers, asking me to take the permanent post of medical officer as the previous medical officer had retired on account of illness. Although I would have preferred to specialize in internal medicine, I had my family to think of, so I began my new duties right away.

A new chapter had opened in my life, overshadowed by the coming war. But there was a ray of light in the descending darkness: Chaim's prophecy that the road to Palestine would lead through Britain was to be fulfilled.

4

Early Friendships : Prelude to War

THE year 1913 brought many changes into our lives. It saw the start not only of my professional medical career as a fully-fledged British doctor (I had taken out naturalization papers in 1910), but also the beginning of many new friendships which enriched our lives and, in some measure, affected the whole course of Zionism. But before I touch on these friendships, I ought perhaps to put my own story into perspective.

My medical career in Manchester was something of a rarity. When I began my studies in that city, there was only one practising woman doctor in Manchester, a gifted, intelligent woman who, like me, was of Russian origin. She was many years my senior.

The seven nursery clinics to which I had been appointed permanent medical officer on my return from Lugano were taken over by the local council and I had to resign my post and re-apply formally. I was appointed official medical officer of the clinics by the local authority.

My main concern in the three years in whch I worked in the over-crowded slum districts of Manchester was to develop improved methods of diet-and-weight control for the babies under my care. During a vacation, I paid a special visit to Paris to investigate social welfare methods there, and when I returned I introduced the relatively simple system of Professor Marfan of Paris which consisted in weighing children before and after feeding. The difference, if any, between the actual weight and what the child should have weighed was made up by artificial feeding. This discouraged premature weaning and, at the same time, ensured that the babies received adequate nourishment.

For myself, I greatly enjoyed my work among the working-class mothers and children in one of Britain's largest industrial cities and can testify to the selfless work done by the sisters in charge, as well as by numerous social workers, many of whom became my friends. In addition, the extra income I was able to bring to our slender budget was very welcome. Moreover, when the war came, I was anxious to play my part in the war effort of Britain, a country with which I was to be associated for more than thirty years. The consequences of this association for Chaim, myself, and our two children were far-reaching. Whatever 'alienation' we may have felt subsequently during the struggle for Jewish statehood, neither Chaim nor I ever lost our feeling of special affection and admiration for Britain and the British people. That during the period of the Mandate our affection may have been misunderstood by our own people was a penalty we both accepted in silence.

Chaim's disappointment at not securing the Manchester professorship soon mellowed and then disappeared as he was called more frequently to London to be in the centre of Zionist affairs and, later, to work for the British Admiralty. These activities led to prolonged separations although Chaim travelled backwards and forwards as often as possible between London and Manchester. I found delight in five-year-old Benjy who was a constant source of amusement and of some anxiety to me. He was a precocious and witty child—an attribute he carried into manhood—whose development I tried to encourage by always telling him the truth. I never pretended, for example, that babies were brought by storks! As a result, when Benjy's German governess told him shortly before Christmas that storks brought babies through the chimney, Benjy was amazed and told her she was ignorant! His governess, profoundly shocked, repeated her version, and convinced Benjy she was right. He said to me reproachfully, 'Mummy, you told me a lie'. When I held my ground, he rushed off to his governess and announced gleefully, 'I told you—you're wrong'! The flustered woman insisted on her fairy-tale; so Benjy finally gave up. 'Well,' he said, decisively, 'it may be so in Germany, but not in England.'

On another occasion, he was enchanted with the story in Exodus of the punishment of Pharoah for his cruelty. A week or so later Benjy went to a nursing-home to have his adenoids removed. When he came to from the anaesthetic, suffering greatly, he exclaimed bitterly, 'Oh, God, God, come down from Heaven and punish the wicked doctor as you punished Pharaoh!'

Perhaps the most revealing of all these family anecdotes shows not only his acute sense of personal dignity, but also his innate feeling for justice. I reproached him for fighting a little boy of his own age during a holiday at Chamonix. 'Benjy', I asked, 'which of you hit the other first?' I waited for his reply, knowing full well that he would tell me the truth. Benjy thought for a while. 'But, Mummy, he hit me first—after I hit him', he said. The poor child was sure he was in the right.

When Benjy was five, he had a special friend at his Kindergarten. One day he came home, and said that this child was his friend no more. Surprised, I asked why. He answered, 'He killed a fly'.

His natural sharpness of wit endeared Benjy to his father. The bond of affection between Chaim and his elder son never slackened although it was often subjected to strain, particularly in later periods when Chaim's frequent absences from home gave his children the erroneous impression that his devotion to Zionism was stronger than his love for his family. But in the early part of Benjy's development, Chaim played an important, almost maternal role. Benjy reciprocated every act of gentleness shown him by his father. Indeed, Chaim and Benjy had many traits in common: not only was there a marked physical resemblance between them, on which strangers often remarked, but they shared many gifts, such as clarity of mind, application, a gift for languages, and a sharp perception of character. Just as our younger son Michael revelled in his father's greatness, so Benjy suffered through his father's great task which took him from his family so often.

We all shared a fondness for Benjy's favourite uncle—my brother-in-law Joseph Blumenfeld, or Ossinka, the Russian diminutive by which we called him. Ossinka was a unique, irreplaceable character whose kindness, advice, and sympathy were always at the service of his numerous friends. Indeed, Ossinka was often so absorbed in helping others that he unwittingly neglected his wife and children! In the five decades of our friendship, I think Ossinka brought us more joy and worry than any other member of our closely-knit family. With Chaim, Ossinka shared a passion for chemistry, over which they would be absorbed together for hours at a time.

Ossinka was a noted specialist in rare metals such as cerium, thorium, and uranium, having worked for many years with the brilliant French chemist Professor Urbain. It was in this branch of inorganic chemistry that Ossinka rendered great services to the French Government during the First World War. Later, for many years up to his retirement, he was Managing Director of the Société des Terres Rares. He came to Israel after the formation of the State to promote excavations of rare metals in the Negev. He was most successful, and a company—the Israel Mining Company—was formed which brings in profits to the State of Israel.

We often stayed with Ossinka and my sister Rachel in their home in the south of France. In later years, our boys also paid frequent visits to their deeply loved uncle whom we all called our Benevolent Dictator. No one could, or dared, disregard his orders and instructions!

Ossinka died a few years ago from sheer self-neglect. He never made any effort to look after himself, and was always annoyed if my sister or I suggested that he should visit a doctor. His death was a sad loss not only to his immediate family, but also to his numerous friends. His memory lives not only in our hearts, but in the laboratory at Haifa which now bears his name. His widow, my charming, elegant and other-worldly sister Rachel, visits me in Rehovoth each year. She is exceptionally musical and a great patron of Impressionist art.

If I place Ossinka at the head of my 'early friendships', a group of devoted friends follows closely, most of whom have passed into the annals of Zionism which they served with generous and unsparing enthusiasm. I would mention particularly Simon Marks (later Sir Simon and then Lord Marks), Israel Sieff (now Lord Sieff), and the extensive Rothschild family. Chaim and I first met the two dynamic directors of Marks and Spencer in the summer of 1913. It came to their ears that Chaim had spoken at a mass meeting at Cheetham Hill. They wrote asking if they could see him. On the appointed day two young men appeared at our house. They were happy-go-lucky and looked as if they hadn't a worry in the world. Having lived for five years in Geneva, among students who never knew where their next meal was coming from, I did not take Simon Marks and Israel Sieff seriously. Neither Simon, who was about twenty-five years old, nor Israel Sieff, who was about a year younger, knew anything about Zionism; but they were genuine, sincere, devoted human beings.

Chaim and I discussed the possibility with them of raising funds for the *Keren Kayemeth* (Jewish National Fund), devoted to the purchase of land in Palestine. Chaim said that this land should be purchased with the 'pennies of the people', and Israel Sieff promptly countered by suggesting that it was 'pounds', not 'pennies', that were needed.

When Chaim and I had further opportunities of meeting these young men, we discovered that, despite their youth, they were practical men of affairs who knew very well how to convert pennies into pounds. Before long, from pupils they became apostles and started to contribute to the Jewish National Fund, a course they followed over many years so that the list of their donations for public and private charities grew with their experience of Zionism. It would be a needless embarrassment to list all their good works, the fruits of which may be seen everywhere in Israel, no less than in Britain. Closely joined in all these endeavours was Simon's wife, an attractive, generous woman, with whom I have spent many happy, sad, and intimate days.

The recent death of Lord Marks in 1964 brought an inestimable sense of personal loss to me. Our friendship, begun so superficially in 1913, blossomed into intimacy during the period when Simon Marks worked as my husband's political secretary in the latter years of the First World War. Israel Sieff came into prominence as the secretary of the Zionist Commission which visited Palestine in 1918.

My husband's acquaintance with the many-branched Rothschild family began when he was a lecturer in Geneva. He has written at length of his first meeting with Baron Edmond de Rothschild, who lived in Paris.[10] Baron Edmond was very much the *grand seigneur* whose eccentricities, like his virtues, were on an enormous scale. Despite opposition from all the members of his widespread family, Baron Edmond had sunk some tens of millions of francs in land development in Turkish Palestine at a time when the franc was twenty-five to the pound—money not always wisely spent, but without it the early efforts of Jewish pioneers might have come to nothing.

Chaim developed a great liking for Baron Edmond, with whom he had many a verbal battle. The Baron had heard that crazy young Russian Jews, disappointed at the non-fulfilment of the promise of Emancipation—instead a dreadful pogrom had taken place in Russia in 1881—had abandoned their universities and gone to Palestine to settle on the land. As Jews had never been permitted to own agricultural land in Russia, these students had never held a spade or a scythe. In Palestine many of them starved, many went down with malaria which raged in a country of marshes. Puzzled and impressed by these youthful efforts, Baron Edmond sent an expert to investigate—the expert, it was rumoured, his best orchid grower! In the end, Baron Edmond built many Jewish settlements. But the farmers did not do the work themselves; they became gentleman farmers, hiring Arab labour to do the work. Chaim did not approve of this method of settlement. Palestine, he emphasized again and again, did not need overseers of hired Arab labourers, but Jewish men and women who were prepared to work the land with their own hands. 'The trouble with us', Chaim would tell me, 'is that we always build the first and second floors, but forget all about the foundations. Now, for the first time, we Jews have the opportunity of starting with the foundations. . . .'

Happily, the influence and ideas of Arthur Ruppin, one of the moving spirits of the Kibbutz movement and a close and greatly-loved friend of ours, managed to restore the imbalance between Baron Edmond's rarefied ideas and the practical needs of the young Jewish community in Palestine. The poor, straggling settlements of the ill-housed and ill-fed pioneers who had come in trickles from Russia and Poland in the 1880s grew into self-reliant, proud colonies of working farmers, supported by the unfailing generosity of Baron Edmond. Much later many of his relatives came forward, as well as the countless thousands of other donors to the various land-purchasing funds and schemes to which Chaim devoted much effort.

*

In 1931, rich *effendis*, many of whom lived in Monaco and Monte Carlo, wished to sell their lands worked by Arab settlers for a sum running into many millions. It was then that Chaim brought his begging bowl to the Baron, asking for a sizable donation. The great financier smiled and said, 'Do you know the definition of a rich man?' Chaim answered, 'I have never been rich so I cannot give you a definition'. The Baron then gave the answer himself: 'A rich man is one who lives on the income of his income. If I agree to give you such a large sum, I shall not continue to be a rich man'. Later, when the Zionist exchequer was depleted, he presented Chaim, who was ill at the time, with a cheque for forty thousand pounds, remarking, 'This should bring your temperature down'.

Many stories of Baron Edmond's *largesse* and witticisms have been recorded and require no repetition. Less, however, is known about the numerous scions of his family who came to an understanding and appreciation of Zionism as slowly and painfully as I did myself. My favourite, possibly unrecorded, story took place some time after Chaim's first meeting with Baron Edmond in 1913.

Nothing, as has so often been said, succeeds like success, and some of the Baron's contemporaries pricked up their ears when they learned that his manifold undertakings and investments in Palestine were at last beginning to bear fruit. Henri de Rothschild, a physician and playwright, asked Chaim to a dinner to which many distinguished guests had been invited. Chaim was to make an after-dinner speech about Zionism. Henri's daughter, the lovely, charming Madame de Thierry, whose husband was a Secretary at the French Embassy in London, acted as hostess. She expatiated with great charm and eloquence on the history of Baron Edmond's colonizing efforts in Palestine. Chaim remained silent. Towards the end of the discourse, she exclaimed, 'Et vous, Monsieur, est-ce-que vous vous intéressez à Palestine?'

'Vaguement, Madame, vaguement', Chaim replied.

I need hardly comment on Madame de Thierry's reaction when Chaim was called on to make his after-dinner speech in which he described the first idealistic pioneers to reach Palestine who became, with their descendants, the future citizens of Israel!

Many years have gone by, bringing their toll of changes and up-heavals: the doyen of the House of Rothschild has long been dead; but the present generation of Rothschilds has followed closely in the footsteps of their illustrious forebear. The Baron's grandson Edmund, son of Maurice, has devoted all his energy and financial skill to building up numerous enterprises in Israel. My old friend Victor, third Baron Rothschild, a fine scientist, a humanitarian, and a thoroughly inter-esting character, made numerous anonymous donations to that country. He is a frequent visitor to Israel, and only recently brought his fifteen-year-old daughter to see me in Rehovoth. She had won a scholarship to Cambridge, a rare and perhaps unique achievement for a girl of her age.

Victor's parents, Charles and Rozsika, played a notable part in Chaim's preparatory work in laying the foundations of the Balfour Declaration. But our greatest friends on the British side of the Roths-child family were James de Rothschild and his brilliant and enchanting wife Dolly. I have known them both since their marriage in 1913.

Chaim and James did not always agree, but they were very attached to each other. Tall, with a strikingly original face, made more dis-tinguished by a monocle which he wore in one eye after a golfing accident in Normandy, James once said to Chaim, 'I never had a chance to earn half-a-crown in my life. If I had had that chance, I might have become a great man. . . .'

James, who served with great distinction on the Zionist Commission which went out to Palestine in 1918, died some years ago, but my friendship with Dolly—she is a J.P. and the president of many Jewish and non-Jewish institutions—has continued to this day. She not only gave much of the land and enterprises built up by the old Baron Edmond to the State of Israel, but provided funds to build the new Knesset, the Israel house of parliament. Two or three years ago Dolly, knowing my great love of dogs, sent me a little pug—which had been nicknamed Bother because he had been brought into the world by Caesarean section. He was sent first-class like a V.I.P. to Tel Aviv airport on an El Al plane. On being led out of the plane, he immediately broke away and ran towards me, promptly winning my heart and affection. I changed his name to Bambi. I love Bambi dearly. He has brightened my existence with his clever, eloquent eyes.

If I digress at this point, it is simply to remind myself of the dangers and pitfalls which await anyone who tries to set down his or her earliest reminiscences of kind friends, past and present. Baroness Moura Budberg, that highly versatile and cultured personality who once worked with Alexander Korda, and has made many fine translations of books and plays, once remarked to me when I urged her to write her memoirs, 'But then no one would talk to me again!'

It is a risk that must be taken in such an endeavour. It is not possible to write a catalogue of one's friends as if they were a laundry list! Many of their names will happily come alive in the course of my narrative, but many others must remain hidden in my heart and memory. I love them no less, even if the exigencies of time and space prevent me from enumerating all of them. I can only ask their forgiveness.

Before I return to the main body of my narrative, I should mention one friend whose liveliness and devotion have been a source of great delight and wonderment to me ever since our meeting in 1916. I refer to Flora Solomon, a woman of rare ability, drive, vision, and paradox whom I first met a few weeks before the birth of my second son Michael. Flora is the exact opposite of me: she is very gay, does not miss anything in life, is a perfect friend in need—who forgets you in between!

Flora's early 'irresponsibility' will, I think, delight every collector of anecdotes. Flora, whose father had been a very wealthy financier, lived in the lap of luxury: she even had a maid who put on her silk stockings! It was not surprising, therefore, that shortly after her marriage, when she acquired a cheque book, she began to issue cheques with gay abandon, until the bank manager sent a warning note to her husband, asking that her withdrawals should be covered by deposits. When questioned by her husband, Flora replied in all innocence, 'So what? I'll write another cheque to cover the overdraft!' She had imagined that a bank existed solely to provide money, an illusion she lost when faced with the severe financial crisis of 1931 which struck so many wealthy families. It was then that she found employment with Marks and Spencer, where she devoted herself to creating one of the most enterprising and far-sighted welfare departments in the whole of Britain. As a pioneer in the field of company welfare, which in pre-war Britain was something of a radical venture on which many aspects of the so-called Welfare State came to be patterned, Flora Solomon stands pre-eminent. No anecdote of her early eccentricities can diminish the imagination of her welfare enterprise, in which she was supported by Simon Marks. But I cannot resist commenting on her indiscriminate curiosity over people and causes, her lavish entertainment, and the numerous instances in which she promoted the Zionist cause as an unofficial Zionist public relations officer.

My intimate friend Rosette, Baroness de Menasche, a beautiful, witty woman, used to refer, in her French accent, to Flora and her two sisters as—'the Sisters Kar-ramazov', a description which could hardly be bettered. Each of these sisters is a personality in her own right: Flora's 'American sister' Fira runs a fashion house in New York, and her equally imaginative, sensitive sister Manya is a well-known publisher and translator.

Of Zionist friends and acquaintances in this early period I have said little or nothing, largely because they played an intimate part in the events which I shall describe later. But I must mention that enigmatic, highly flamboyant but nevertheless sincere Zionist Vladimir Jabotinsky with whom both Chaim and I were on terms of close amity, until events and political divergencies separated our paths. The record of our friendship with 'Jabo' has become overclouded with much misunderstanding among well-wishers and opponents of Chaim's 'gradualism', which is contrasted favourably or unfavourably with Jabotinsky's 'activism'.

It would also be fruitless for me to search the caverns of memory so as to write extensively on such an important formative influence on Chaim's development as that of Achad Ha'am (Asher Ginsberg). I have neither the training nor the inclination to engage in philosophical digressions on the meaning of Achad Ha'am's 'cultural Zionism', which Chaim occasionally criticized as 'a soul without a body'. But Achad Ha'am, who was some twenty years older than Chaim, did much to provide the spiritual basis of a lot of Chaim's thinking. And Chaim was greatly attached to the small, lean, ascetic Achad Ha'am who always spoke slowly as if speaking for eternity. They argued frequently and sometimes bitterly because Chaim, the statesman, dealt with immediate problems to which Achad Ha'am, the philosopher, had a more abstract approach. Yet somehow a synthesis occurred in these two attitudes, and Chaim frequently turned to Achad Ha'am for his sage advice. I myself found Achad Ha'am a rather remote, sceptical character—in contrast to myself who am more inclined to optimism—and the few times that I met him in his Golders Green house did not bring me much closer to him.

Of far greater importance in my own Zionist development was the instruction I received from Zvi Aberson, our 'eternal student', as we called him. It was Aberson even more than Chaim who brought me to a closer understanding of the significance of Zionism. I do not propose to record here our long arguments in Geneva and elsewhere, but it would be unpardonable for me not to pay tribute to Aberson's restless and questing spirit which did so much to lead me on to the path I was to follow.

*

If the year 1913 brought an influx of new friends and acquaintances, some of whom I have mentioned, the succeeding year 1914 carried us in the full flood of events even closer to the distant goal we had set ourselves. It also brought us more friends, together with unforeseen forces affecting that complex road of halt and progress towards the Balfour Declaration.

In June 1914, Chaim and I went to Berlin, little knowing that this would be our last contact with our German-Jewish friends for some years. Chaim attended a committee meeting to discuss the management of the newly opened Haifa *Technikum*, or technical institute, a meeting which was somewhat acrimonious because 'pro-German' and 'pro-British' cross-currents rocked the proceedings. The money, about £10,000, for the construction of the Institute had been given by Mr. Wissotzky, a Russian tea-magnate. The actual ground on which the Institute had been erected had been the subject of negotiation between the Turkish Government and the then German Under-Secretary for Foreign Affairs, Dr. Zimmerman.

Zimmerman and the 'pro-German' wing of the management committee insisted that instruction given in the *Technikum* should be conducted in German, while Chaim and other ardent Zionists insisted on Hebrew. The full story of this rather indecorous tug-of-war has been fully related by Chaim.[11] Nevertheless it foreshadowed the more serious divergencies which occurred between Continental Jewry and pro-Allied Zionists, a split which time healed but could never entirely obliterate. It did, however, lead to the 'wooing' of world Jewish opinion by the contending governments, something Chaim, with his usual foresight, had anticipated.

A further meeting of the management committee of the *Technikum* was arranged to take place towards the end of July in an attempt to resolve all these differences, but the outbreak of war on the Continent on 28 July put an end even to this slender hope. Despite all the signs and portents of war of which we had been aware, Chaim, Benjy, and I went to Switzerland for our annual holiday in the blissful hope that we should be back home before the conflict actually started. It broke out two days after we reached Switzerland, and it was some three weeks before we could start making our way back to Manchester; we had to struggle through dense crowds of agitated people in the Paris stations, and into and out of crowded trains and cross-Channel steamers.

A week or two after our return to Manchester, I had my taste of the more comic side of the artificially widened gap between the contending 'patriotisms' of pro-German and pro-Allied Jewry. If there were some German Jews who had made common cause with the nationalistic aspirations of Wilhelm's Germany and were at great pains to demonstrate their 'super-patriotism' on every possible occasion, there were pro-British Jews of German origin who went to absurd lengths to show their opposition to all things German, a fever they shared with their Gentile friends.

At the risk of offending the memory of Mrs. Charles Dreyfus, a good friend of mine, wife of the man who introduced Chaim to Balfour in 1905, I will tell a story which also shows a lack of 'diplomacy' on my own part! Mrs. Dreyfus had invited me to tea to meet her sister Mrs. Simon. Both these ladies, long domiciled in Britain, were of German-Jewish origin. They wanted me to tell them something of my early life in Russia, and listened with rapt attention to what I had to say. Then the conversation drifted to the war. Mrs. Dreyfus and her sister declared in unison that they had turned their backs on Germany for ever and would never so much as read Goethe again. I may have been simple-minded, but I began to argue, saying I found it difficult to accuse Goethe of starting the war. A shocked silence followed: it was not polite to argue with one's hostess. But we turned to less controversial subjects and our friendship was preserved.

Yet it was at one of the big wealthy German half-Jewish homes in Manchester that Chaim and I made the acquaintance of C. P. Scott, the powerful, famous, controversial editor of the *Manchester Guardian*

(now the *Guardian*). A few weeks after my gaffe at Mrs. Dreyfus's
tea party, Chaim and I were invited to another afternoon ritual, this
time in the home of Mr. and Mrs. Eckhard. She was the chairman of
the clinic for mothers in which I served as medical officer before it
was taken over by the local council. Chaim and I went to this tea
without an inkling that it would mark a momentous turning-point in
Chaim's political career and, indeed, in the fortunes of the Zionist
movement.

Chaim did not catch the name of the elderly man with piercing eyes
to whom he was introduced in the usual perfunctory British manner.
Almost immediately, Chaim launched into a severe criticism of
Czarist Russia's anti-Semitic policies, a somewhat foolhardy venture on
his part since Russia was now the ally of Britain. He even quoted the
remark of a Russian poet about his country: 'You are fated to have
noble intentions, but to achieve them is not given you. . . .' Chaim's
eloquent exposition of the plight of Russian Jews and intellectuals
impressed Mr. Scott, and he invited Chaim to call at his office where
they could continue their conversation.

'And what is your office?' asked my husband.

'The *Manchester Guardian*', Mr. Scott replied.

It was only then that Chaim realized that he had made contact with
the influential editor who had had the courage to support the Boers
during the South African War. I, too, was impressed by this distinguished looking man with the intelligent eyes whose newspaper had
provided me with my first stumbling exercises in English.

Some months later Scott invited Chaim to breakfast in London with
Lloyd George, then Chancellor of the Exchequer in Asquith's administration. The breakfast took place in December 1914 at nine o'clock at
Lloyd George's house; others present included Josiah Wedgwood and
Herbert Samuel, then President of the Local Government Board; and
Chaim has left an account of it in his autobiography.[12] Lloyd George
asked him a number of questions about Palestine and the Jewish
colonies there, and Chaim found to his surprise that Herbert Samuel's
attitude was helpful—he had assumed that Samuel, like Edwin Montagu, then Under-Secretary for India, belonged to the assimilationist
side of British Jewry. Chaim was getting closer to those centres of
power where human destinies are disentangled from the morass of
politics.

I shall not repeat what my husband has already told of his early
meetings with Lloyd George and Balfour; but there is one unrecorded

story I want to tell of the fiery, eloquent Welshman who played such an important part in the destiny of the world and in the future State of Israel. He was at times much confused by the highly vocal discussions and arguments which raged between 'assimilationists' like Montagu and out-and-out Zionists like my husband. 'I can't understand you Jews', L. G. remarked sadly one day. 'I have a war on my hands, but when problems get me down and I become depressed, I take my little bag and go to Wales. We all come together, sing songs, and I become so elated that all my problems fall away from me. Why don't you take the same attitude?'

It was not easy to explain to L. G. that we had no 'little bag' to pack, and no 'Wales' to go to! In spite of his sympathy with Jewish aspirations, based on his own deep religious feelings and his understanding of a 'small people' (so like the Welsh, he used to say!), he didn't understand that the Jewish people required a period of recuperation, of patient rebuilding to discover their strength and to test their capacity for nationhood.

With the war, there came changes in our personal lives. My husband has told how, on receipt of a circular from the War Office inviting any scientist in possession of any discovery of military value to report it, he offered his fermentation process, but got no reply. Some months later, however, he was summoned to the Admiralty where he saw the First Lord, Winston Churchill (whose acquaintance he had made in 1906 when Churchill was contesting N.W. Manchester), and was entrusted with the task of producing the immense quantities of acetone needed by the Navy.[13]

Chaim's work for the Admiralty had its comic side. A processing plant had been put up for him at Putney and the architect presented him with a bill amounting to some thousands of pounds. Chaim sent this bill on to the Admiralty but received no response. A little later the architect threatened him with legal proceedings, and he went in person to Whitehall to remonstrate. A sympathetic official consoled him by remarking, 'Please don't worry, Dr. Weizmann. Only now are we settling the bills of the Boer War!'

From the start of his work for the Admiralty until some time in 1915, Chaim travelled backwards and forwards between London and Manchester until, worn down by the constant travelling, he took a small apartment at Number 3 Justice Walk, Chelsea, which he shared for a while with Vladimir Jabotinsky. I continued my medical work in Manchester since a replacement could not be easily found in wartime.

But early in 1916 I came to live in London. We set up house first in Campden Hill Road and a year later at 67 Addison Road.

Chaim's salary at this time was in the region of £1,500 a year, but with the expenses of two households we had little money to spare. The Admiralty asked Chaim what salary he wanted for the work he was doing for them. He answered that he required the salary he had received at Manchester University plus my salary as a medical officer, and an additional fifty pounds a month to cover the difference in the cost of living between Manchester and London. He also asked for fifty pounds to move all our belongings from one city to the other. This last bill, like so many others, was not settled for three years.

On my arrival in London, I promptly fell ill with 'flu and Chaim was left to look after Benjy, which he did with his usual patience and good humour. He himself was deeply immersed in his political and scientific work, both offering their usual frustrations. Chaim had warned the Admiralty that he would need large amounts of maize for his acetone process, but as maize had to be imported the quantity required could not be provided under wartime conditions. He then tried horse chestnuts, arranging for regiments of school children to do their patriotic duty by scouring the countryside for nuts. No less a personage than the beloved Queen Mary herself joined in this war effort.

With my arrival in London, I found myself in the not entirely unexpected role of a political social hostess. It is at this point that my diaries begin. . . .

5

Talking to Myself: Diaries,
March 1916—December 1916

I BEGAN to keep a diary early in 1916 in a somewhat desultory
way, and I continued it with many fits and starts up to the death
of my husband in 1952. I cannot explain what prompted me in
this effort. I had no secrets to impart to its pages, nothing to hide from
prying eyes, and no particular literary aspirations. In re-reading my
diaries half a century later, I have come to the conclusion that I was
merely 'talking to myself . . .'.

The earliest entries consist in the main of jottings, scraps of conversation, ideas and comments, together with a record of the social
and political events in which Chaim—and I myself when I moved to
London—were increasingly involved.

These diaries, with the exception of a few scattered quotations, have
not seen the light of day before, and I offer the extracts that follow for
whatever interest they may have for the general or specialist reader.
Beyond correcting mis-spellings, I have not attempted to 'improve'
either the style or substance of these diaries. Their abruptness and
immediacy—they were written shortly after the events they describe—
may contain errors of fact and of judgement, but these must not be
amended by the benefit of hindsight. I can at least say that I spared
neither friend nor foe! The abrasion of time may have softened the
outline of my strictures on both.

I will begin with my first entry:

15 March 1916

Chaim was invited to lunch at the Astors' in St. James's Square to discuss
Zionist problems. Others invited to lunch were Mr. Oliver Lyttleton, Mr.
[later Sir Alfred] Zimmern and Mr. Balfour, whose professional occupations
prevented him from being present. But he rang up and expressed the wish
to meet Chaim next Sunday evening. [My diary does not record if this

particular meeting took place. Dr. Weizmann and A. J. B. were meeting frequently at this time.] Chaim gave an account of the history and present state of Zionism. Mrs. Astor was very interested and confessed that she had been rather prejudiced against Jews, as she had never before met Jews with such views and attitudes; her Jewish acquaintances were people like the Rothschilds and Montagus.

Despite Nancy Astor's somewhat ambivalent attitude towards Zionism and her rather patronizing remarks about Jews in general (of which more later), both she and her husband were clearly impressed by Balfour's wish to meet Chaim. Chaim himself was delighted, since he telephoned this news to Mrs. James—Dolly—de Rothschild, in whose house we met later that evening. Charles de Rothschild, who was also present with his wife,

> expressed the opinion that uncle Leopold R. will get to know that he [Chaim] discusses Zionism with Cabinet members. Mrs. James cunningly asked him if he *always* tells *everything* to his uncle.

The words in italics were underlined in my diary entry, and indicate the extent of the pro- and anti-Zionist attitudes within the large Rothschild family.

On the following day, we were invited by Mrs. James de Rothschild for lunch, together with Lady Crewe and Mr. and Mrs. Reginald McKenna.

> Mr. McKenna criticized Lord Derby's scheme, and the calling up of married men now. He said they have already over 400,000 men and don't need any more, and called Lord Derby an idiot.

After this burst of ministerial confidence, the ladies retired. McKenna (who in May 1916 was to become Chancellor of the Exchequer) then asked Chaim 'whether it is possible to make nitric acid from the air'. Chaim answered that he thought it possible, though it was not in his line, but he did not see why it couldn't be done, if the Germans could do it. McKenna then asked Chaim

> if English students are a good material for scientific research and said that Chaim has now a lot of new things, which could be the nucleus of the chemical industry after the war. He was well informed on Chaim's last discoveries of acetone and benzol and toluene etc.

Chaim did not mince matters. He told McKenna that although the human material was excellent, the whole English system is wrong; they are not encouraged to do research and therefore don't get the same chance as the Germans. To that McKenna replied, that as long as he lives, he will keep up the laboratories started now and will make them national companies; he asked Chaim to call at the Treasury any time to discuss it.

When the McKennas and Lady Crewe left, Dolly turned to Chaim, saying that

Lady Crewe is not as snobbish or mondaine as she looks; she is very good-hearted, serious and a very brilliant woman, but her manners are so objectionable that she puts everybody at a distance and people generally feel shy in her presence.

Both Chaim and I came to share Dolly's estimate of the Marchioness, her close friend, in whose 'wonderful house in Curzon Street' we enjoyed hospitality. Because of Chaim's inveterate hatred for Czarist oppression, Lady Crewe suspected him of 'pro-German' leanings[14] but all these difficulties and misunderstandings were smoothed over in time. A few days later (according to my diary entry of 20 March) Dolly de Rothschild told Chaim that she had overheard a conversation between Lady Crewe and Lord Robert Cecil, Parliamentary Under-Secretary for Foreign Affairs, in which she asked him what he thought of Zionism. She also said, 'We are all "Weizmannites" in this house', and asked him whether the time was ripe to start a Zionist campaign.

Although Dolly Rothschild did not 'overhear' Lord Robert's reply, Chaim had no difficulty in assessing the climate of opinion which prevailed in the Cabinet and government circles at this time. Apart from Lloyd George and Balfour, other leading personalities such as Lord Milner, General Smuts, Philip Kerr (later Lord Lothian), and General Sir Henry Wilson were also favourably disposed towards some kind of Allied declaration of intent concerning the future of post-war Palestine. They were supported in this by both Wickham Steed, foreign editor of *The Times*, and our good friend C. P. Scott, editor of the *Manchester Guardian*.

But despite the friendly 'intelligence' which we received from Zionist friends, neither Chaim nor I knew that Sir Edward Grey, the British Secretary of State for Foreign Affairs, had sent out feelers to Britain's two major Allies, Russia and France, suggesting that in the event of Allied victory 'the prospect of an autonomous Jewish Commonwealth in Palestine, subject only to the exclusion of Jerusalem and the Holy Places', should be offered to the Jews. The object of this exercise was 'to find an arrangement which would be so attractive to the majority of Jews as to enable us to strike a bargain for Jewish support'. Nothing came of this *démarche*, as my friend Leonard Stein has pointed out.[15] But it was a straw in the wind which was later converted into a kite, if I may mix my metaphors!

It should also be noted that great efforts were being made at this time to gain the support of American Jewry, which in turn would exert pressure on the United States to enter the war on the Allies' side. There was much talk of calling a Pan-Allied Zionist Conference to 'launch a Zionist Campaign', as Lady Crewe had remarked to Lord Robert Cecil. Chaim, who was broadly in favour of such a move, met with opposition from the American side. According to my diary entry of 20 March, a letter had reached him from Julius Simon, a leading American Zionist representative, in which he declared his opposition to such a Conference. 'The fact that Czarist Russia was a member of the Entente was enough of itself to alienate the sympathies of American Jewry', is how Leonard Stein explains the motives behind this reluctance.[16] New stresses and strains were constantly appearing on the surface and beneath the surface of Zionist aspirations, which Chaim—although he had as yet no official status on the Executive—tried to check, palliate, and overcome. 'To conduct internal Zionist politics during the First World War was to walk on eggs', as he himself put it ruefully.[17]

*

At the risk of indulging in this risky operation myself, I now propose to say something about our friendship with Vladimir Jabotinsky. Early in 1916, I had moved from Manchester to London, joining Chaim and 'Jabo' in their bachelor establishment at 3 Justice Walk, a few days before our removal to our first Kensington address.

Looking back over fifty years, I think I may say that my friendship with Jabotinsky reached its peak in the early period of the First World War; but we remained friends even in the most difficult and harrowing circumstances when our friendship was sorely tested in the crucible of political differences.

My friendship for Jabo sprang from admiration of his charm, his personality, his ability, and his wide knowledge of history and world affairs. In spite of our continual disagreement on almost all matters concerning Zionist policies, my admiration for him remained undimmed until his death in 1940, at the lamentably early age of sixty.

Jabo, who was well-known as a correspondent of the leading Russian newspaper *Russkiya Vyedomosti*, had a superlative command of many languages, and I found him a compelling orator in most of them. Not only had he an extensive vocabulary, but his delivery on a public platform was brilliant. I always felt that he should devote himself to exposition as a publicist rather than to political polemics whose realities he did not always grasp, and I never failed to tell him so.

I recall that I once pleaded with Jabo to leave politics alone. It seemed to me, I told him, that he would do better to put his talents unreservedly at the service of Zionism generally, and not to just one partisan aspect of it. With his great eloquence, vivid style, and skilful way of dealing with people, I felt that he could be instrumental in converting many non-believers to the Zionist ideal. Jabo was shocked when I made this suggestion, and I remember with what dramatic fervour he said to me, 'But, my dear Vera Issayevna, politics is my greatest talent and virtue!' We agreed to differ on this also.

Despite these differences, Jabo had sterling qualities which he placed at the service of the Zionist cause. In 1915, for example, he conceived the idea of forming a Jewish Legion raised from young Jewish refugees who had fled from Palestine to Egypt. Before this Legion was formed, these Palestinians served as the nucleus of the famous Zion Mule Corps formed by Trumpeldor which gave notable service during the Gallipoli Campaign. Colonel Patterson was the Commanding Officer, a great sympathizer with the Zionist cause and a brilliant soldier.

On Jabo's arrival in England, he lived with us in Manchester for some time. He then joined the British Army and began his historic, if contentious, struggle to form the Jewish Legion, in which endeavour both Chaim and I were his fervent supporters. He enlisted in the Royal Fusiliers as a private and rose to the rank of sergeant. For a time, while he was promoting the Legion, he lived with us in Kensington.

A furious storm of controversy broke over Jabo's and our heads over the whole issue of the Jewish Legion. Even pro-Zionists thought such a force was unnecessary and positively harmful to the Jewish cause since many Jews were already enrolled in Allied armies: Achad Ha'am, Chaim's closest friend, went so far as to castigate the scheme as an 'empty demonstration';[18] but Jabo, with my husband's support, continued to press the idea, and both Chaim and I followed his recruiting campaign with the deepest interest.

Later, when the plan was accepted and recognized by the War Office, Jabo was given a room of his own in the building. As is by no means unusual during a war, when different interests are involved, Jabo's work for a Jewish Legion was not widely known even among the high-ups in the Army Command. I recall Jabo's telling us of an incident which occurred one morning when a General called Jabo to his office and, in the presence of Lt.-Colonel Patterson, angrily charged him with working in the War Office without authorization!

Poor Jabo, who was only a non-commissioned officer, could not answer back to a General, and all he was able to say was, 'Yes, sir', 'No, sir'.

Colonel Patterson afterwards explained to the General that Jabotinsky was not an ordinary conscript, nor had he moved into the office without higher authorization. 'He is a most exceptional person', said Colonel Paterson. 'He is a volunteer in the British cause, with a great name in Russian journalism. He is here to help us to win the war and to ensure that the Jewish people are brought in on our side'.

The General was greatly taken aback.

'Good heavens!' he exclaimed. 'I thought he was a Laplander!'

But Laplander or no (Jabo's appearance *was* somewhat Mongolian), Jabo persisted and eventually succeeded in forming the Jewish Legion. Later, when he asked me to assist in organizing welfare work among the Legionaries in England, I did so willingly. I became a voluntary waitress in the Jewish soldiers' canteen in Wardour Street, in the heart of London's West End. There I met many of the men who later served in Palestine.

Shortly afterwards Jabo was commissioned as a lieutenant and went out to Palestine. There another characteristic episode occurred. During a bout of disagreement, the aristocratic 'Jimmy' de Rothschild, who was irritated at Jabo's apparent intransigence, exclaimed, 'I am your Colonel!' Jabo, without a moment's hesitation, replied, 'But I am your *General*!' He meant this, of course, in the widest sense of the word, since he was the founder of the Jewish Legion.

Where Jabo's private affairs were concerned, he was highly impractical and neglectful. In his dedicated work for the Legion, he forgot all about his own and his family's welfare. He did not, for example, arrange for the allowance to which his wife was entitled to be paid to her. So I took both her and their son Eric into our home in London until I was able to make necessary arrangements for her to receive her allowance.

Although after the war, as the split grew in Zionist ranks, our relations with Jabo became overclouded by partisan differences (Jabo formed the Revisionist party and the so-called New Zionist Organization), he remained for us a genuine and dedicated idealist, a perfect gentleman, and an orator of remarkable eloquence. No matter how much Chaim's views differed from his, and how unconditionally opposed Chaim was to his methods, he always retained a deep admiration for Jabo's singular personal gifts and his devotion.

But to return to my diaries. . . .

On 25 March 1916, in the afternoon, Mr. Leopold Greenberg, editor of the *Jewish Chronicle* (who never forgave Chaim's political opposition to Herzl), arrived at our house, bringing with him the correspondence between 'Monsieur l'Oncle' (Baron Edmond de Rothschild of Paris) and certain American Jewish financiers and Pope Benedict XV concerning Jewish life in Poland. The Committee of the League for Liberty and the American-Jewish Committee had addressed a letter to the Pope, who had written a sympathetic reply, stating that in the event of Poland's achieving independence after the war, the Jewish population ought to be given all civil rights. Jews who had lived in the country for ten years should have the right to become naturalized and Yiddish should be used as an auxiliary language. Pope Benedict XV also offered to act as arbitrator between the Jews and the Polish authorities. The diary entry continues,

> As regards Palestine, it is proposed that it should be neutralized, with the Pope's representative in the government. We discussed what was to be done with all these documents, and what attitude Zionists should take to them. There is no doubt that if the Pope got the upper hand in Palestine, it would be unacceptable.

Greenberg and Chaim agreed that there was some difficulty in presenting these documents to the British Government since

> the Pope is considered here as pro-German. Mr. Greenberg decided to show the documents to Lord Robert Cecil and to ask his opinion.

At seven that same evening Chaim went to see Mrs. James de Rothschild.

> She warned him to be very discreet and careful with McKenna who is ready to wring Lloyd George's neck. Concerning Palestine, she heard that the English are afraid to take it on account of France and France takes the same attitude towards England; therefore there is a notion in the Foreign Office of offering it to America.[19]

Asquith appeared concerned at a possible 'Unionist intrigue', designed to use the Jews to support their policy in acquiring new territories after the war. Charles de Rothschild 'thought we must be careful not to fall between two stools and not to play up any party interests'. This was wise counsel indeed, since it was generally agreed that 'Balfour is sure to become Prime Minister soon', an opinion generally shared at this time. A luncheon was arranged at Dolly Rothschild's house the next day for Chaim to talk to McKenna, ostensibly to continue their previous discussion on nitric acid, but at which Charles de Rothschild was to take the opportunity of bringing up the whole issue of Zionism.

My husband had become friendly with the Astors during the war, but he never spoke of his private life in the numerous coversations he had at their hospitable table until Mrs. Astor once asked him whether he was married. Chaim said yes, adding that we had two children. 'Why didn't you tell me?' she asked. 'Do bring your wife to lunch'. Thereafter I was a frequent visitor at their lovely house, 4 St. James's Square. Later that same evening of 25 March 1916, Chaim and I went to dinner there where we met Balfour, Philip Kerr, and a few American journalists. I wrote in ironic vein:

> Mrs. Astor tried with success to bring the conversation with Balfour round to Zionism. She very indiscreetly then said to Balfour, 'you really must speak about Zionism to Dr. Weizmann', and made the situation rather awkward.

Nancy's intervention, however well meant, was not necessary, as Chaim had had many opportunities to 'talk Zionism' with Balfour! I suppressed my irritation on this occasion, though I had the temerity to explode later.*

> The rest of the conversation was for the most part gossip about the present Government. The Premier was called 'Squith' and much fun was made of Asquith's reception of the King and Queen.

Mrs. Asquith (it was said) had taken the Queen upstairs to her husband's bedroom to show the Queen how 'simply Henry lives'.

Whether or not Asquith was much concerned about Unionist intrigues, I cannot say. But his authority over the Government was becoming increasingly precarious, as salon gossip was quick to grasp. On 2 June 1916, my diary records 'news of a great Naval battle with heavy English losses. We were all frightfully depressed, and were

* See p. 68.

afraid that it was the beginning of the end . . .', an over-pessimistic assessment on my part. On the following day McKenna telephoned to Chaim to tell him that he had seen a report from the Admiralty which showed that Chaim's 'acetone process proved to be a complete success on a large scale, and that the plant for the toluene and benzene process in Poole will be ready to start next July'.

On the afternoon of the 3rd, Chaim went to Lady Crewe's where he learnt further details of the Battle of Jutland, which had been fought on 31 May-1 June between the British Grand Fleet under Admiral Jellicoe and the German High Seas Fleet under Admiral von Scheer. Lady Crewe told Chaim that 'the Government is delighted with the naval position. Although we have lost 17 ships, the German Fleet is disabled for six to eight months and that has saved the Russian position, as the Germans intended to go to Riga, which would have been fatal to Russia'.

Two days later, on 5 June, the *Hampshire* went down off the Orkneys. Lord Kitchener, who was on an official mission to Russia, was drowned. When Chaim asked C. P. Scott, a month or so later, if this had been a great shock, Scott replied (my diary of 13 July), 'Yes, he was sorry for the *Hampshire*; as for the old man [Lord Kitchener], he could not have done better than to have gone down, as he was a great impediment lately'. Scott also agreed that the Battle of Jutland was a great victory which might have rivalled Trafalgar 'if Beatty hadn't engaged the Germans so quickly, but had allowed them to come nearer to Jellicoe'. As to the alarming news which had been reported on 2 June, this was due to the fact that Jellicoe had sent no official report, fearing that a radio message would give away the position of the British Fleet if the message were intercepted by the Germans. The 'alarming news' had been spread by the Germans, it seems, who also claimed 'a great victory'. The Germans had, in fact, retired behind extensive mine-fields which made pursuit impossible, but they did not venture to challenge British naval supremacy again on the High Seas.

My 1916 diary goes no further—not surprising since I myself was engaged in a 'battle' of another kind. On 16 November 1916, my second son Michael was born, an event of considerable importance in all our lives. This increase in our family made us very happy, but his birth left me tired and not too well for a time.

We had only one telephone in the house, in Chaim's study. When in February 1917 Chaim had become president of the English Zionist Federation, an honorary post designed to give him status in his negotiations with British statesmen, journalists, and foreign visitors, he found that his small city office was not ideally suited for the work this post involved. Apart from nursing the baby, I acted as Chaim's secretary, and this meant continual running up and down the stairs to answer the telephone. So I went on strike and put my foot down, insisting that he should find himself a more suitable office and a paid secretary.

After much consideration and heart-searching, we decided to open an office of the Zionist Organization at 175 Piccadilly, and Simon Marks, who was released from military service for the purpose, took charge of it.

Chaim also obtained the services of a highly efficient and perfect secretary, Miss Lieberman, of whom I have the warmest and friendliest recollection. One day after ten years of service, when we were all travelling by train, Miss Lieberman suddenly announced, rather timidly, that she was going to get married and would have to give up her job. Chaim was horrified: 'Then I will have to resign my presidency!' he exclaimed. She later settled in Israel.

This threat to resign the presidency of the English Zionist Federation was repeated by Chaim on many more serious occasions, and was a warning sign of the overwrought state of his mind. There was little opportunity to whisk him away for a much-needed holiday abroad in war-time but happily his scientific work was beginning to show results, and he had more time to devote to Zionist affairs. These became intensified with the arrival at the end of 1914 of Mr. Nahum Sokolow, a prominent member of the Zionist Executive which now had its headquarters in neutral Denmark.

I myself also found some relief from my domestic and nursing responsibilities: a few days before Michael's birth, I had engaged Jessica Usher as his nurse, on my doctor's recommendation. Miss Usher was a pleasant-looking, slender person of decided views, cast in an old-fashioned mould, a great disciplinarian, and an excellent children's nurse in every way. Despite temperamental differences which appeared later, we were all very fond of her, and I gladly surrendered much of the day-to-day running of our establishment into her capable hands. I began looking round for a larger house, where we could entertain on a wider and more relaxed scale.

But the 'fateful' month of November 1916 ended with a change of Government in the offing. Early in December, Lloyd George (who had become Secretary of State for War in June following Kitchener's death)—and not Balfour as had been assumed in 'well-informed' circles—became Prime Minister: A. J. B. went to the Foreign Office. Winston Churchill was brought in as Minister of Munitions in July 1917. The arrival of this triumvirate at the pinnacle of power brought an intensification of Chaim's political activity.

6

The Great Declaration

TO a large extent through Chaim's initiative, with the backing of such loyal friends as Norman Bentwich, Harry Sacher, Dr. Gaster, and Achad Ha'am, a memorandum was submitted in January 1917 to Sir Mark Sykes, at this time attached to the Foreign Office as chief adviser on Near Eastern policy. The complexities of this memorandum have been fully described by my husband, who said that it represented 'the efforts of a group of amateur state builders, members of a people which had for many centuries been separated from this type of activity'.[20] Chaim's modesty about this document has been challenged by the brilliant British historian Sir Charles Webster, who paid ample tribute to his skill as a diplomat and negotiator.*

This January memorandum may be reduced in essence to two main points: it asked for the recognition of the Jewish nation, and for the right of this nation to settle in Palestine with full civic, national, and political rights. It appeared to him in retrospect that 'the memorandum does seem to have anticipated the shape of things to come'. Yet it is precisely this shape of things to come that British assimilationists like Edwin Montagu, Minister of Munitions in Asquith's government, June–December 1916, and later Secretary of State for India, resisted most bitterly. Montagu, for all his fine qualities as a government servant, was afraid of what we call today double loyalty. To him, the idea that the Jewish people could constitute a nation seemed absurd. Who had ever heard of such a thing? They were simply a religious community! Chaim considered that the Cabinet, and even Lloyd George himself, attached undue importance to the opinions held by so-called 'British Jewry', and in a full and frank letter to Lloyd George went on to explain that the majority of Jews settled in Britain were in favour of Zionism. Only the minority of wealthy, half-assimilated Jews who had been

* *See* Appendix A, p. 270.

living in the country for three or four generations were dead against Zionism. His letter continued:

> But here is the tragic misunderstanding. Zionism is not meant for those people who have cut themselves adrift from Jewry, it is meant for those masses who have a will to live a life of their own and those masses have a right to claim the recognition of Palestine as a Jewish National Home. The second category of British Jews will fall into line quickly enough when this declaration is given to us. I still expect a time, and I do so not without apprehension, when they will even claim to be Zionists themselves. Some Jews and non-Jews do not seem to realize one fundamental fact, that whatever happens we will get to Palestine. . . . No amount of talk by Mr. Montagu or people like him will stem the tide.[21]

The ranks of the 'assimilationists' were far from united, however. Here and there attitudes softened as time went by. I remember Chaim's telling me after he had had a particularly chilly interview with Lord Reading that he ended it by saying, 'All the intelligence you have, you give to the British—and the little "stupidity" that is left, you give to us'. I do not know how Lord Reading reacted to this taunt; but Chaim has put it on record that even this distant, magisterial pro-Consul was half won over by the practical achievements which followed in later years.[22] His son Gerald, the second Lord Reading, married Eva, daughter of Sir Alfred Mond, first Lord Melchett, and they became our friends and Zionist supporters. Mond was a financial genius—and an active supporter of the Palestine to be. He bought large tracts of land, a few thousand dunam, and called it Tel Mond, his object being to parcel it out and make it possible for various people to buy enough land to settle on.

Numerous other Jewish and non-Jewish friends also entered our lives at about this time. I think with particular warmth of Leopold Amery who gave us much encouragement and advice, and was particularly incensed when the leading Jews in 1917 openly attacked the scheme of a Jewish homeland under British protection.

The process of influencing and winning people over to the Zionist cause, as well as softening 'the doubters', continued to be our main task at this period, as an entry in my diary indicates:

13 March 1917

Chaim dined at the Astors' where Balfour and L. G. were present. No sooner did L. G. come in than he asked Chaim in the presence of everybody if he liked the situation and the campaign in the East. Confidentially, he informed Chaim that British troops were already in Gaza. He said he must see Chaim to discuss Eastern affairs, and when Chaim remarked that he was afraid to take up his time, L. G. simply said that Chaim must come and inflict himself upon him. L. G. left early, and the rest of the evening Balfour discussed Zionism with Chaim, merely academically. All the secretariat who were present were thrillingly interested in it.

When Chaim saw James de Rothschild next evening, he was much impressed by this conversation of Chaim's with L. G.

On 15 March 1917 Chaim and I were invited to lunch at the Astors', together with Philip Kerr (later Lord Lothian) and other distinguished guests. In the course of the lunch, Nancy suddenly remarked from nowhere that before she met Chaim she had disliked Jews and now Dr. Weizmann had entirely altered her views.

The Astors always had a large table for people who had been invited and a smaller table for those who dropped in on their way to the House of Commons. On one occasion a number of American guests had been invited who probably were not aware that Nancy invariably interrupted people talking at the other end of the table. Chaim was speaking to some of these American guests when Nancy suddenly exclaimed (referring to Chaim).

'Don't believe him! He's a great charmer. He will convert you to his point of view. He is the only decent Jew I have met'. She certainly did not mean this but it was her way of being entertaining.

There was dead silence in the room. All the guests looked down at their plates. My husband did not know what to do.

I felt faint. But I said, 'Mrs. Astor, are *all* Americans as charming as you are?' Mr. Astor said, 'Bravo, Mrs. Weizmann! Nancy, you asked for that!'

Dear Nancy, there were many such clashes between us. Some years later when a friend of hers forwarded a letter of introduction from her —I was already living at Rehovoth—I read this odd sentence, 'You must feel very sad to live in Jerusalem after you had lived so long in Liverpool (*sic*). . . .'

I wrote back immediately to Lady Astor, as she had now become, saying,

It is very strange that you who are an American and have lived so many years in England should think I am sad to live in Jerusalem, which I do not. I live in an orange-growing country, with a beautiful view of Jerusalem and the Judaean mountains, after having lived not in Liverpool but in Manchester. . . .

That, I think, concluded our correspondence.

*

I now reach one of those hidden shoals of secret diplomacy which had to be negotiated at this time.

Early in 1917 my husband, with the concurrence of Sir Mark Sykes and others, asked Nahum Sokolow to find out the French attitude towards a Jewish Palestine under British protection, a plan which Chaim supported resolutely. Sokolow's first reports, as my diary of 21 April indicates, were 'most pessimistic':

> The French will not hear of a British protectorate; they want Palestine for themselves. They will give Jews 'rights' but not autonomy or a charter.

Then followed a shower of enthusiastic telegrams saying that all was well. After a fortnight without letters, at last a long letter came which explained the changed attitude of the French and their sudden understanding of Zionist aims: the French, we were told,

> are very sympathetic and agree to adopt our programme as the British are willing to do. Sokolow thought that in three weeks in Paris more was achieved than in three years in England. James Malcolm, a London Armenian who acted as a go-between, arrived yesterday and confirmed these facts, and added, by the way, that the British bargained for Haifa and Acre for themselves. On the other hand, Mr. Scott heard from Lord Milner that some pledges to the French exist about Palestine. Vicomte de Caux of the *Journal des Débats* mentioned to Mr. Scott that it was settled that north Palestine will be French and south—an Anglo-French condominium. All these facts undoubtedly point to the existence of some pledges.

The settlement mentioned to C. P. Scott by the Vicomte de Caux was one of the Asquith administration's less glorious chapters—so far as Zionism was concerned. It was the so-called Sykes-Picot Agreement which had been signed in May 1916 although its existence was not known until April of the following year. Under this agreement, Palestine was to be divided by a line running from Acre to Tiberias: the northern part was to be included in France's 'Greater Syria' and the southern part, as rumour correctly had it, was to be placed under a Franco-British condominium. Palestine, if it survived at all, was to be bedevilled by two masters!

69

Fortunately, nothing came of this scheme, largely through the efforts of one of its signatories, Sir Mark Sykes, who became a convert to Zionism and was called by Chaim 'one of our greatest finds'. Sir Mark evinced warm feelings of sympathy for all subjugated people—the Jews, the Arabs, the Armenians; he also saw that in the grand pattern of imperial design (imperialism was not then the word of opprobrium it was to become), the creation of a Jewish homeland in Palestine would help to secure Britain's position in the Near East. When it came to a choice of colonial masters, the British were infinitely to be preferred to the French, a point Chaim hammered home on every possible occasion. After some wavering, Sykes gave sincere and whole-hearted support to Zionism: he was, in every sense, a fair-minded and generous person, and his attributes passed to his son Christopher.[23]

But in April 1917 the Sykes-Picot Agreement was still secret, and as my husband had been urged by British official quarters to go to Egypt, whence he was to go on to Palestine (then being won from the Turks), with the object of raising world Jewish opinion in favour of some kind of nebulous scheme the full terms of which he himself did not know, the position had to be clarified before he started. Chaim and all those in the inner circle of British Zionist affairs were in a state of consternation over the position.

My diary continues:

> All unanimously agree that Sokolow's presence in Paris any longer is dangerous and all connexion with the French ought to be severed. Telegram to that effect sent to Sokolow who was then in Rome.

Chaim had an interview with Herbert Samuel, on the morning of 25 April, and put all the known facts before him. I noted:

> H. S. could not divulge the arrangement made between the two powers, as he was a member of the Cabinet at the time, but he said it was not satisfactory from the British point of view. He advised Chaim to see the F.O., and also promised to go to L. G. with him.

Later that afternoon, Chaim went to see Sir Ronald Graham, a senior official at the Foreign Office. Chaim told him that

> he couldn't go to Egypt unless he has a definite mandate to raise public Jewish opinion for British Palestine. That it will carry tremendous weight if he starts this agitation from Jerusalem. Chaim also told him there were three possibilities: (1) French North Palestine and International South; (2) French North and British South; (3) British Palestine. The last is ideal, but if there are any pledges the second best would be British South. Chaim said that the

situation now is entirely different; democratic Russia[24] and America will never allow annexation pure and simple, and the division of Palestine is much worse than annexation. This policy could happen in Persia five years ago, but could not happen now, and we Jews will raise the whole of Jewry against the division of Palestine. Sir Ronald Graham was most sympathetic, said he didn't think the situation was satisfactory and that a few days ago already he presented a memorandum to the Foreign Office to that effect. He made Chaim understand that though some pledges exist, there is nothing definite; he strongly advised Chaim to go to Egypt and work there with Mark Sykes. Chaim asked him to arrange an interview with Lord Robert Cecil.

The interview with Cecil, then Assistant Secretary for Foreign Affairs, was arranged for next day. Chaim has paid tribute to Lord Robert Cecil as 'one of the great spirits of modern England'; like Balfour, Milner, and Smuts, he 'was deeply interested in the Zionist ideal. . . .' My diary for 25 April 1917 gives a summary of the meeting:

> Interview with Lord Robert Cecil which lasted an hour. Chaim put the whole situation before him. He said that Chaim ought to go to Egypt and Palestine to raise Jewish opinion for British Palestine. Chaim asked him if he would confirm the interview in writing and whether Lord Robert Cecil would sign it. The answer was affirmative.

The Sykes-Picot Agreement, or 'semi-official treaty', as my husband called it, began to recede into the background. The French themselves were under heavy pressure from President Wilson, whose principle of 'open covenants openly arrived at' would have stifled the Sykes-Picot arrangement almost at its birth.

Simultaneously with these Zionist activities in London, American Zionists headed by Justice Brandeis impressed on Mr. Balfour, who was visiting the United States, the willingness of American-Jewish opinion to support a British-protected Palestine. Balfour appeared to be gratified by this support. Slowly but inexorably events were pushing the British Government to make some declaration of its intentions.

Nothing, however, came of the project for Chaim to visit Egypt and Palestine in 1917, despite the encouragement he received from the British Foreign Office. Instead, an interlude which Chaim called an 'opera bouffe intermezzo' divided the year at its middle. Early in June, he received word from Brandeis that a special American mission was travelling to the Near East and Chaim was asked to get into contact with it. The object of this mission was wrapped in mystery. Its purpose was explained to Chaim by Sir Mark Sykes and Ormsby-Gore, at that time M.P. for Denbigh. Henry Morgenthau, former American Ambassador in Turkey, had conceived a plan by which Turkey might be detached from Germany's side and encouraged to surrender its suzerainty over the hapless Jews, Armenians, and Arabs included in the ramshackle Turkish 'empire'. This extraordinary project had the support of the high-minded President Wilson, whom the British Government had no desire to offend. But it was quite clear to Chaim from his conversations with Foreign Office officials that they would like nothing better than to torpedo the whole business and turn the mission back before it reached Egypt, and it was proposed that Chaim should go as a quasi-official representative of the British Government, without of course disguising his Zionist affiliations!

Chaim himself entered into the opera bouffe spirit of this enterprise, which, I think, he realized would provide him with a little relaxation while he acted in the unfamiliar rôle of a secret diplomatic agent. I cannot read my diary entry of 29 June without a great deal of amusement:

> Chaim, accompanied by Captain Kennerley Rumford, left Waterloo at four p.m. for Gibraltar to meet the American Mission consisting of Morgenthau, Levin-Epstein, and Frankfurter. The purpose of the mission is not quite clear. It is supposed to conduct separate peace arrangements with the Turks. Sir Louis Mallet, late British Ambassador in Turkey, was at first suggested as British representative; but Balfour subsequently decided to send Chaim alone. From the Spanish frontier they will travel in a military car, accompanied by a detective. At Waterloo Station M.I.D.—the Military Intelligence Department—gave Chaim a military passport.[25]

A letter arrived from Chaim on 2 July telling me that he had reached Paris where he had seen Lord Bertie, British Ambassador in Paris, and Baron Edmond de Rothschild, neither of whom, it appeared, knew anything about this mission! Chaim and Captain Rumford left for Bordeaux the same evening at eight-twenty-five. Rumford, who was a singer of repute, and incidentally the husband of Clara Butt, regaled Chaim with many stories and a snatch or two from the light operas of the day. My husband described Rumford as 'a delightful companion, though somewhat unsuited for a secret mission' since he looked 'every inch a British officer' despite his disguise in mufti!

On 3 July I sent Chaim a telegram and a letter through Sir Mark Sykes. Next day, a telegram came from Captain Rumford to say that they had arrived safely in Gibraltar. On 6 July I had lunch with Carrie Schuster who told me a curious story which was going the rounds:

'Lloyd George had been called up by the King who offered to abdicate if in Lloyd George's opinion it would induce the Kaiser also to abdicate. . . .' I do not know whether there is any foundation for this story; but it was typical of the 'gossip' of the day which relieved the more sombre war news. That same evening I spent with Achad Ha'am, who dismissed the 'double abdication' story as a *canard*.

At four-thirty on the afternoon of 19 July Captain Rumford turned up bringing me a letter from Chaim. I see from my diary that

> he was absolutely in raptures about Chaim who, he said, was the most lovable man he had ever met in his life, adding that he had never enjoyed a trip as much as this.

He and Chaim had been followed

> by German spies all the time and one of them even tried to be in the same sleeping compartment with them. They were warned to be very careful and not to drink water on the train, as spies are up to all kinds of tricks.

Rumford also told me that Chaim had met Dr. Max Nordau, an Austrian subject who had been expelled from France and was now living in Madrid. He had been very cautious in not revealing too much about his 'official mission', but when Chaim turned up to lunch at the British Embassy, he found that 'the British Ambassador had told Nordau all about Chaim's mission'.

A letter which Chaim wrote to me on 3 July gives a graphic picture of his meeting with Nordau, the great Zionist leader, and both his and Captain Rumford's 'cloak and dagger' experiences in Spain:

My dear Verotchka,

Yesterday evening we left Madrid and now Rumford and I are waiting at the railway junction for the connexion to Gibraltar. In Madrid, where we spent the day, I managed to call on Nordau. He was so astonished—he and his wife—to see me that they could hardly recover from the shock. The poor creatures live like refugees in a very small apartment and it looks quite sad.

Nordau is delighted with all our work in England and is absolutely enchanted with everything. He shares our ideas in every way. He considers that attempts made by the gentleman [Morgenthau] whom I am meeting will be exceedingly dangerous for Zionism, Jewry, and generally for the Allies. I was delighted to hear that from him. I could talk only briefly with him. On my return I shall stay longer and then it should be interesting to chat about it. It is unpleasant, however, that I cannot take a single step without being shadowed by some German spy. There was one who followed us from the frontier to Madrid. Yesterday he came four times to our hotel, trying to find out from the reception desk the date of our departure. The clerk, an Austrian, kept asking us all the time when we were leaving. We told him that we were staying another night and did not close our suitcases. Only at the last moment a car arrived with an English guide, and we packed hurriedly and settled the bill and in ten minutes we had disappeared. You should have seen the clerk's fury. Obviously he had told his spy that we were remaining for the night. He was very unhappy to look such a fool. As a result no one followed us. I don't know what's going to happen when we appear in Gibraltar. In any case, it's most amusing and I must confess that the Germans are very clumsy in their shadowing. Even a child could have seen through them.

Tonight we shall be in Gibraltar and will learn something from the others. Tomorrow I will write the details. It is impossible to say how long we shall have to stay here. I hope to find news of you. We are now in the heart of Andalusia and the climate, temperature, and atmosphere are absolutely African. The heat is unbearable and the sun is blinding. They say that Gibraltar is a little cooler.

My companion Captain Rumford is very pleasant and quite unacquainted with secret service methods. It was a nice trip. I write to you on the off-chance because it seems incredible to me that this letter will some time somewhere reach you from this station.

If I can get a guide, I shall go to Granada just to look at the Alhambra and other Moorish monuments. And how is everything with you, my dear, and the children? I do hope that you don't feel lonely. What strikes one is the enormous quantity of olive groves here. I wonder whether it will be like this in Palestine? I always feel sad and envious if I happen to be in the south.

I kiss you and the kiddies many times.

Your loving, Chaim.

When Chaim wrote this letter he had not yet reached Gibraltar, but by the 19th I was able to enter in my diary,

Chaim and Captain Rumford did not stay in Gibraltar but went every morning in the steamer from Algeciras. *Chaim's mission was very successful and he managed to stop the Mission from proceeding farther towards Eygpt.*

It may not have been a famous victory, but at least it was a triumph for common sense: Morgenthau and his lukewarm American Zionist 'advisers' had abandoned the idea of appealing to the Turks to pull out of the war and had gone home. It did not make Chaim popular in certain American circles, but it did save some people from making fools of themselves!

Later that evening I received a cable from Chaim, who had reached

Paris, telling me to expect him home that same day. The opera bouffe was over and there was more serious work on hand.

*

I do not wish to go into the details of the negotiations immediately preceding the issue of the Balfour Declaration. The conversations, persuasions, promises, disillusionments, frustrations and meetings which took place up to the day on which agreement was reached; the protestations of misguided opponents of the Declaration, the attitude of various anti-Zionist British Jews—all this has been told before. But a few points taken either from my diaries or my memory seem to me to be worth re-telling.

I remember, for example, that when one such opponent declared that the idea of a Jewish homeland was a mad solution propagated by mad European Jews, Chaim answered on one occasion, 'It is not necessary to be mad to be a Zionist, but it helps!'

Madness, however, was not only one-sided. When Mr. David L. Alexander, the president of the Jewish Board of Deputies, and Mr. Claude G. Montefiore, President of the Anglo-Jewish Association, published a long statement in *The Times* attacking the Zionist position, Chaim immediately went to Lord Rothschild—Walter—and persuaded him to counter this statement. They drafted a letter which Lord Rothschild signed, and Chaim and I went with it to the foreign editor of *The Times*, Mr. Wickham Steed, who published it in the next day's issue of his newspaper together with letters from Chaim, from Dr. J. H. Hertz, the Chief Rabbi of the British Empire, and from Dr. M. Gaster. It had a tremendous effect on the public.

This was on 24-25 May 1917, shortly before Chaim's Gibraltar 'mission'. When he returned from this adventure, he found that anti-Zionist sniping had intensified. The new target for attack was Jabotinsky and his Jewish Legion. Chaim's feeling of loyalty towards Jabotinsky was outraged, and he twice offered, in August and in September 1917, to resign from the presidency of the English Zionist Federation and from the Political Committee among whom disagreements about the Jewish Legion had appeared. Achad Ha'am, to whom he wrote proposing his resignation, replied, 'To whom do you offer your resignation? Who has appointed you? Fate has appointed you, and only to Fate can you offer your resignation'.

It was perhaps this feeling of 'fate' which guided my husband to declare in London in August 1917, at the Twentieth Anniversary of

75

the First Zionist Congress, 'However sheltered this port, and however calm these waters, we Zionists cannot anchor here, however welcome the hospitality that surrounds us'.

On 18 October 1917, I recorded in my diary, 'For the third time the War Cabinet has had the Palestine Declaration on the agenda, and for the third time it was put off owing to our Jewish opponents'. A draft resolution had been submitted twelve times before an acceptable formula could be found! The issue frequently hung on the insertion of a word or a phrase.[26] Anti-Zionists such as Edwin Montagu fought hard to delay or emasculate the Declaration, and found support in the powerful figure of Lord Curzon, then Lord President of the Council. My diary records:

> On the eve, Lord Curzon came in to say that the question is too important and he would like to postpone it in order to present a memorandum on the subject. Sir Mark Sykes, Ormsby-Gore, and Sir Ronald Graham were infuriated and saw nothing in this but obstruction. Chaim went to Philip Kerr and insisted on seeing Lloyd George. He told Kerr—and repeated it to the Prime Minister—that either the declaration has to be put on to the agenda in the next few days or taken off altogether; that Chaim's position before the Jewish people is becoming intolerable; they had trusted Chaim blindly for the last three years, but there must be some statement from the Government. The Prime Minister promised to have it put on the agenda.

A text which received the approval of the War Cabinet was presented on 27 October, a date which has not received the historic emphasis it deserves—it was overshadowed by the actual date of the issue of the Declaration, a week later. My diary makes good this omission:

27 October 1917

> Poor Chaim was overjoyed, and all our Zionist friends looked positively silly from joy. Aaronson and Tolkowsky came to dinner unexpectedly to celebrate the occasion. Colonel Patterson, the officer commanding the Jewish Legion, came later. He said that now was the time for the Zionist Organization to associate itself openly with the regiment. Chaim has undertaken to obtain the support of the Political Committee and secure the collaboration of the Zionist Organization for the Legion. . . .
>
> No end of telegrams of congratulation. Everybody is most enthusiastic except Dr. Tchlenow, who still advocates Jewish neutrality and the policy of sitting on the fence. But behind these snipings there was, I fear, pure jealousy. . . .

Perhaps I am being unduly hard on Dr. Tchlenow, but his behaviour during these historic days was both inept and clumsy. He kept insisting on every occasion that he spoke in his capacity 'as a member of the Zionist Executive'.

On 2 November the last of the twelve drafts of the Declaration came before the Cabinet at a meeting at 10 Downing Street. Apprehensive and downcast, Chaim went to 10 Downing Street and saw Philip Kerr, Lloyd George's private secretary. 'Do you foresee any chance of my being called into the meeting?' he asked. Kerr smiled ironically and said, 'Dr. Weizmann, never in the history of England has an outsider been called into a Cabinet meeting'. Unwanted and crestfallen, my husband went into an adjoining room to await the decision. Meanwhile the Cabinet must have run into rough water as the Prime Minister (Lloyd George) suggested that Dr. Weizmann should be called in for consultation. So, contrite, Philip Kerr telephoned to our home in Addison Crescent, to the Acetone Experimental Plant at Putney, and to the Lister Institute where the laboratory was located. But they could not find Chaim—he was sitting only a few yards away, tense and brooding, awaiting the outcome.

When the Ministers dispersed, my husband heard them in the corridor and came out of the room. Upon seeing him, Sir Mark Sykes came forward and exclaimed, 'Dr. Weizmann, it's a boy!'

Chaim greeted the arrival of this 'boy' with some misgivings. The motives underlying the famous Declaration have been subjected to much analysis, much argument, and the debate on its merits has never ended. Yet I do not think I need apologize for providing a fuller version of how my husband came to hear of it, or for re-stating its main contents for the reader who may not be familiar with the text, which has, I think, been engraved on every Jewish heart. It read:

> His Majesty's Government view with favour the establishment in Palestine of a National Home for the Jewish people, and will use their best endeavours to facilitate the achievement of this object, it being clearly understood that nothing shall be done which may prejudice the civil and religious rights of the existing non-Jewish communities in Palestine or the rights and political status enjoyed by Jews in any other country.[27]

Like most diplomatic documents, it tried to please too many people —and succeeded in pleasing too few! Yet it represented the beginning of the great adventure which brought the Jewish people home after almost two thousand years: the first glimmer in the sky of the Land of Israel, still thirty years away! As such, the Balfour Declaration was carved on Chaim's heart and mine. Balfour, our philospher friend who signed it and whose name it bears, did not direct it to my husband. It was sent at Chaim's suggestion to Lord Rothschild, the Honorary President of the English Zionist Federation.

Some days later, prompted by Chaim, the English Zionist Federation sent a letter of appreciation to Balfour. But, as with all historic occasions, the issue of the Balfour Declaration and the subsequent reactions to it were not without their moments of high drama.

Chaim, the moment he heard from Sir Mark Sykes of the birth of this 'boy', reached for the telephone to give me the news. He then rushed off to Achad Ha'am and broke the news personally to him. Up to a fortnight before the issue of the Declaration, Achad Ha'am told Chaim it would never be achieved! Afterwards my husband came home with a small group of friends, and we all joined in a circle and danced a Chassidic dance in his library. Three days later I noted, 'Lately Chaim has had nothing but worry and trouble'. Dr. Tchlenow had behaved in a high-handed manner to Aaronson who complained that he had been excluded from meetings of the Zionist Political Committee when 'the attitude of the organization to the Balfour Declaration was discussed'. Aaronson, who had done notable service for the Allied cause as an intelligence officer, was very much upset.

Then on 15 November, at a reception held in London, at the Princes Restaurant, Lord Rothschild was given an opportunity to read the Declaration. Chaim, who presided at this meeting, made one of his best speeches, tactful and dignified. Sokolow, however, spoke very inappropriately, stating that the Declaration had been 'sent to the Lord and not to the Jewish people because they had no address, whereas the Lord had a very fine one'. I sat opposite Lord Rothschild, and I could see that he thought Sokolow's 'joke' in very bad taste. Then it was Dr. Tchlenow's turn to speak: he spoke in bad German and his 'whole speech was a slavish glorifying of Lord Rothschild'.

On the other hand, Chaim's reception by the East End Zionist Society on 17 November was 'very nice and cosy':

> A cheque for £400 towards the political fund was presented! There were lots of speeches: Abraham Tulin, who spoke on behalf of American Zionists, said they had come to look on Chaim in America as their leader, after Herzl. Tchlenow sat sulky and glaring and was the only dissonant note in the festivities.

Thus the year of the Great Declaration ebbed to its end. The fateful November of 1917 brought not only the Balfour Declaration, but also on the 7th of the month (N.S.) the Bolshevik Revolution in Russia. The old world was changing, and the new, with its unfathomable troubles, was upon us. Early in 1918 Chaim went with the first Zionist Commission to Palestine, and I followed him a year later. It was the beginning of a new and fulfilling experience of my life, the beginning of my own journey back to my own people. . . .

7

Palestine: 1918-1925

EARLY in 1918, it was proposed by the British Government that Chaim should go as chairman of a Zionist Commission to Palestine. The object of this commission was to review the political and economic conditions in this small corner of the Turkish 'pashalik' which was still being wrested from the Turks, and to make recommendations 'in the spirit of the Balfour Declaration'.

It was Sir Mark Sykes, I believe, who suggested that it would enhance the prestige of the Commission, and strengthen Chaim's hand as its chairman, if Chaim, before his departure, were received by King George V. This produced great excitement. Chaim bought a top hat—the only one, I think, he ever possessed—and went off to the Foreign Office looking very smart in his morning suit. Here, he found everything in confusion. An atmosphere of mystery prevailed. Sir Mark Sykes told my husband that telegrams had arrived from the British authorities in Cairo hinting that there might be trouble from the Arabs if Dr. Weizmann went to see the King. My husband was flabbergasted. The idea of his seeing the King had not come from him. He said that if notice had to be taken of Arab reactions every time, there would be no point in his going to Palestine. He added with dignity that the cancellation at the last moment of his reception by the King would be bound to have an extremely detrimental effect on his prestige and his influence with World Jewry. Major Ormsby-Gore shared Chaim's opinion.

At that moment Balfour walked in slowly, knowing nothing of this change of plan. 'What's the matter? What's going on?' he asked. On hearing what had happened, he rang up Buckingham Palace, and in his quiet but irresistible manner apologized that a mistake had occurred over the appointment with the King because 'he had arrived late in the office'. He asked that the appointment should be arranged for the next day.

Next day Chaim went to Buckingham Palace in a taxi—'I went to visit the King in a taxi so that my future Ambassadors should go by royal carriage', he remarked to me later. The first thing His Majesty said as my husband walked in was, 'This mistake often happens because Balfour always comes late to the office'—a tactful and gracious thing to say.

His Majesty was most friendly and was well informed as to the work of the Commission. He evidently knew of Chaim's Russian origin because, holding my husband's hand, he said—referring to his cousin Czar Nicholas II. 'I always told Nicky—"You will end badly"'.

The Commission left that same afternoon.

On 10 March 1918 I wrote into my diary the text of the first letter I received from Chaim. It was from Rome where, he said,

> One does not feel the war here. People are smartly and elegantly dressed: they crowd the streets as if these were normal times. It is difficult, my dear, good child, to describe my feelings as I approach Palestine. The task is immense: shall we have enough strength and wisdom not only to assume it, but also to start it on the right track, so as to solve the difficulties through our united efforts? . . .
>
> And you, my dear, good Verotchka, don't be sad. Remember that this is my military service for the good of our Fatherland. You, as well as I, will bear the separation, remembering the most beautiful and noble task that has fallen to us. We are paying a high price, but that is inevitable! I think of you and our little children, Benjy and Michael, of our home, of all the complex and complicated life behind us, which was only a preface to the chapter now beginning. Be strong and courageous! Those were Joshua's words on approaching Palestine. With deep love, I commend those words to you. In your strength is my strength.

On 14 March he again wrote, saying that he found Rome 'oppressive'. Everything was alien to him, reminding him of all the tribulations the ancient Jews endured at the hands of Rome. On the 15th, the members of the Commission found themselves marooned at Taranto: they had to wait for a naval escort to take them to Alexandria through the submarine-infested waters of the Mediterranean. The Commission had had a couple of meetings; nothing definite had been decided, but they had, said Chaim, 'cleared the ground and eliminated misunderstandings'. Professor Sylvain Lévi, the French representative on the Commission, was a well-known anti-Zionist, 'far from our point of view', Chaim thought 'it was a mistake to have him on the Commission'. All the others seemed likely to work quite well, though

James de Rothschild 'was somewhat sulky and aloof, and last night I had to tell him this wouldn't do: he must put his heart into the work or we should simply leave him to himself. I think my talk did him good'.

'Jimmy', for whom I had a sincere affection, was constantly stressing his 'Englishness', which was never in dispute. Indeed, before the Commission went out, I had said to my husband, 'Look, Chaim, perhaps Jimmy is being difficult because he wants to be chairman of the Commission instead of you. Offer the position to him. You'll do all the work anyway'. Chaim followed this advice; but Jimmy, too nervous to accept so much responsibility, refused. Ormsby-Gore, on the other hand, was 'splendid', Chaim confided. The Commission itself was somewhat apprehensive about meeting the Arab Committee in Palestine—'nobody seems to know clearly whom this Committee represents, but it is noisy and speaks on behalf of a people it claims to know and understand'. During the days spent in Taranto there was a sorting out of plans which could not be formulated because everything would 'depend on what we shall find in Palestine'. But the more Chaim talked with Sylvain Lévi, 'the more I came to the conclusion that he will not co-operate with us'. The American representative Walter Meyer 'is very superficial and I'm afraid he won't be much use, in contradistinction to Aaronson who will, I think, be a very valuable collaborator, if other Palestinians get on with him'.

On 29 March I received a cable from Chaim telling me that they had arrived in Cairo, and that he had talked with 'the Arabs, the Duke of Connaught, with Jews, and with government representatives, and all went very well'. He also received an invitation from General Allenby to spend the day with him. The military news from Palestine was far from comforting, as Allenby's small forces had been depleted to meet German attacks on the Western Front.

In a letter which left Cairo on 24 March, Chaim told me of the delirious welcome which had been accorded to the Commission by the Zionists of the ancient community in Alexandria where they were met 'with music, banners and a parade and such great ado that I was almost ashamed'. There was so much to be done before indulging in such junketing was Chaim's implication. Despite the personal friendliness of such high officials as Sir Reginald Wingate (a cousin of Orde Wingate) who was the British High Commissioner in Egypt, Chaim was quick to detect that much anti-Zionist propaganda had been subtly directed at the Commission, and even the most well-meaning officials had been affected by it. He wrote, for example,

All the authorities here were sure of one thing and that is precisely that the Jews intend to create a Jewish State *immediately* [his italics], and that their first step would be to confiscate all the land and enslave the Arabs. It is hard for me to define as yet who has been spreading such rumours and notions which have percolated into the minds of the Arabs and have been nurtured by the local authorities.

Even the sympathetic Sir Reginald and General Clayton, the political officer, were somewhat taken aback by Chaim's disclaimers:

When I told Wingate of the project for a British Protectorate over Palestine and explained why we and other Zionists consider it necessary, he opened his eyes wide. Both he and General Clayton, with whom I spoke briefly, assured me that if this was the case, then there will certainly be no serious difficulties with the Arabs.

But it was still too early for Chaim to assess the kind of 'difficulties' he and other Zionists would have to face from the Arabs. Nor did the local Jewish-Egyptian community impress him although, as he remarked,

they enjoy great influence in all spheres of life, chiefly in the financial field. They are all related to each other and constitute, so to speak, one family. One or two are exceptionally clever men. One such is Harari Pasha who occupies an important position in the administration of the country, and another is Victor Mosseri. There are innumerable Mosseris here of all kinds . . . All these people are millionaires and get richer daily. I would not like to *condemn* them, but when one looks at this crowd, one feels positively chilly and eerie. They are indifferent and maybe will remain so. Some of them may become interested in Palestine, but only under one basic condition—that Palestine should become a continuation of Egypt so that these gentlemen could spread their influence and Egyptian expertise over the country. I shudder at the thought of such a possibility.

Chaim was naturally more impressed by the Palestinian Jews who had streamed as refugees into Egypt and who were now waiting for an opportunity to return to Palestine. But the disorganized state of affairs, and the fact that British control had not yet been established in the country, made this a complex operation. Chaim foresaw that a special organization would have to be created to repatriate these Jews from Egypt. 'Meanwhile', Chaim wrote to me, 'the whole burden falls on Victor Mosseri, who works honestly, but who cannot cope with it all'.

Two days later, he had a two-hour talk with General Clayton and came to full agreement with him. 'He sees no difficulties for our work', stated Chaim. 'I ask you no questions, but wait for your letters—like manna from heaven'.

Chaim found little manna in Palestine in 1918. Indeed, as he told me later, he found the most terrible fear in the country. The Turks were still only two miles from Jerusalem, and Arabs were going round with handfuls of British gold—the British had paid them not to join the Turks and the Turks paid them not to join the British! The few military who were about were suspicious of Jews. If anyone was seen walking from one room to another carrying a lighted candle, that person was liable to arrest, accused of signalling to the Turks. It was difficult to explain that few Jewish homes at this time could afford any curtains! Nor were the Arabs over-fond of the British. Most of the Jews in pre-war Palestine, moreover, had fled to Egypt, to Europe, anywhere, rather than remain under Turkish domination. I do not believe there were more than thirty thousand Jews left in the whole country, and most of these were what we called *Challukah* Jews: that is, Jews who had come to die in Palestine and be buried in the Holy Land; they lived almost exclusively on charity. American and British Jews sent money for this purpose and there had been a good deal of exploitation in the distribution of these funds, which were now left to be disbursed by the Zionist Commission. It fell to Dr. David Eder to handle this difficult problem, and he cut down the individual allowance so as to make distribution more equitable. He also withdrew allowances from younger people in an effort to persuade them to find work, but they came back in a week of two saying they did not want to work. When asked why, they said that when they worked they became hungry and had to eat much more, and that they wore out their clothes and their shoes! Of course they complained to the Americans that the Zionists were pocketing their money.

My husband mentioned another Palestinian sidelight to me. He had taken with him a pair of field-glasses, which seemed to exert an uncontrollable fascination on one of the Arab guides who had never seen such an object before. Brandishing a fistful of gold in his hand, he asked to be allowed to try the glasses; but Chaim, the bacteriologist, was not unnaturally terrified of trachoma, then prevalent in Palestine and the whole Near and Middle East.

My diary notes and my quotations from Chaim's letters to me should, of course, be read in conjunction with his own 'positive' account of the work of the Zionist Commission of 1918, which he wrote many years later and which was published in *Trial and Error* (page 290 *et seq.*). But of special interest is a personal letter Chaim sent to Balfour on 30 May 1918 which was not published until close on forty years later when it appeared on 4 April 1958 in the *Jerusalem Post**. This moving document reveals the mood, as well as the complex web of intrigues and circumstances, which faced both the Commission and Chaim himself.

A letter Chaim wrote to me on 6 April 1918 provides a more direct glimpse of the situation he found in Palestine at this period:

> Before coming to Jaffa, I spent twenty-four hours in an apartment of the General Staff, not far from here, at the invitation of General Allenby. The meeting with him was very interesting. I met Lady Allenby in Cairo and she had obviously got in touch with him. This has been very helpful to us. Allenby is a great man, intelligent and well-read; very straighforward and interested in many problems. Not that I can say that he profoundly appreciates or understands the moral and political significance of the Movement, but there is no doubt that he expressed goodwill in trying to understand us and help us.

Lower down the hierarchical ladder 'the local military authorities do not understand the meaning of the Declaration and hadn't, to some extent reckoned with it'. Jewish demands, Chaim found, 'even the most modest, meet with great difficulties: and Arab requests are unceremoniously treated, and without being discussed'.

Allenby's reception heartened Chaim, and he felt he had made a good impression on the General; but the problem of bringing relief to the Palestinian Jews remained paramount. 'The work is bottomless', Chaim admitted. 'The material situation of the population is on the whole better than one expected. But the terrible past has left its marks. . . ' The military front was still too close for any normal life to be established. 'One can still hear the sound of guns clearly. Palestine is surprisingly beautiful now, but something sad and grave hangs in the air and all that is so senseless . . . this war among the lemon and orange groves'.

After he had seen Allenby, Chaim and the Commission were to spend a day in Jerusalem and the following week were to tour the Jewish settlements. 'Jimmy went to Rishon yesterday and made a speech in Hebrew', he reported to me, asking me to keep him fully informed on what was going on in London.

On 24 July 1918, a 'modest but memorable ceremony' took place when the foundation stone of the Hebrew University was laid on

* *See* Appendix B, p. 272.

Mount Scopus, in the presence of General Allenby, his staff, and other dignitaries.

On the way there, a hot hamsin* was blowing and the atmosphere was unbearable. The Sudanese cavalry riding in front of Allenby's carriage raised an unholy dust which made Allenby choke. He exclaimed: 'Dr. Weizmann, you are a very intelligent person. Do you really believe that any damn Jew will come to this bloody country?'

My husband replied: 'General, come here in ten years'.

General Allenby came in seven years when he attended the opening of the Hebrew University.

The Hebrew University was the first physical realization of Chaim's dreams. But there was also another event and one friendship with which I should like to close this account of my husband's visit to Palestine in 1918. Chaim had been invited to stay at General Allenby's headquarters at Bir Salim. As fate would have it, there is a wonderful view of Bir Salim from the spot where my husband and I built our home at Rehovoth.

Among the officers to whom my husband was introduced was Colonel Wyndham Deedes, later General Sir Wyndham Deedes, a small, sensitive, intelligent man who never married in spite of his attractiveness to women. My husband spent the whole of the night talking with Deedes in his tent. In the course of the conversation, Deedes produced a copy of the notorious 'Protocols of the Elders of Zion'. It was the first time Chaim had ever seen this 'document', which he described as 'utter rubbish'. Wyndham Deedes answered that he would be wise to read it carefully as it was likely to cause a great deal of trouble in the future. Copies had been brought into Palestine by the members of the British Military Mission which had served under the Grand Duke Nicholas in the Caucasus.[28]

Deedes's prophecy that a great deal of trouble would be caused in the future by this revolting document—a forgery which claimed that Jews used the blood of newly baptized Christian infants in the preparation of their unleavened bread at Passover—was only too true: it was later circulated in Germany, and in Vichy France, and became one of anti-Semitism's prime exhibits. A deep and abiding friendship sprang up between Wyndham Deedes and my husband, a friendship I was privileged to share. Two years after Chaim's death, I wrote to Wyndham asking whether he had any letters or documents of my husband's arising out of their association which could be deposited with the

* A desert wind.

Weizmann Archives at Rehovoth. His reply, dated 28 February 1954, reveals the depth of their friendship:

My dear Vera,

In answer to your letter I don't think—indeed, I am sure that I have not any *correspondence* from Chaim. As you know, our communications were all so personal and verbal on those—oh, how many!—occasions when he, you and I met and had a meal together.

Ah, what precious memories.

Au revoir, my dear Vera, et adieu,

Your devoted old Friend,

Wyndham

When, in preparing these memoirs, I re-read this letter, it brought back so many memories—Wyndham at our home at Addison Crescent, the week-ends he used to spend with us in Kensington, our long conversations sometimes lasting far into the night, his mature mind and penetrating observations on men and affairs, the asceticism he practised no less than he preached, and which eventually led to his decision to go to live and work among the under-privileged in Bethnal Green in London's East End.

Naturally we were all eager that Wyndham should remain in Palestine as long as possible, if not as High Commissioner, then at least for a second term as Civil Secretary. But he resisted all persuasion: he said he had a duty to perform for his own people. It was then that the idea of returning home and working among the poor in the slums of London began to form in his mind. We often spoke of his mission during the long hours he spent with us at Addison Crescent. He felt that this was his true calling. He also wanted to teach the people among whom he lived and worked the highest principles of integrity and moral values, to raise their civic pride and patriotism, to infuse them with the belief that, materially poor as they were, they were rich in being individually part of a great Empire. He worked selflessly and incessantly, without any thought for his physical welfare or strength.

Our conversations also constantly touched on the future of Palestine. He believed profoundly in the Jewish people, in its moral heritage, in the Bible, and the new Word which he was certain would one day come forth again from Zion, the Jewish State.

Frugal in his material wants, but generous to a fault in his spiritual gifts, completely devoid of self-interest, deeply attached to the welfare of his fellow-men, consecrated to his ideals of service and human betterment all his life, Wyndham Deedes was a saintly personality such as we find but seldom in a generation. He was not too well known beyond his own orbit and the circle of those who loved him; but although he never attained, because he never sought, the level of renown reached by the historic figures under whom he served as soldier and administrator, and later as social worker, he had no less the attributes of greatness by which great men are remembered. Wyndham Deedes died on 2 September 1956, and these are some of the reflections I set down at that time.

*

One of the most significant things that happened to Chaim on his 1918 mission was his meeting with the Emir Feisal, friend of T. E. Lawrence and one of the most powerful Arab rulers of his day. Because the Turks were still in control of the Jordan Valley, Chaim had to go to Suez and pick up a boat there instead of making the relatively short road journey which would have taken him to Amman in four hours. Major Ormsby-Gore, who travelled with my husband, was unfortunately taken ill with dysentery and had to be left behind in hospital at Suez while Chaim and another British officer and their Arab guide travelled to the Emir's encampment. The journey took Chaim and his companions some eleven days, but he found these travels through the deep desert spaces and rocks of the Bible country a fascinating experience.

He told me that after his friendly meeting with Feisal, who seemed anxious to establish a basis for Arab-Jewish co-operation,[29] Chaim took a stroll at twilight. His mind traversed three millennia in a second: 'Here', he thought to himself, 'three thousand years ago stood our great leader and ancestor Moses. Here he saw the Promised Land which he never himself reached. . . .' Lost in his dreams, he suddenly heard the gruff voice of a British sentry, 'Sorry, sir, I'm afraid you're out of bounds'.

Chaim also met Colonel T. E. Lawrence, later to become famous as 'Lawrence of Arabia'; he found Lawrence's alleged anti-Zionism to be untrue. In fact Lawrence, like Emir Feisal, thought that 'the Jews would be of great help to the Arabs, and that the Arab world stood to gain much from a Jewish Homeland in Palestine'.[30] I met Lawrence on one occasion. I cannot remember the exact year. He had come to dine with us; Herbert Samuel and, I think, another soldier were present. I listened to the conversation attentively, taking no part in it. Suddenly Lawrence said, 'The Jews in Palestine are all pro-German. . . .'

I was taken aback, and could not restrain myself from asking him what made him think so. 'They all speak German', he answered. 'Do you speak Hebrew?' I asked. He admitted that he did not. Then I explained, 'Some of the Palestinian Jews speak Yiddish, which is a mixture of German and Hebrew'. But by then all hope of Arab-Jewish accord had receded when the Hashimite dynasty, to which Emir Feisal belonged, was forced out of Syria and later out of Iraq. Arab 'unity' itself became a fiction, although Chaim never ceased to hope that time would heal Arab-Jewish differences, and to that end he always made contact with Arab leaders, Moslem and Christian, whenever he could.

*

On my husband's return to England after eight months in Palestine, one of the first things he said to me was, 'Verotchka, I can't serve two mistresses—Science and Zionism. Which shall it be?' While I pondered, my brilliant but naïve husband went on, 'After a year or so, I shall return to Science. The American Jews have the money: the Russian Jews need the land. The American Jews will buy the boats and transfer the Russian Jews to Palestine'. But American Jews did not react sufficiently to this idea, and after the Bolshevik Revolution the gates of Russia were closed against Jewish emigrants who wanted to reach Palestine. And it was not until 1931, when he was turned out of the presidency of the World Zionist Organization, that Chaim was able to return to his beloved science. Science, of course, did not wait for him, and he used to sit cross-legged on the floor, like a schoolboy, surrounded by the latest scientific books which he read endlessly in his efforts to catch up with the latest advances. My younger son Michael, who studied science at Cambridge, used to help his father a great deal.

When Chaim returned home in October 1918, he rang up Philip Kerr to ask if he could make an appointment for him with the Prime Minister, to whom he wished to give a first-hand report of the findings of the Zionist Commission. A luncheon appointment was arranged for 11 November—without anyone being able to foresee that this would be Armistice Day. When the news was announced, Chaim naturally assumed that his appointment with Lloyd George would be cancelled. He telephoned Philip Kerr, and Kerr said, 'Wait a minute, I shall enquire'. He soon returned to the telephone to say that Chaim was expected.

Chaim sallied out in a taxi through the swarming, rejoicing Armistice Day crowds. It took him two hours to reach Downing Street in which hundreds of people had gathered, and with the greatest difficulty he attracted the attention of a constable and asked to be let through. The surprised policeman asked—why? Chaim told him he was lunching with the Prime Minister. 'So several other people have already informed me', said the man. Perplexed, Chaim produced his visiting-card and said, 'Please show this to the constable at the door of 10 Downing Street; he knows me well'. To the great surprise of the crowd, Chaim was taken into the Prime Minister's residence.

Chaim has related how he found the Prime Minister reading the Psalms and moved nearly to tears. The first thing Lloyd George said to Chaim was, 'We have just sent off seven trains full of bread and other essential food, to be distributed by Plumer in Cologne'.[31]

When Lloyd George came to publish his *War Memoirs* in the 1930s, he said, 'Dr. Weizmann with his discovery [of acetone] not only helped us to win the war, but made a permanent mark upon the map of the world'. My husband commented that Lloyd George's narrative

makes it appear that the Balfour Declaration was a reward given me by the Government when Lloyd George became Prime Minister, for my services to England. I almost wish that it had been as simple as that, and that I had never known the heartbreaks, the drudgery and the uncertainties which preceded the Declaration. But history does not deal in Aladdin's lamps.[32]

Since we are on the subject of 'rewards', it may also be interesting to mention that when Herbert Samuel, Chaim, and I were once travelling together by taxi, Samuel let drop the remark that the British Government would like to offer Chaim a knighthood for his services during the war. It was the last thing my husband expected. 'It does not mean anything to me', he replied, 'unless I get the title for services I rendered the Jewish people. . . .'

It seems likely that the idea of offering Chaim a knighthood had met with objections in some quarters. What would, however, have made Chaim very happy would have been recognition of his scientific work by his being chosen a Fellow of the Royal Society; but that never happened. Chaim was not disturbed by such 'reverses', since he never sought for honours in his service to his people which he found reward enough in itself.

*

My first visit to Palestine was made in the autumn of 1919 and lasted little more than a month. We had wasted ten full days in Marseilles waiting for a boat to take us to Palestine. We arrived at Kantara and went on from there to Jerusalem, where we stayed for a few days with the Eders. Like Chaim, I became very fond of Dr. David Eder, who did great service for the Zionist cause in those early days in Palestine. Edith Eder was a very capable woman, but also very abrupt. Once when she and Mrs. George Halpern were having tea with me, our conversation turned to literature. She was particularly taken with a book by D. H. Lawrence. When I begged to disagree with her praise, Mrs. Eder rounded on me and exclaimed, 'I am a literary woman and you are not!' I smiled ironically, and said, 'I wouldn't go as far as that'.

My visit to Palestine, to which I had looked forward so much, was an abysmal disappointment. The country was desolate and all the trees were grey with dust: there had been no rain for five months, and the heat was unbearable. I could not imagine that I should ever be able to settle in such a country. We travelled a great deal, and the roads were so bad that the life was nearly shaken out of you. On one occasion it rained so hard that water seeped through the back of the little car in which we were travelling and poured down my neck. When we returned to our rooms, we had to undress and sit by a small oil-stove to dry and warm ourselves: conditions in Palestine in 1919 were very primitive indeed!

Mrs. Eder, Mrs. Sieff, and I, as we toured the country, were very impressed by the hard work done in rebuilding Palestine by the devoted *Halutzot*, a new name at that time for our pioneering working-women. But we were no less perturbed, even appalled, by the arduous physical conditions of their lives. Eager and energetic and praise-worthy as they were, they misinterpreted the concept of 'equality' between men and women. We thought these enthusiastic, idealistic women were mortgaging their future motherhood and even risking their health for this principle of equality: they were working ten or twelve hours a day breaking rocks and stones for road-making and mending, carrying heavy loads, performing superhuman tasks. Their bare, simple homes were neglected; their cooking was haphazard at best, and the results of their culinary efforts anything but satisfying; dietary standards were neither known nor even considered. They and their menfolk snatched whatever food they could lay hands on, and often this amounted to little more than bread and cheese, some onions, a glass of tea. Butter was scarce and regarded as a luxury. Meat and fish were generally out of reach of their modest means. They lived a stark existence.

Pre-natal care had not been heard of and the fate of unborn generations was left to chance. Even the most elementary essentials were lacking. Only one central purpose guided them: building, building, building! Nothing else mattered except the future of the new Jewish society.

Before leaving the country in mid-November, I decided to make some graceful return to those who had shown us frugal but cordial hospitality, and I sent them a few flowers. In those days flowers were virtually non-existent, and I had the greatest difficulty in buying any. Who could think of flowers when more urgent matters demanded attention? Bread, housing, trees, roads: these were the staples of a renascent nation.

Coming as the three of us did from so highly developed a civilization as England's, it was not easy for us to adjust our outlook to those rugged physical conditions and the whole situation worried us a great deal until it dawned on us that something drastic had to be done. On our return home, therefore, we decided to form a women's organization, the purpose of which would be to fill the gaps and shortages which had faced us so disturbingly when we were in Palestine.

Thus it came about that in 1920 we three—Mrs. Eder, Mrs. Sieff, and I—enlisted the help of Mrs. Romana Goodman and, later, Mrs. Olga Alman, both of whom were active in the English Zionist Federation, and proceeded to work out our plans. I was commissioned by this small committee to approach an elderly lady who was, at that time, a most enthusiastic social worker in the East End of London. As I was trying unsuccessfully to persuade her to join forces with us, and she was apologetically pleading the weight of her years and the pressure of other commitments to excuse her refusal of our invitation, a charming woman entered the room and was introduced to me as Mrs. Henrietta Irwell.

She listened to the conversation, and suddenly exclaimed, 'Mrs. Weizmann, if you wish me to join your organization, you'd better ask me now, or it will be too late!' I was only too delighted to ask her to join us. Henrietta Irwell proved to be a person of unique qualities, abilities, tact, and ardour, and she worked in any capacity required of her right up to the last days of her life.

Thus was our small initial band of six women formed. The first international meeting of Zionist women's groups in Europe took place in London in July 1920, at the time of the first post-war Zionist Conference. The first steps were taken at this gathering towards the establishment of W.I.Z.O. (Women's International Zionist Organization). Having had some experience, as a medical officer of health, in infant and pre-natal care in Manchester, I read a paper to the women's conference on this subject, an understanding of which was essential in such a primitive land as Palestine was at this time. As a result a home for infants and a domestic science school at Tel Aviv were among the first projects created and supported by W.I.Z.O.

Although we met with a good deal of opposition from men Zionists who were afraid of losing the women members of their Federations to W.I.Z.O., our organization made great strides from the early 1920s onwards. During this period, when the able and dedicated women of the executive committee in London were extending W.I.Z.O.'s scope and enlarging its membership by correspondence, I was fortunate enough to travel with my husband on his Zionist mission to various countries. While he was active in political Zionism and in fund-raising, I had the opportunity to make personal contact with the women in the lands we visited, and was thus able in the course of these visits to sponsor the creation of W.I.Z.O. groups in Canada, France, Egypt, Portugal, Italy, and South Africa.

In 1921 my husband and I, accompanied by Albert Einstein, went to the United States. From the U.S.A. we journeyed to Canada, where I found an excellent women's organization in existence. But for reasons of its own, it had recently seceded from the *Hadassah*, the American Women's Zionist organization. Each of the Canadian Zionist bodies—the Zionist Organization, *Keren Hayesod* (Palestine foundation fund), and *Keren Kayemeth*—was eager to benefit from the services of this unattached women's group and to bring its members into its own ranks.

It occurred to me that I might take the opportunity of explaining to the Canadian women the essence and urgency of the work of W.I.Z.O. and of convincing them that their destiny lay in our fold. I spoke at many meetings of the purpose and objectives of W.I.Z.O. in the creation of a Jewish national homeland in Palestine. In the end I succeeded in winning them over, and the Canadian women joined W.I.Z.O. They later made themselves responsible for the wonderful project of the agricultural and domestic science school at Nahalal. Thus W.I.Z.O. became a great force, and created many progressive welfare institutions in Palestine, and later in Israel.

Some little while after W.I.Z.O. was founded, a group of intelligent and enlightened women in Palestine formed the *Histadruth Nashim Zioniot* (Organization of Women Zionists) which later joined forces with the world body. Mrs. Hadassah Samuel, daughter-in-law of Herbert Samuel, was elected chairman, and under her competent leadership the Palestine group carried out admirably the programme adopted by W.I.Z.O. at its annual conference. Hadassah Samuel, attractive, capable, intelligent, and successful in her work, was a great friend of mine for almost half a century.

I myself was a member of the world executive committee for two decades, from 1920 to 1940. During that time Mrs. Rebecca D. Sieff and I were joint-chairmen, serving alternate years. For some months before I was compelled by pressure of work and other reasons to resign in 1940 from W.I.Z.O., I was joint president of that body with the 1st Viscountess Samuel. Thereafter I devoted myself to Youth Aliyah (rescue and rehabilitation of children and youth organization), of which I became president. When we moved to Palestine, my place in Youth Aliyah was, incidentally, taken over by Lorna Wingate. When she re-married, Lady Wolfson took her place with great success, initiative, and dignity.

Looking back over some forty-five years, I think we have every reason to congratulate ourselves on taking the step in 1919-1920 that led to the inception of W.I.Z.O. If its welfare work has not outrivalled the welfare systems in most European countries, it has certainly equalled them—an achievement of which we can be proud. More than that, W.I.Z.O. has assumed a place and a meaning in Jewish life the world over. It has created social values and established standards which are indispensable for our Jewish existence.

Although the W.I.Z.O. project occupied most of my mental energies in Palestine in 1919, I realized very soon that my visit would have to be cut short: our lease of 67 Addison Road was running out, so I decided to return home and begin house-hunting. I was not altogether sorry, I must admit, to leave Palestine at this time. The howling of jackals at night frankly terrified me. I was also beginning to miss my two children, our friends, and the sight of plants and flowers and the song of birds. In treeless Palestine there was hardly a bird: there was nowhere for them to perch. Today in my garden in Rehovoth, and indeed throughout the country, there are many hundreds of birds of many species—a sure sign of agricultural progress and of irrigation.

To find a suitable house in post-war London was not easy. There had been no building during the war. Edwardian or Victorian mansions of six or seven floors were to be had, but these I could not and would not take. At last I found a house in Addison Crescent which filled our needs. I put down a deposit of four hundred pounds: but where was I to get the rest of the money? My husband was at the peace conference in Paris; so I asked my bank manager if he could arrange a mortgage on the house, to be told that they mortgaged only businesses. So I wrote to Chaim, asking him what we should do. He must get the money from somewhere. Here was a man fighting for a Jewish homeland—without a home of his own, and with no one to give him a mortgage. So Chaim sent Simon Marks, his political secretary, to London. He arranged with someone he knew in Manchester to provide us with a mortgage. When Chaim returned from the peace conference, I had re-decorated the house and put in central heating.

I do not propose to write about the Paris Peace Conference or my husband's part in it—he has written his own account of what happened.[33] But one episode which he recounted to me stays in my memory. To his intense surprise, Baron Edmond de Rothschild, whom he knew to be a good Zionist, had nominated Professor Sylvain Lévi as one of the Jewish representatives at the peace conference. Lévi's lukewarm, even hostile, attitude towards Zionism had been clearly apparent when he was serving as a member of the Zionist Commission in Palestine early in 1918, and at the peace conference he excelled himself in creating as many obstacles as possible. The spectacle of Jewish representatives arguing among themselves would not be particularly edifying, thought Chaim. So when the American Secretary of State, Mr. Lansing, to save the situation, asked Chaim to define what he meant by 'a Jewish national homeland', my husband replied, 'I think Palestine should be as Jewish as England is English, France is French, and America is American'. At the close of this session, Balfour sent his secretary to congratulate Chaim: but when Lévi came up to Chaim and held out his hand, my husband refused to shake it.

★

At the time of my second visit to Palestine in 1925, Balfour, no longer in office, was asked to preside at the opening of the Hebrew University in Jerusalem. Chaim and I were invited to travel with his party, which included Edward Lascelles, Balfour's former secretary, and his wife, a niece of Balfour's. I was rather nervous at the thought of travelling with such a great personality as Balfour; but he had the gift of putting one at ease within a few minutes. He took an interest in the person he was with and, after a few questions, made you feel important. He was a very good-looking man, over six feet tall, with grey hair, and deep, absent eyes full of thoughts. Occasionally, he could be very exact. 'Baffy', another of his nieces, our good friend Blanche Dugdale, once told me that during an excursion in a garden she said she had seen some birds. Balfour turned to her sharply and said, 'You should name those birds. Who are you—Baffy or a girl?'

Balfour, who was not a good sailor, joined our boat at Naples, whilst Chaim, myself, Benjy, and Professor William Rappard, the permanent secretary of the Mandate Commission, had boarded it at Genoa. I remember that on his way to the boat Balfour lost his gloves and walking-stick. As his circulation was poor, he invariably wore fur-lined gloves. We asked his valet to describe these gloves to us and got him a new pair, together with a walking-stick, all of which we placed in Balfour's cabin, without his knowledge. After his death Mrs. Lascelles returned the walking-stick to us as a memento. It has its permanent place in the building at Rehovoth holding the Weizmann Archives.

Balfour and Mr. and Mrs. Lascelles were having lunch in the hotel in Naples and invited Chaim and me to join them. Mrs. Lascelles took an instant dislike to me. Not only were Chaim and I the only Jews she had ever met, but she was greatly put out because I was wearing a Molyneux suit exactly like one in her possession which she was, therefore, prevented from wearing! We gave Balfour the best cabin, my husband and myself took the second best, which left the third best for Mrs. Lascelles and her husband. She immediately objected, and I was on the point of yielding our cabin to her, but Chaim would not allow this.

The first evening on board ship we were invited to dine with Balfour. Professor Rappard, in the course of conversation, said that a certain member of the League of Nations, when asked if he had met Dr. Weizmann, had answered, 'I would not dream of it! He is a charmer and I fear may convert me to his point of view!' Balfour went quite red as he said indignantly, 'What's the name of the scoundrel? He has no business to sit on the League of Nations!'

We had another clash with Mrs. Lascelles soon after we arrived at Kantara. The High Commissioner, Herbert Samuel, came out to meet Balfour: Balfour went off in his car, Chaim and I in another, and Mr. and Mrs. Lascelles in a third. Mrs. Lascelles objected to the car which they had been allotted, so I promptly suggested that they should take our car. Mrs. Lascelles graciously accepted my offer; but I kept her at arm's length thereafter. When she complained to Chaim about my apparent coldness, he said, 'Are you surprised? You have treated my wife very badly although she has tried to give way to you on every occasion'.

Later, Mrs. Lascelles and I became firm friends, which, I think, proves how impermanent such trifling irritations can be. Apart from being a great lover of hunting, Mrs. Lascelles was an omnivorous reader and I frequently lent her books.

The formal opening of the Hebrew University on Mount Scopus took place on April Fool's day—1 April 1925; but the creation of the University was far from being an act of folly, although it brought its toll of headaches and worries. Chaim's dream of almost three decades had taken physical shape. Arthur James Balfour, General Allenby, Professor Rappard, Nahum Sokolow, and hundreds of civic and university dignitaries, dressed in their picturesque, colourful academic gowns arrived in Jerusalem to be present on this unique occasion. A picture of the event was painted by the Jewish artist Leopold Pilichowski.

At a big party which followed the opening, I turned to General Allenby and asked, 'Did you think my husband completely harebrained when he asked your permission for the laying of the foundation stones in 1918?' Allenby was thoughtful for a moment. 'No, Mrs. Weizmann. When I think back to that day—as I often do—I come to the conclusion that the short ceremony inspired my army, and gave them confidence in the future'.[34]

But the last word or two should belong to Balfour. During the opening ceremony, over which Chaim presided, there were too many speeches as usual. Balfour himself made a moving address which was translated into Hebrew by Rabbi Abraham Isaac Kook. Somehow, the translation proved surprisingly long. Balfour, with his inimitably subtle sarcasm, remarked to Chaim, 'I always thought the Hebrew language was concise!'

On our return to London, Chaim attempted to apologize for an incident which had occurred in Beirut when some Arabs made a rowdy demonstration, for which, of course, my husband was not responsible. Balfour smiled and said to Chaim, 'Oh, I wouldn't worry about that—nothing compared with what I went through in Ireland!'[35]

Palestine had, in fact, taken the place of Ireland as the major trouble spot in the vast British dominions.

8

The Troublesome Decade

THREE main problems dominated the troublesome decade 1921-1931: our relations with Britain, the Mandatory Power in Palestine; the growing conflict with Arab Nationalism; and our own internal divisions. The problems were obviously interconnected, and they rested on an uneasy triangle of immigration, land for development, and—that root of all evils and blessings—money. The Zionist organizations had made little provision for land purchase: it had been assumed that the Mandatory power would place land owned by the Government at the disposal of immigrants. But such dreams were soon shattered: as Chaim wrote in his autobiography, 'We found we had to cover the soil of Palestine with Jewish gold. And that gold, for many, many years, came out of the pockets, not of the Jewish millionaires, but of the poor'.[36]

The story of the growth of the two funds—the *Keren Hayesod* and the *Keren Kayemeth*—makes fascinating reading. In human terms, both Chaim and I knew what the farmers representing a 'homeland' of about eighty thousand souls were enduring in that hungry period. We had seen them subsisting on potatoes, and on tomatoes when these were the only staple crop. Chaim was often cast down. When asked if they had enough to eat, they answered, 'Dr. Weizmann, that's not your business; leave it to us. You go to the United States and get us the funds to expand, to improve, and to become self-supporting'. The dignity, courage, and pathetic self-sufficiency of these men and women was deeply moving.

We made our first trip to the United States in April 1921: but before I describe it, let me go back in my narrative. I returned from Palestine to London in the autumn of 1919; Chaim followed some two months later, in January 1920, but was again drawn back to Palestine. He and Benjy, now twelve years old, planned to spend Passover with Chaim's mother in Haifa that same March. Before setting out, tragic news of the first Arab pogrom reached Chaim. On 1 March two Jewish settlements, at Metullah and Tel Hai in the northern part of the country, were almost entirely destroyed, with the loss of seven defenders, among them that devoted Zionist and fine soldier, Captain Joseph Trumpeldor. A month later, on the eve of Passover, when Chaim and Benjy were already in Palestine, six Jews were killed in the Holy City, and our old friend Vladimir Jabotinsky, now a captain, who came out with a small body of youths to defend the Jewish quarter, was promptly arrested by the British military authorities. A savage and totally inexplicable sentence of fifteen years' hard labour was passed by a military court on Jabo. It was some consolation that Jabo was amnestied a few months later when Herbert Samuel came out as the first British High Commissioner of Mandated Palestine. Jabo—the leading spirit of the Zion Mule Corps and the Jewish Legion which had fought so gallantly on Britain's side during the First World War—never entirely forgot or forgave the insult of that sentence and refused to accept the amnesty as it included also Aref el Aref, the chief instigator of the riots, Amin el Husseini (later Grand Mufti of Jerusalem), and several others. Instead Jabo appealed against the sentence, which was duly quashed.[37]

★

It seemed that the soil of Palestine would have to be covered not only with Jewish gold, but also with Jewish blood, as well as the blood of the Arabs, whom Emir Feisal had, in 1918, called cousins by race of the Jews.

April 1920 found Chaim at San Remo, where leading French and British politicians were playing with the fate of Palestine as if it were a diplomatic game. A letter my husband wrote to Wyndham Deedes on 20 October contained the passage:

> We are not particularly happy about the Mandate. It has been altered again, not in our favour. So much water has been poured into the wine that I am quite sure there will be great disappointment when the Mandate is published. . . .

Although the British had won from the French the recognition of Britain's paramount interest in Palestine, they too had to make many concessions, and Chaim's letter continued,

> If we could say that we begin colonization on a fairly extensive scale in the new area, be it round Gaza or Rafa or Beersheba, that would put us in a position to go out to the people and to demand from them a great effort. . . .

I cannot help repeating what I have already said in my letter and what I consider to be the *crux* of the situation at present. Give us 'sand' and we shall be quite all right. With sand in my pocket, I would go to America and I am sure we would find a good deal of money.

My husband was referring to the sand of the Negev, and this, I think, was the very first occasion when the Negev was mentioned as an objective of practical Zionist effort. Chaim's offer to transform the sand of the Negev into gold was certainly no idle one, nor indeed was Chaim's effort in the final stages of the drama when, more than twenty years later, he obtained the Negev, through President Truman, as part of the young State of Israel.

But as yet Chaim had little 'sand' in his pocket to distribute among the pathetic contingent of some five thousand five hundred Jewish immigrants who came to Palestine in 1920.[38]

*

Other troubles soon loomed on the horizon at the first post-war Zionist Conference held in London in July that year, and the Congresses which followed at Karlsbad in 1921 and 1923.

Apart from the jealousies and rivalries which exist in any political organization, the London conference brought a rift in the ranks of American Zionism which affected the entire body politic of World Zionism. The chief protagonists were—as every student of this period will know—Chaim and his American supporters headed by our friend Louis Lipsky, and the 'Brandeis group' led by Justice Brandeis. Despite their mutual admiration for each other, the differences between Chaim and Brandeis were too fundamental to disguise. It rested on their interpretation on how the Jewish National Home should be built. Chaim was for public enterprises as represented by the Keren Hayesod and the Jewish National Fund, whereas Brandeis and his group supported what they called private initiative. In other words, Brandeis believed that Palestine should be built up on the basis of private capital rather than public funds. The other main issue was the question of federalism. Brandeis was in favour of a federal system of the Zionist Organization, based on the concept of 'States' Rights'. Each country's Zionist Organization would be sovereign and independent, and not subject to the Zionist Congress. If this view had prevailed, it would have meant for all practical purposes, the dissolution of the World Zionist Congress.

I recall a particular episode which illustrates some of the particular bitterness which divided the pro-Weizmann and pro-Brandeis groups at this time. When Justice Brandeis complained that Palestine was full of malaria, and therefore it would be wrong to encourage immigration into Palestine until malaria had been eliminated, our much admired friend and magnificent orator, Schmarya Levin, burst out ironically, 'So you mean, Justice Brandeis, that the first immigrant should be allowed into Palestine only when the last mosquito has left it?' Attempts to heal the breach between the Brandeis minority and the pro-Weizmann majority failed. At the London conference, an attempt was made to cement unity by electing Brandeis as honorary president of the World Zionist Organization, while Chaim became its president, and Nahum Sokolow the chairman of its Executive.

In one of Chaim's first statements as president of the World Zionist Organization, he said in Jerusalem in January 1921, 'A state cannot be created by decree, but by the forces of a people and in the course of generations. Even if all the governments of the world gave us a country, it would be only a gift of words. But if the Jewish people will go and build Palestine, the State of Israel will become a reality'. Yet despite these words, there were people at the Thirteenth Zionist Congress at Karlsbad in 1923 who believed that a Jewish State was already in existence! There were others—may I be forgiven—who were rather jealous that one man from the little village of Motol should have secured the Balfour Declaration. The Polish Jews in particular felt like this since they would have preferred Nahum Sokolow, the father of the Hebrew press, to have been the initiator of the Declaration. To smooth over their ruffled feelings, Schmarya Levin, who was never lost for words, told the story of two Jews who were arguing as to which was more important—the sun or the moon. At length they decided that the moon was more important: the sun gives light in the day-time, when it is light anyhow, whereas the moon gives light when it is dark!

*

But to return to our first trip to America in April 1921. Chaim took Leonard Stein with him. I shall never forget Leonard Stein's unparalleled devotion, his wisdom, sincerity, and serenity. Not that there were no disagreements between him and Chaim. There was, for instance, a serious difference of opinion over the Brandeis attitude.

Chaim lost his temper and said, 'Leonard, I take political decisions here. . . .'

After my husband's defeat over the Passfield White Paper Leonard Stein went into private practice. He also accompanied Chaim, as his political adviser, to the Peel Commission in 1936. He deserves a great tribute on all these scores. He is the author of a successful book on the Balfour Declaration, and a distinguished lawyer.

Our voyage to America—the first of innumerable journeys Chaim made across the Atlantic Ocean as 'the commercial traveller of the Jewish people' (as I used to call him)—was spent in the delightful company of friends, among whom were Professor Einstein and his wife, whom we met at the Hook of Holland whence we travelled together. Einstein was young, gay, and flirtatious. His wife, I recall, told me that she did not mind her husband's flirting with me as 'intellectual women did not attract him; out of pity he was attracted to women who did physical work'.

Our immediate impression of the reception awaiting us in America was far from heartening. Very few of the 'notables' were there to greet us; but thousands of Jews from Brooklyn and the Bronx came on foot to the harbour to welcome us, and we stayed there for a few hours until Shabbath was over.

Chaim, Einstein, and I travelled through America like a gipsy caravan. Einstein's job was to speak on the future of the Hebrew University.

While we were staying in Boston my husband had to go to another town to address a meeting, and Professor Einstein and I spoke to a *Hadassah* Women's meeting in Boston. His English was very poor, but he made the best of it. To be really truthful, we were both fed up with meetings, speeches, and crowds. He turned to me and said, 'Let's run away, somewhere we don't have to see anyone'. He suggested taking a taxi and driving out of town, so that we could go for a long walk. It was a lovely sunny day and we both enjoyed being relaxed for once. As we walked, from time to time something dropped out of Professor Einstein's hand, making a tinny sound, to be picked up again and again by him. Curious, I asked the Professor what it was. Whimsically, he answered, 'Oh, it's a secret. My wife wasn't well when we left New York, so I came away without any luggage except a tooth-brush and a tin of tooth-powder'. And that explained the tinny noise! I never thought a great genius could be so childish!

During this visit of ours to the United States, I received a most charming tribute from him; a signed photograph on which he had written in German: 'To our witty queen, in friendship and unbounded respect. Einstein'.

Einstein had neither pomposity nor self-importance. He had the great gift of being simple and direct, a quality which is often lacking in lesser men. I think that, without any prejudice on my part, it was this quality which Chaim shared with Einstein that drew them together. But Chaim knew how to harness this quality and use it judiciously as the following episode shows.

As the president of the World Zionist Organization, he had to have frequent and important dealings with the British Colonial Office, particularly when significant questions arose in connexion with immigration, the acquisition of land, and the establishment of relations, based on the Balfour Declaration, with the Palestine Administration. Chaim was prepared to support any fair and reasonable measures that the Palestine Administration undertook. Many of his colleagues saw no good at all in that Administration and blamed him for this. And some of his closest colleagues on the Zionist Executive often could not understand the need he felt to press home one or two major points and not to weaken the attack by bringing up too many points at one time. Some members of the Zionist Executive, for example, insisted on accompanying my husband on his visits to the Colonial Office; but Chaim knew only too well that he could express his displeasure with the Palestine Administration in the Colonial Office far more firmly and bravely if he was alone. On one occasion, he expostulated with Lord Moyne, saying, 'Your floor is littered with broken promises!' If Chaim had brought another Zionist with him to this interview, he could not have expressed his views in this manner.

It was in this moral and frank side of Chaim's work, in and out of Zionist Congresses, with British statesmen and administrators, that his wisdom and patience were most apparent. As he wrote, the opportunity for creative work in Palestine had been provided by the Churchill White Paper of 1922: it was up to the Jews—of Palestine and of the World—to find the means to accomplish this. 'Constructive criticism was needed: not belittlement of the terms of the White Paper, but indication of methods by which those terms could be taken advantage of in order to expand the Jewish Homeland.'[39]

I was a little surprised, therefore, when, returning home one afternoon to 16 Addison Crescent, I saw a newspaper placard announcing 'Mysterious Chaim . . .' I bought the newspaper—it was the *Daily*

Express of 28 October 1922—but could make neither head nor tail of who this mysterious Chaim could be, this Chaim who appointed and dismissed Governments, who decided on the destiny of nations and of political leaders—until I realized that this 'mysterious Chaim' was none other than my husband: I was both rather shocked and amused. When, a couple of hours later, someone on the Beaverbrook press telephoned to ask Chaim for an interview, he replied, 'What kind of interview can I give you? You seem to know everything'.

A sadder, and perhaps not altogether unexpected, development followed the issue of the 1922 White Paper. Like other members of the Zionist Executive, Jabotinsky signed the letter of acceptance; but some time afterwards he resigned from the Executive in protest over the document. Later Jabotinsky explained that he had signed the letter of acceptance under pressure because he thought that otherwise the Mandate would not be confirmed. Jabo also began to attack what he called my husband's 'Fabian' tactics and decried his lack of energy and enterprise. 'We have always to fight the Brtish Government', he declared.

Yet in August 1922, a month after the League of Nations ratified the British Mandate in Palestine, Jabo sent this lyrical letter to my husband, which I have translated from the Russian:

August 1922

Dear Friend,

I have re-read the Mandate very carefully; a colossal document and absolutely ineffaceable. Its failings you yourself know, but on the other hand there is nothing in it, not a single sentence which in a severe judicial analysis could exclude our most remote goal—even a Jewish State. This Mandate is almost an idealistically elastic receptacle for our energies. No matter how much we put into it, how much we fulfil, it will not burst. When I remember the beginning: Manchester and Justice Walk in London, and how all this was built up like children's toy bricks—and *sucked out of the thumb of one man*—I must say to you—and I flatter myself that I know a little of history—that this process is without parallel as a personal performance. You need neither congratulations nor compliments.

I wish you a good rest and embrace you warmly; also Vera Issayevna and the children if they are with you.

My family sends you its warmest regards and congratulations. Yours, V.J.

Criticisms continued to he heaped on Chaim's head from both the right-wing 'Revisionists' and the 'leftists'. Another resignation followed at the Thirteenth Zionist Congress at Karlsbad in August 1923. This time it was Menahem Ussishkin, the one-time leader of Russian Zionists, who used to call himself 'the man of iron'. When Chaim asked him what he would have done with regard to the 1922 White Paper, Ussishkin answered, 'Demand! Protest! Insist!' But my husband realized even then that in order to get the goodwill of the Government, Zionists had to hasten the work of development, while in order to hasten the work of development they desperately needed the active goodwill of the Government.[40] And in his address to the Thirteenth Congress, my husband put the issue squarely when he said,

> The political successes you would like to have must be created in the Emek*, in the swamps, and on the hillsides, and not in Downing Street. It is enough if your diplomatic representatives—if they are already entitled to that name— can hold their ground. . . .
>
> I have taken careful note of all the measures proposed here to influence the British Empire, . . . how demonstrations could be held in Warsaw or perhaps in New York. . . . but if you could have brought two hundred thousand Jews into the streets of Jerusalem, then you would not have asked me; you would have done it [i.e. organized the demonstration] yourselves.

This rapier-thrust was aimed directly at the heart of the problem: the immigration of Jews into Palestine for the year 1923 amounted, according to official Government figures, to 7,421 persons. A serious economic depression was also looming on the horizon. The need for money, for land, for jobs became an overwhelming preoccupation with my husband. In 1924, Chaim again went to the U.S.A. on a money-raising expedition. The famous banker Felix Warburg invited him, not to his house—that would have been too much of an honour—but to his office. As soon as they met, the banker plunged into the current gossip: that out of each dollar given for Palestine, ninety-nine cents remained in America and only one cent went to Palestine.

My husband kept silent while Mr Warburg reported more gossip of a similar kind. When he had at last exhausted this theme, my husband asked quietly, 'Mr. Warburg, supposing I were to tell you the sort of gossip that goes on about your Kuhn Loeb Bank—what would you have said?'

Mr. Warburg answered, 'I would have thrown you out of my office'.

---

* The Emek Jezreel lands, about twenty thousand acres, bought in 1920 from an Arab family named Sursuk: (*see Trial and Error*, pp. 316-317.)

'That's exactly what I feel like, but as I am in your office, I'm not in a position to do so', said my husband.

Felix Warburg, embarrassed, offered Chaim ten thousand dollars for Palestine.

My husband said, 'I won't accept it until you go to Palestine and see for yourself that of each dollar given, ten per cent remains in America and ninety per cent is used in Palestine. And when you are convinced of this let me know—and it will cost you much more than ten thousand dollars'.

Felix said he would go, and was as good as his word. He went with his family to Palestine and sent us a postcard: 'I have seen what is being done and I feel like throwing myself on the ground and kissing every inch of the soil'.

That was the beginning of a great and permanent friendship not only with Felix, but also with Freda, his beautiful and angelic wife, who never missed an opportunity of doing something useful. My husband liked beautiful women, but they had to have brains as well, which she had in abundance. Both Felix and Freda showed great interest in the establishment of the Hebrew University, to which they made sizable donations.

The year 1924 saw two developments affecting the history of the Jews. Hitler, the obscure Austrian corporal of the First World War, had come to the fore as a leader of anti-Semitism in Germany; his notorious book *Mein Kampf*, with its open invitation to an onslaught on the Jewish people, was written in 1924. Chaim, unlike many of his contemporaries, recognized this as a sign of the horrors to come, and repeatedly warned Jewish and non-Jewish friends of the possible developments.

In 1924 also appeared, in October, the first report of the League of Nations Mandates Commission, which—if it did not say so implicitly—criticized the Balfour Declaration and the British Mandate, and emphasized the 'inevitable clash' between Zionism and the Arab majority in Palestine. Chaim reacted spiritedly in a characteristic letter to Professor W. E. Rappard, secretary of the Permanent Mandates Commission, who showed a better grasp of the meaning and significance of Zionism than did its president, the Italian Count Theodoli. Chaim not only castigated the report for its omissions, but reminded the League that the White Paper of 1922 had made it clear that the Jews were in Palestine as of right and not on sufferance.*

* For text of Dr. Weizmann's letter to Professor Rappard, *see* Appendix, C, p. 279.

The next three years saw the deepening of the economic crisis in Palestine, with unemployment rising to six thousand persons in 1926. In the previous year, however, some thirty-three thousand Jewish immigrants had entered the country, the highest number to arrive in the 'troublesome decade', and by 1928 the Jewish population had increased over the 1922 figure by some eighty-three thousand. Much had been done to improve economic conditions in the country, with benefit not only to the settlers but also to the Arabs.

★

When his political activities permitted, Chaim took the children and me for annual holidays, and we spent many days rock climbing. When our younger boy Michael was only fourteen, we climbed to the top of the Jungfrau where an unforgettable view met us.

Four years earlier, Michael, then a child of ten, was staying with Benjy at Tiberias while Chaim and I had gone to spend a few weeks with my brother-in-law Ossinka in the south of France. I feel I must quote a letter Michael sent me at this time. It is dated 13 July 1926:

Dear Mumy,

I am 2nd in class with 75½ marks out of hundred. Waller was top with 76, so he beat me by only a half mark. I got 20 out of 20 for the oral Latin test; that is a good house mark.

I hope you are not lonely, never mind we shall soon be together again only about another fortnight. . . .

He signed his letter 'your beloved and important son' Michael. He was, indeed, both beloved and important. He also enclosed a delightful and well-executed drawing of the *Leonardo da Vinci*, the ship on which he and Benjy had travelled.

The second half of the Troublesome Decade saw frequent departures by Chaim from 'Oakwood', our London home, of which we had all become very fond. I had managed to establish a comfortable, smooth-running household which included not only Miss Usher, the children's 'nurse' who—although the children had now outgrown their baby-hood—remained with us for many years, and our splendid butler, Payne. The French statesman Léon Blum, when he visited us much later, always referred to Payne as the 'Admirable Crichton'. 'Do you know, when I go up to my room, my evening clothes are out on the bed, and when I go to bed, there are no clothes visible, and I never knew who did it!' Léon Blum remarked on one occasion. Payne was a wonderful servant; spoke with an 'Oxford' accent and adored music. I used to buy tickets for Albert Hall concerts for him. He stayed with us for fifteen years and married one of our housemaids. When we went to live in Palestine, Payne and his wife opened a little grocery shop. But whenever we came to England, he would come back to us for a few months, until we settled definitely in Palestine. Payne was very superior, but we were very friendly, although always at a certain distance, as you have to be with English people.

From Chaim on his travels came the usual abundant crop of beautiful letters. In one written to me in 1927 aboard ship—he was travelling yet again to the United States—he wrote that he had found comfort in a book on Jewish history. While the masses danced round the Golden Calf, there were a few who abstained and who were responsible for Jewish culture. He recalled that in Nehemiah's time too the rich stayed in Babylon, and only the poor came to Israel. At that time also we had enemies . . . 'But the Torah was saved and given to us'. But from New York he wrote, 'I am weary of the constant round of speeches, fund-raising and so on'. The inexorable wear-and-tear of political life was beginning to leave its mark on Chaim.

In 1929 the Jewish Agency was established, and Chaim recruited the services of a very able personal secretary, Miss May, a graduate of Oxford. Miss May, a devout Catholic, had been Leonard Stein's secretary for some time before coming over to the offices of the Agency at 77 Great Russell Street where she devoted her manifold talents to the work she did for Chaim. We all loved her dearly and appreciated her many fine qualities.

Chaim's political secretary at this time was the brilliant historian, Professor (later Sir) Lewis Namier. Of noble character, he had a sense of duty that knew no limits. But the political memoranda he prepared on my husband's instructions usually had to be returned to him two or three times for re-writing as, in the form he originally wrote them, they would have been unacceptable to the British Government.

On one such occasion the text was derogatory, so my husband said to him, 'We can't send such a thing to the Government. I didn't ask you to do that. I gave you the exact points of what I wanted to say'. Lewis protruded his lower lip and said, 'I worked the whole night on the thing. . . .' Next day, he brought another memorandum: this time it was libellous! Chaim took it and wanted to tear it up. Offended, annoyed, and disgraced, Lewis went home—and returned on the following day with a brilliant memorandum! Chaim was very fond of Namier; but Namier was not very popular with the Zionist Executive because of his intolerance towards them.

In August 1929, Chaim was far from well, and we went for a brief holiday to Wengen in the Bernese Oberland, where we were joined by Michael. Following a couple of peaceful, relaxed days, on 25 August Chaim received a lengthy telegram from an under-secretary at the Colonial Office, with news which stunned him: savage riots had broken out in Palestine, with the loss of numerous Jewish and Arab lives. One hundred and thirty three Jews had been murdered, some three hundred and thirty nine wounded in this first large-scale pogrom in Palestine, which cost the Arabs almost as many lives in fighting with British troops and police. Religious fanaticism had been the mainspring of this riot, which followed a pattern that was to be repeated again and again. The Holy Places of the world's three great religions were desecrated with the blood of the guilty and of the innocent.

All thought of holiday-making was forgotten and we hastened back to London. Chaim gave a full account of his meetings with leading Government personalities, including a particularly unsympathetic encounter with Lord Passfield—the former Sidney Webb—who was then Colonial Secretary in the Labour Government. That staunch humanitarian his wife observed to Chaim, 'I can't understand why the Jews make such as fuss over a few dozen of their people killed in Palestine. As many are killed every week in London in traffic accidents, and no one pays any attention,'[41] a remark that, a classic of its kind, remained engraved on our hearts. Ramsay MacDonald, the Prime Minister, despite the representations made by his son Malcolm, who was not, at this stage, unfriendly to our cause, declined to meet Chaim. But a flurry of commissions were sent out to Palestine to investigate and report. The first of these, the Shaw Commission, merely established the already known fact that the Arabs were the instigators, but made no recommendations as to how further outbreaks could be avoided. The second commission, under Sir John Hope Simpson, published its findings in October 1930, simultaneously with the publication of the Passfield White Paper. According to my diary, Chaim received a copy of the White Paper on Friday, 17 October, four days in advance of its official issue. Much as we had anticipated, Passfield recommended suspension of further Jewish immigration into Palestine, the introduction of restrictive land legislation, and the abrogation of the Jewish Agency's slender authority. On Sunday, 19 October, my husband sent a formal note to Lord Passfield, telling him of his resignation as president of the Jewish Agency: this was followed later by the resignation of Lord Melchett from the chairmanship of the Council of the Jewish Agency and of Felix Warburg from its Administrative Committee.

The stage was now set for the struggle over the Passfield White Paper. Of the many crises which faced us, this was one of the most serious, a bitter climax to the troublesome decade which we had lived through. Yet another climax followed close on its heels, the curt dismissal of Chaim Weizmann from the presidency of the World Zionist Organization at the 17th Congress in Basle, July 1931.

*

But meanwhile, early in March 1930, our good friend Arthur James Balfour had passed away. 'Baffy' Dugdale gives this account of Chaim's parting with his friend:

> A few days before the end he [Balfour] received for a few moments a visitor from outside the circle of his family. This was Dr. Chaim Weizmann, the Zionist leader. No one but myself saw the brief and silent farewell between these two, so diverse from one another, whose mutual sympathy had been so powerful an instrument in the history of a nation. . . . No words passed between them, or could pass, for Balfour was very weak and Dr. Weizmann much overcome. But I, who saw the look with which Balfour moved his hand and touched the bowed head of the other, have no doubt at all that he realized the nature of the emotion which for the first, and only, time showed itself in his sick-room.

> When great men die,
> A mighty name, and a bitter cry
> Rise up from a nation calling.[42]

Finally Balfour stretched out his hand to his night-table on which stood a vase of flowers, indicating that Chaim should take the flowers. That was their parting moment. I dried and preserved those flowers, and they now lie on a table in the Weizmann Archives at Rehovoth.

9

In the Wilderness

THE reports of commissions which investigated the cause of the riots in Palestine in 1929 came out like an avalanche. They created considerable agitation in Zionist circles and in the councils of Britain's Labour Government,* but, ironical as it may seem, they brought few positive results. It is something of a futile exercise—rather like writing on sand or water—to try to recapture the fever of those half-forgotten days. But the consequences of the Passfield White Paper had far-reaching results which affected Chaim, myself, and our children. We found ourselves, not entirely unexpectedly, in the midst of storms and upheavals, alternating with welcome periods in the doldrums.

My diaries throw some light on the events which followed and it is from these that I propose to quote. On Saturday, 18 October 1930, the day after Chaim received an advance copy of the Passfield White Paper, Harold Laski, a prominent member of the British Labour Party, rang up to say that he had received a call from America from Professor Felix Frankfurter, who suggested that he and Felix Warburg should come immediately to London to make representations against the White Paper.

When Laski turned up later that Saturday, he said, according to my diary, that Passfield 'was the only old civil servant in the Government and had the mentality of one'. The few survivors of the wartime coalition government which had brought about the Balfour Declaration immediately dissociated themselves from the ill-fated document which bore Passfield's name. In December 1929, not long before his death, Balfour, together with Lloyd George and General Smuts, had

---

* The Conservatives lost their majority in the General Election of May 1929, and Stanley Baldwin was succeeded as Prime Minister by Ramsay MacDonald whose administration included Lord Passfield (Sidney Webb) as Colonial Secretary and Arthur Henderson as Secretary of State for Foreign Affairs.

written a letter to *The Times** warning the Labour Government not to go against the major premise of the Balfour Declaration. The forces ranged against Passfield's well-known anti-Zionism were formidable and not exclusively drawn from the ranks of world Jewry.

My husband reported to me a remark made to him by Lord Passfield, a practical man and an economist, 'Dr. Weizmann, do you realize that there is not enough room to swing a cat in Palestine?'

By the time I came to set down these memoirs, some two million immigrants had been brought into Israel.

My friend Colonel Meinertzhagen provides an illuminating aside on his uncle, Lord Passfield: after he had seen him in London early in October 1929, he wrote:

> I had a long interview with Sidney Webb today at the Colonial Office. He seemed rather tired of Zionism, having been subjected to ceaseless bombardment of complaint and suggestion for the last few weeks. He told me what steps were being taken to enquire into the recent troubles. I tried to impress on him that the two essentials were, a friendly Administration and adequate security. Any commission of enquiry sent to Palestine could be only a sop to public opinion. We all know the causes of the trouble, we all know that the administration is not sympathetic to Zionism and we all know that the Jews have been denied security. Sidney promised he would do his best to remedy matters and appeared to realize the situation, but he struck me as being a tired man and particularly apathetic towards Zionism.[43]

This 'apathy' towards Zionism and a complete misunderstanding of its aims were written large all over the Passfield White Paper.

A copy of Chaim's letter of 19 October 1930 to Passfield was taken over by hand to the Prime Minister. Next day, Chaim telephoned to Passfield 'trying to postpone the publication of the White Paper, but Passfield said that nothing could be changed now'; and on the 21st the White Paper was officially published, together with the news of Chaim's resignation. At the same time Chaim received a letter from Ramsay MacDonald which showed that he had not as yet read the copy of Chaim's letter to Passfield which had been forwarded to him. Things now began to hum for the Government. On 22 October, Blanche Dugdale, who was closely associated with the Jewish Agency, rang up Leopold Amery and went to see him. She told him—according to my diary—that 'something must be done to dissociate the Conservatives from the White Paper. Amery agreed with her, but must consult Baldwin'. Blanche thereupon went to see Baldwin, who said, 'Now

* Published 20 December 1929.

wait, I think slowly'. Blanche replied, 'I know, but we can't waste time. Something must be done at once'. Baldwin then said that he wished to consult Austen Chamberlain. Blanche returned to Amery, and together they drafted a letter, protesting against the White Paper; it appeared the next day in the press.

Chaim also received a sympathetic letter from Mrs. Philip Snowden, wife of the Chancellor of the Exchequer. She told him that 'Passfield had definite instructions not to publish the White Paper without Chaim's acceptance'. On 23 October, Chaim went to see Lloyd George who told him that he would refer to the White Paper in a speech he proposed to make in the House of Commons shortly. Lloyd George had received a cable from General Smuts asking him to see Chaim. Smuts had also, it appears, sent a cable to Ramsay Mac-Donald castigating the White Paper as 'a betrayal'.

Our telephone line at 16 Addison Crescent was besieged by callers from all directions. Harold Laski telephoned to say that the Prime Minister had asked him to cable Justice Brandeis to calm American opinion, but Laski had refused. 'The P.M. had the shock of his life', I observed in my diary.

On 27 October, Chaim addressed a mass meeting in Whitechapel where he spoke bitingly and made no effort to spare the Government. Later, Major Marcus* came in. He had been to see the Prime Minister, who appeared to be very shaken and had said that 'Passfield and Chancellor† (the British Commissioner in Palestine) must resign'. According to Marcus, MacDonald had also said that he 'intends to write Chaim a public letter inviting him to negotiate. The P.M. says he will invite Marcus, Hopkins‡, a few of our parliamentary friends, and Passfield. They should attack Passfield in such a way that he should be compelled to resign'. This was a most extraordinary outburst for a Prime Minister to make about his Colonial Secretary; but Ramsay MacDonald was greatly taken aback at the reaction to the White Paper and was now trying to rid himself of the encumbrance of both the Paper and its author. A day previously Passfield had tried to safeguard himself by writing to Chaim, asserting that Chaim had been consulted before the White Paper had been drawn up.

On the 29th, Einstein dropped in. He was much amused 'at the

---

* Major Michael Marcus M.P.

† Sir John Chancellor, British High Commissioner in Palestine, 1928-1931. Ramsay MacDonald was obviously 'kite flying' in suggesting that Chancellor should resign.

‡ Daniel Hopkins, M.P.

O.R.T.* dinner, where, he says, people made the impression of a monkeys' assembly. They were mostly concerned over whom to shake hands with first—Lord Rothschild or Einstein himself'.

A letter of 31 October 1930 from the Prime Minister to Chaim suggested that Chaim should present any points he had to his son Malcolm, who was the secretary of the Cabinet Committee dealing with Palestine policy. Chaim lunched with Malcolm MacDonald and told him (my diary of 3 November) that the American Jews would not negotiate until the White Paper was withdrawn. 'Malcolm, who was very grieved, said he has told his father that he will vote against him' in the coming House of Commons debate: the split on the White Paper in the British Cabinet was widening to include members of the Prime Minister's own family. But there were also rumblings within the Zionist movement as my diary entry of 5 November shows:

> Not only Revisionists and Radicals but also some of the Centre and all the Polish delegates and some Mizrachist† are ready to accept Chaim's resignation. Speeches were made in the Actions Committee of the Zionist Organization accusing Chaim's policy of bringing about the White Paper. Chaim is very worried and says he won't accept a small majority in his favour.

To add to all these accusations and counter-accusations, Harold Laski telephoned on 5 November to say that he had seen Lord Passfield, who repeated that there had been no breach of faith, that immigration into Palestine had not been stopped, and that fifteen hundred certificates of immigration had been granted. He also made the novel statement that 'there is no embargo on land purchase' in Palestine, whereas this was precisely one of the bones of contention which had been laid bare by the White Paper!

The cumulative result of all this was that Chaim was invited to a lunch with Ramsay MacDonald at 10 Downing Street, on 6 November, at which Malcolm was also present. My husband did not deal with this event in his published autobiography and I feel there is some justification for quoting extensively from a report Chaim subsequently wrote and which I transcribed into my diary: after the passage of nearly forty years, its confidences will hardly appear world-shaking. This is the report, exactly as Chaim wrote it:

> The Prime Minister, who looked very tired, came in immediately after the conclusion of a Cabinet meeting. He complained that the world was very

* Organization for Reconstruction and Training of Jews in skilled trades and agriculture.
† Religious Zionist party.

difficult and that a great many of the difficulties would not have arisen had he been able to give time to the matters they represented. He was overworked and overwrought, and therefore could not himself attend to business.

Then the Prime Minister said, 'I shall tell you something in great confidence, which you are not to mention to anybody. When I read Lunn's* answer yesterday, which he gave in the House with regard to the Round Table Conference, I was infuriated and terrified; for it was not true, I gave repeated instructions to the Colonial Office—and they did not carry them out. What the instructions were, I need not tell you'.

He then passed on to the question of Palestine. He said the Cabinet have been considering this question this morning and have come to the conclusion they will appoint a Cabinet sub-committee which is to invite you and your friends (the Jewish leaders, those are the words he used) to consider the situation in Palestine.

At this stage Mr. Malcolm MacDonald remarked, 'Is it to consider the White Paper?' The P.M. replied, '*There is no White Paper*.'†

The Prime Minister went on to say, 'I understand there are errors in this White Paper'. I told him there were two groups of things: infringements of the Mandate; and interpretations which cause considerable difficulties and misgivings.

Malcolm said, 'There are about four infringements, and fifteen other points'; to which the Prime Minister replied, 'The errors have to be put right, and the misunderstandings to be cleared up; and any new statement which is to be issued is to be issued in agreement with you'.

I answered, 'In that case, Mr. Prime Minister, we can relieve you from discussing the details; but you know my position: I can give no answer. You know the attitude of our American friends, that they do not want even to enter upon negotiations as long as the White Paper stands'.

The Prime Minister remarked, 'We cannot simply withdraw the White Paper or be expected to do so'. I said nothing to that. I said I would communicate to my friends what he was good enough to say. I would also try to get in touch with America and would let him have an answer as soon as I could.

He said, 'Could you do it in twenty four hours?' I told him I would do my best.

He said he would issue a communiqué after having agreed upon a conference. It would naturally cause trouble among the Arabs, but the Administration in Palestine would have to look to that.

We then abandoned this subject altogether, and I said, 'Now, Mr. Prime Minister, even if an agreement is reached, it could never be carried into effect unless the Administration in Palestine is completely overhauled. To put it

* Dr William Lunn, M.P., Colonial Under-Secretary.
† My italics V. W.

vulgarly: this Administration has been sabotaging the thing for years. They have been preaching two pernicious doctrines: first, that if you do something good for the Jews it must necessarily be evil for the Arabs, which is not true. The other follows from it: it is that there exists an inherent conflict which can never be bridged over. They [the Administration] have been trying to lend colour to their doctrines by causing all sorts of difficulties'.

To this the Prime Minister said, 'I quite see what you mean, but you will permit me to listen to you and not give a reply'.

Then he went on to speak about Passfield. He said Passfield was old, in some ways very efficient, but that he had the mind of a German professor and an indestructible belief in the experts who sit in the Colonial Office. No imagination. To which I answered, 'You will permit me to listen to you and not give a reply'. Then he said, 'It should not be beyond human ken to find the proper people for Palestine'.

That concluded the interview exclusively on Palestine.

I told him there was one other thing I wanted to mention, which had something to do with the question of Moslems. With regard to the Indian Moslems here, a good deal of play has been made with them. I was quite sure they were not interested in the economics or in other problems of Palestine: their general interest lay in the Moslem Holy Places. No doubt they have been told that we have burnt down the Mosque of Omar and committed other acts of that kind.[44] If Irwin*, at the time this propaganda was spread, had issued a statement categorically denying what the Mufti had said, as he could have done, they would have believed him rather than the Mufti. That was not done. Since the P.M. would be in contact with them [the Indian Moslems], he could easily find an appropriate moment to say a word to them about it.—We shall try on our side to get in touch with them. He promised and said: 'Whenever you wish to meet the Indian Moslems, I could arrange it'. He thanked me very much for having come. I said I would be always ready to help.

One interesting point emerged from this luncheon with the Prime Minister which Chaim does not mention in his 'secret' report. According to my diary entry of 6 November, the day he met Ramsay MacDonald and Malcolm, the P.M. said,

'Balfour was always ambiguous in his statements; the Colonial Office always speaks of some secret documents in its possession about the Declaration'. Chaim answered, 'Arthur James Balfour was always clear about the Declaration in his public statements, although his original declaration was quite different from the final version'. He added, 'In any case the Cabinet took part in the formulation of it'.

* Edward Frederick Lindley Wood (1881-1959), created Lord Irwin 1925; Viceroy of India 1925-1931, 3rd Viscount Halifax 1934, 1st Earl of Halifax 1944.

Balfour's 'ambiguities' about the Declaration which carried his name belong to the many myths which surrounded this famous testament, to which talk of 'secret documents' in the possession of the British Colonial Office added fuel without providing much fire. I must leave it to historians to make what they can of it.

On 9 November, Chaim informed Malcolm MacDonald that the American Jews had agreed to a conference, and that Felix Frankfurter had been suggested as a representative; and Namier spent some time with Malcolm working on the text of the Prime Minister's letter which was to appear in the press. On 12 November, my husband saw Henderson, Secretary of State for Foreign Affairs. It was agreed between them that a communiqué should be issued to the press, after Henderson had cabled the Palestine Administration telling them 'that they will be held personally responsible for any trouble'. Later that evening Harold Laski called. He said that he had spoken to Lord Passfield and had told him bluntly that he was an obstacle and invited him to resign!

A week later Chaim went for a brief two-day visit to Paris, where he had a very interesting interview with Blum and De Jouvenel. 'They are very keen on Jewish colonization in southern Syria', I wrote in my diary (16 November). The French Government was prepared

> to put a large stretch of territory at the disposal of the Jews. There are only two thousand Arabs there. The French Government would approach the British Government offering this co-operation, in view of the difficulties they are faced with in Palestine.

The French had other than purely altruistic reasons in making this offer. They were anxious, as M. de Jouvenel told my husband, to encourage Jews to develop the sandy area in part of the Euphrates region—'the Jews were the only people who could develop Syria'; but Chaim considered that the idea 'had no practical value for us'.

On the day following my husband's return from Paris, a fierce debate took place in the House of Commons on the Passfield White Paper and the Government's policy in Palestine. The mood of the House was highly critical, and a large part of the Prime Minister's own party was opposed to the anti-Zionist attitude of the White Paper. From my diary, 17 November:

> Lloyd George was rather violent and not dignified. Herbert Samuel was excellent, but could not forget himself. Walter Elliot was wonderful and spoke on a very high level. The Government's defence was very poor. Certainly this was a Jewish day.

On 18 November, Chaim was invited to address the Cabinet Committee. According to Harold Laski, Chaim spoke very movingly, honestly and masterfully. On his return home, I found Chaim in a nervous state. The unremitting strain to which he had been subjected was beginning to tell and we again thought of refreshing ourselves by a visit to Palestine.

Chaim's labours over the autumn and winter months of 1930 came to a climax with a letter he received from Ramsay MacDonald, which the Prime Minister had read on the floor of the House of Commons on 13 February 1931: it effectively retracted the Passfield White Paper. There was not only a marked improvement in the attitude of the Palestine Administration towards Jewish aspirations, but Jewish immigration into the Holy Land rose from nine thousand odd in 1932, to the unprecedentedly high figure of some sixty-two thousand persons in 1935.[45] In addition, a highly capable and sympathetic administrator in the person of Sir Arthur Wauchope, the new British High Commissioner, replaced Sir John Chancellor. To show the sincerity of his good intentions, the Prime Minister went so far as to consult Chaim on the new High Commissioner's appointment. A notable victory had been won for common sense on both sides, and Arab disturbances abated under Sir Arthur Wauchope's administration, although they never entirely ceased. Chaim said of Wauchope, 'We remember him in Palestine as a friend, an intellectual, a soldier, an administrator and a statesman', a tribute to which I can add but little.

On 23 February 1931 we left for Egypt to visit our dear old friend Lola Hahn-Warburg *en route* for Palestine. It proved to be a leisurely and pleasant interlude which lasted some two weeks. It was a regular 'Cook's Tour' and took us on steamers up the Nile, with desert rides on donkeys, and sight-seeing excursions to Luxor with its magnificent temple and giant statues of Rameses II, to Thebes and the Valley of Kings, and to Karnak. My diary in this period was quite apolitical. We had given politics a rest, or so it seemed. In mid-March we arrived in Haifa and proceeded to visit our friends, rejoicing in the marked improvement in the living standards of the settlers. On our visit to Tel Mond, I was thrilled with the new orange groves, farms, and houses. And at the Bet Alfa kindergarten I was struck by the neat, healthy appearance of the children, and the plain, good food which was served to them. I also attended W.I.Z.O. functions and negotiated contracts for nurses and teachers. Towards the end of our stay in Palestine, Chaim and I were invited to lunch at Government House with the Earl of Athlone and Princess Alice. On 10 April, we returned home to London.

Although Chaim's health had shown some improvement, he was warned by his doctors to slow down the pace of his activities. But by this time preparations for the Seventeenth Zionist Congress were under way. It was to meet in Basle, a city of pleasant associations, reminding us as it did of our many holiday trips to Switzerland, our rock-climbing expeditions, and our earliest meeting in Geneva. And it was here in Basle that the first major rupture between Chaim and the World Zionist Organization took place.

The drama has often been told, but its pain lingered long in our memories, too painful it seems even to record in my diary. There had been warning signs in plenty—rumours, hidden disagreements, the inevitable clash of strong political personalities, to which harsh accusations were now added. Saddest of all, perhaps, was the violence and bitterness with which our old friend Jabo had now begun to attack Chaim. He and his Revisionists had been waiting patiently in the wings of history for an opportunity to subvert Chaim's patient policy of building from the foundations, brick by brick, and dunam by dunam. They also had old political scores to pay off, the remembrance of old hurts. Chaim, who had never been personally offensive to Jabo, was interrupted by him on some other occasion during a speech with a loud interjection, 'I said that ten years ago and you turned down my suggestion!' My husband replied, 'I will answer you with a true story. I had a cousin whose daughter was about to marry. As she and her fiancé stood under the bridal canopy, her little sister burst into tears. "I want to be under the canopy too", she sobbed. The mother quietly soothed the child, "In ten years time you will be under the canopy"'.

In July 1931 the full fury of the Revisionists and their allies, the Mizrachi group, fell on Chaim's head. He was told that he had committed an act of folly in accepting Ramsay MacDonald's letter earlier in February, instead of demanding a new White Paper. The Revisionists, in particular, clamoured for the maximum concession, that is to say, a Jewish State on both sides of the Jordan, with all the dangers which this implied. Chaim defended his policy with determination and vigour in a speech in the course of which he said, 'I have been unfortunately unable to descry in the speeches of the opposition any hint as to how the existing discrepancy between the possible and the desirable is to be removed'. And Chaim's last words to the Seventeenth Congress rang out like a bell when he declared:

We Jews have always had to suffer from being misunderstood. Zionism and its realization in Palestine is an attempt to remove this misunderstanding. It is perhaps one of our difficulties, and it would be naïve to believe that ten years of work suffice to overcome such obstacles.

I do not believe that Palestine can be obtained through a short-cut. What I believe is that we shall attain our National Home through hard, tedious work and deep suffering. We are all bound up together in strong faith in the Zionist idea and its realization. But deep faith in a cause is not manifested through heroic phrases but through the patience with which daily difficulties are met. In this spirit we must continue on our way without hesitation.

When the roll-call ballot was taken Congress passed, by a small majority, a vote of 'no confidence' in Chaim. Only the Labourites and the General Zionists supported him.

I was sitting in a box, fuming, while Chaim sat on the platform like a Buddha, without any reaction on his face. I was dying to go out and light a cigarette, but I did not wish to make any obvious demonstration. Then Jabotinsky sent me a piece of paper on which he had written, 'I am proud of my friends'. I turned the note round and scribbled, 'Thanks for condolences, we are not dead yet'.

Jabo had come to the Congress in the certainty that he would be elected president in Chaim's place. His wife arrived dressed in the clothes she thought would be suitable for a president's wife. But the Congress elected Nahum Sokolow as the new president of the Zionist World Organization. It was a bitter pill for Jabo to swallow.

An official British observer, Rennie Smith, who was present at this Congress, later reported to Ramsay MacDonald that 'the Zionists are furious with the British Government over the Passfield White Paper, but since they cannot throw the Government out, they have thrown out Dr. Weizmann'. Our old friend, the poet Chaim Nachman Bialik, gave a more mundane explanation which may have been nearer the mark. He said, 'Do you know who voted against you? People you hadn't invited to your lunches. People with whom you did not shake hands'. Such is the stuff of politics, and such is the irony of life which pushed Chaim Weizmann into the wilderness at a time when he himself had contemplated resigning the presidency because of the strain his years in politics had imposed on him. But the wilderness in which he was to wander for the next four years as a private soldier of Zionism was no lonely place. He was able to return to his beloved science, see more of his children, and gather his physical and spiritual resources for the battles to come. For us both, his dismissal was a blessing in disguise.

10

The Gathering Darkness: 1931-1933

M Y husband's dismissal from the presidency of the World Zionist Organization in 1931 hurt him deeply: he would have been more than human if it had not. But, strangely enough, it affronted our two sons, Benjy, now twenty-four, and the fifteen-year-old Michael, even more. Michael voiced this dissatisfaction when he said, 'It is Zionism and the Jewish people who constantly deprive us of our father. The reward poor Daddy receives is this vote of no-confidence! Please, Daddy, promise never to go back'. But when, in 1935, Chaim was urgently and unanimously pressed to return to the office of president, both boys were in favour of his doing so.

Still, this act of political ingratitude in turning Chaim out of the presidency in 1931 had its own rewards. Chaim was not the sort of person to nurse a grievance for long. Such pain as he felt he pushed into his subconscious. He was too active in body and in spirit to allow any disaster to overwhelm him. In 1918 he had cried out in a moment of pent-up emotion, 'I cannot serve two mistresses—politics and science. I must choose between them. Which shall I give up?' I knew then in my heart that he would give up neither! Like other men of talent and genius, he would combine the two seemingly impossible rôles and emerge as one of that rarest of phenomena—a scientist-statesman.

Immediately after the débâcle of his rejection at Basle in 1931, like the good soldier he was, Chaim stayed on for a few days to help in the re-organization of the Executive Committee and then we set off in a car for a contemplated holiday in Yugoslavia. We collected our children and the nurse on the way and when we reached Abbazia on the Italo-Yugoslav frontier, we picked up our travel visas. The next day who should appear but our friend Joseph Cowen, who had arrived to persuade my husband to return immediately to London to settle some Zionist problems which had suddenly cropped up for the third time. I protested. After the unfortunate Congress, Chaim had already had to return twice within two weeks to London to settle Zionist financial difficulties. It was more than I could stand. But how could I resist Chaim's wishes? So off he went to London for the third time while the children, nurse, and I turned the car towards Spain. I was afraid to go to Yugoslavia with two young boys and without Chaim: it was a primitive country in those days, with poor roads and few touring facilities. So we motored towards Barcelona, staying for the night at a small hotel *en route*, where we learnt that revolution had broken out in Spain, with firing in every direction. Nurse did not want us to go on, but I, having suffered so many disappointments and frustrations, decided to ignore the revolution. Nurse then spent the whole night making a large Union Jack, which we were to display on the front of the car to serve as a talisman to deflect any stray bullets!

By next day when we reached Barcelona, the revolution was over. King Alfonso XIII had abdicated and Spain had been proclaimed a republic. Chaim joined us a week later, and for a change we had ten quiet days with the family.

*

Shortly after his dismissal from the presidency of the World Zionist Organization in 1931, Chaim had written to the Hebrew University, saying that he would like to move to Palestine to conduct scientific experiments there, and that all he would need would be a laboratory and an assistant. We were now financially independent as Chaim had sold his acetone process in the United States after the First World War. The answer from the Hebrew University came like a cold douche: there was no room in its budget to comply with Chaim's request! My husband immediately began to look for suitable premises in London. He found such a place in an old house (6 Featherstone Buildings, off Holborn) where he set up a modest laboratory with a small staff consisting of an assistant chemist, a foreman, and a laboratory boy.

When we returned from Spain my husband started the uphill task of 'catching up on science'. Except for an occasional chance visit, he had not been inside a laboratory for more than thirteen years. He was in his fifty-eighth year, and much work had been done in world science during his long absence from research. He was turning over in his mind the writing of an autobiography for a London publisher (a project subsequently abandoned for the time-being). But he had barely settled down to work when he was again asked to pack his bags and go off on a money-raising expedition to South Africa. A Zionist delegation came and told Chaim that, as usual, the movement was short of funds. Unwillingly but dutifully, he once more abandoned science.

Before we left for South Africa, I called at *The Times* bookshop and asked what they would recommend me to read about South Africa. They said they had an excellent book called *The South Africans* by Sarah Gertrude Millin, an author of distinction who had written *God's Step-Children* and was later to write biographies of General Smuts and Cecil Rhodes.

We embarked for our five-months trip on 31 December 1931. The voyage to that distant land took some seventeen days and was a miserable, painful trip. Crossing the Equator, it was unbearably hot; I was covered in a rash and could not get up out of my bed. We arrived in Capetown in January—in the middle of their summer! It was so hot that I wanted to run away. It was far worse than Palestine! But there were some 'compensations' to flatter my vanity. I was told that there had been great excitement among the womenfolk in the sizable Jewish communities in South Africa, and that much time and money had been spent on dressmakers and modistes making new clothes and hats for the various receptions which had been prepared for us. Dr. Alexander Goldstein, who went ahead of us as an official Zionist propagandist and organizer, told the women, 'I shouldn't worry so much about your clothes! You will all be put in the shade by Mrs. Weizmann when she arrives!' Which was at least a pleasant tribute to my dressmaker!

At first we travelled chiefly by night train, to save time, but we could never sleep because the trains were so shaky. Then we decided to make our tours by car, stopping along the way. I do not think there was one single town in South Africa which we did not visit. It was a beautiful country, very beautiful, but the condition of the African population appalled us. The train stopped at every station and always naked children came round, their tummies distended from hunger, their little legs crooked from rickets.

The Africans did not know how to cultivate their land properly. Their farms did not grow in size with the increase in the size of their families. The young generation had to go to the big towns to make a living. Emigration into the larger cities such as Capetown, Durban and Johannesburg became a problem. Africans were not allowed to come into shops: except by the back door!

It is hardly necessary to emphasize these things; but there has always been a bond of sympathy between the Jewish people, themselves deprived for so long of their natural rights, and other peoples seeking to emerge into nationhood, and I am glad to say that many members of the Jewish population in South Africa have played a notable part in trying to alleviate and improve the lot of those in that country less fortunate than themselves.

South Africa was full of pleasant and less pleasant surprises. In Durban we were invited to a banquet on a Saturday. The food, however, had been prepared the previous day. On Sunday, Chaim felt very ill: he had been sick most of the night. All he had eaten was a chicken sandwich! Then a few moments later Dr. Goldstein came in, unshaven, without a collar, and looking very dilapidated: he too complained of feeling very ill. But I said I was sure it could not have been the dinner since I felt all right. I had spoken too soon! A delayed reaction set in. For the next ten days, the three of us were confined to our beds, trying to breathe through thick mosquito nets, attended by a very inefficient nurse. My gums became swollen and my teeth very shaky, but fortunately I did not lose them.

However, there were compensations. When we returned to Johannesburg, we stayed with Sarah Gertrude Millin, who was a delightful hostess. Like us, she was of Russian-Jewish origin, as was her charming husband. We had already met Ethel Hayman and her husband, with whom we formed a close and intimate friendship which has lasted to this day. Ethel has remained as she always was: very thin, very active, very intelligent, very well read, understanding and sympathetic. After the death of her husband, she settled in Israel.

In Johannesburg we met many leading people, among whom one of the most impressive personalities was General Smuts, with whom Chaim had become acquainted in London during the First World War and whom we met frequently in Johannesburg. He had been one of the prime movers and supporters of the Balfour Declaration, a loyal friend of the Jewish people and of Israel. As a one-time Boer leader, he understood the futility of perpetuating ancient hatreds and misunderstandings, and did much to patch things up on the diplomatic and political level between Britain and Israel, working as always in the background. He was a man of iron will, subtle, with deep, kind eyes and a little grey beard. He was also a great climber. While we were in Johannesburg, Smuts said, 'I don't want you to see only the Jews of South Africa'. Knowing that I was fond of mountain climbing, he invited me to climb Table Mountain with him; but the excessive heat of

Capetown daunted me, and I had regretfully to decline his invitation. So he took us to Pretoria instead and showed us the house where Kruger had lived. When you entered this typical Dutch house, you could see right through it to the garden where there stood a tree four hundred years old. It took ten men to span its enormous trunk. I also recall that Smuts brought his little granddaughter with him, a delightful, sweet little girl who said that she did not understand why my lips were so red!

Some years later, when the persecution of Jews in Germany was in full flood, we formed the Youth Aliyah, of which I later became the president. Rather timidly I asked Smuts, who was in London at this time, if he would become the patron of this organization. His immediate reply was, 'Of course'. Before I knew what I was doing, I jumped up and kissed him on both cheeks. When, in November 1949, Smuts was invited to come from South Africa to London to attend a banquet in celebration of Chaim's seventy-fifth birthday, he replied to Chaim, 'It is not easy for me to travel—I shall soon be eighty. But how can I refuse to honour the modern Moses?' A cherished photograph of General Smuts, together with those of Lloyd George, Balfour, and Winston Churchill, decorates my husband's library at Rehovoth.

There are other memories of South Africa.

While we were in Johannesburg I was taken by Mrs. Smuts, whose husband had previously been Prime Minister, to call on Mrs. Herzog, wife of the Prime Minister at the time. We had an interesting conversation, interrupted now and again by Mrs. Smuts's pointing out that the cupboards, couch, and chairs were standing in different places from those they had occupied when she was in the house. I was much amused.

We were to go on to luncheon at Government House with the Earl and Countess of Athlone (Princess Alice). Mrs. Herzog remarked casually, 'We don't need to hurry. It doesn't matter if you are a little late'. Being accustomed to English formality and etiquette, I was a little shocked. As we set off for Government House, I was shocked for the second time to see that the charming and intelligent Mrs. Smuts was wearing no stockings!

But the most important part of our work in South Africa was to raise funds for the *Keren Hayesod*, and in this Chaim and Dr. Goldstein were most successful. Some hundred thousand pounds were collected. This was the period of the world economic crisis, and the sum raised represented a great deal of money, especially as the pound was worth a good deal more in those days than it is now. I myself had a considerable measure of success in forming a branch of W.I.Z.O. in that vast country but, as usual, I came across stubborn resistance from the menfolk in the Zionist Organization who were afraid of 'losing' their most active women supporters. After my similar experience in Canada, I was able to cope with the situation. Nevertheless, I was considerably affronted and hurt when Mr. Lazar Braudo, the Chairman of the South African Zionist Federation, came up to me after one well-attended W.I.Z.O. meeting saying, 'Mrs. Weizmann, you have ruined Zionism in this country!' I said, 'Thank you very much'. Meanwhile Chaim was on the telephone, asking what was keeping me so late. When I rejoined him, he upbraided me. I was feeling far from well—as a result of our wonderful banquet in Durban! and Chaim said, 'You are feeling ill, but you stay out to all hours of the night. You are killing yourself!' I burst into tears, and said to him, 'The Zionists say I have ruined Zionism in South Africa, and when I come home my husband reproaches me because I stayed late at a meeting!'

On the following day, Mr. Braudo visited us and made me a handsome apology, but Chaim was extremely angry. Not long before, I had been asked to accept a painting of the Transvaal, but Chaim insisted that I return the picture. However, after Mr. Braudo's apology, things were patched up, and the painting, a most colourful landscape of the eastern Transvaal by Ruth Haden, now hangs in my dining-room in Rehovoth.

*

When we got back to London in May 1932, Chaim again immersed himself in his beloved science. But he did not cut himself off from his Zionist activities. Apart from his work as the president of the English Zionist Federation, he was the chairman of the Central Bureau for the Settlement of German Jews.

In December of the same year, Chaim went to Germany. He wanted to warn the leaders of the Jewish community of the dire fate which he felt was awaiting them, and he urged them to make immediate preparations to forestall the inevitable disaster by leaving for Palestine. At a dinner held in the house in Munich of Eli Strauss, one of his old Zionist friends, Chaim was bombarded with numerous questions by those who had been invited to meet us. What was going to happen, Chaim was asked; how did he envisage the situation—was it really going to be so bad?

'Hitler means every word he wrote in *Mein Kampf*', Chaim answered. 'Get out of Germany as soon as you can. If you can't leave immediately, transfer your money to Palestine. I don't want it. Keep it for yourselves so that when you do come to Palestine, you will have something with which to start'.

My husband felt the occasion to be one of the saddest evenings of his life. These men he was meeting had built up fine lives, had taken part in German public affairs, had contributed to the greatness of German culture and economy. Yet now they sat there, helpless in face of the coming tragedy, not knowing what to do, with the sword of Damocles hanging over their heads. This was Chaim's last journey to Germany and was particularly moving for him. He, who had received his early education there and visited it so many times, could never bring himself to go back after the fearful tragedy that overwhelmed the Jews of Germany and of Europe.

I think no more poignant prophecy was ever uttered in our times than the statement which he made to the Peel Commission in Jerusalem in 1937. This is what he said:

> Six million Jews are pent up in places where they are not wanted; and for them the world is divided into places where they cannot live and places which they may not enter. For these people a certificate for Palestine is the highest boon. One in twenty, one in thirty may get in, and for them it is redemption.

As the ghastly events in Europe during the Second World War were to show, this was more than a bitter prophecy: it was an epitaph over the grave of European Jewry.

*

By the end of January 1933, when Hitler was installed as Chancellor, Chaim had left Germany with forebodings which he communicated to me on his return to London. The first sad trickle of German-Jewish scientists, intellectuals, and others who had the vision and the means, began going to Mandated Palestine. The new dispersal brought talent and spiritual enrichment not only to Palestine but to the whole civilized world; it also brought new administrative and financial problems to the Zionist movement, many of which fell on Chaim's shoulders. When, early in 1933, Meyer Weisgal telephoned and cabled to my husband offering him a hundred thousand dollars for the German-Jewish settlement fund if Chaim would speak on the 'Jewish Day' at the Century of Progress Fair in Chicago, Chaim promptly agreed to break off his work in London and take a trip to the United States and back—in those days, by land and sea—to address one meeting in Chicago.

Benjy and I went down to Southampton to see Chaim off. It was a particularly cold and foggy night when we went aboard ship. There were only two tables occupied in the dining salon. We had just settled down to dinner when the steward came up to say that the ship would not be leaving that night because of the fog, and that passengers could go ashore if they wished. He asked us to finish our meal as quickly as possible as the staff were going ashore. All of a sudden, a little man who looked exactly like a Jewish tailor came into the dining-room. He came up to my husband and began to talk. He did not appear to know who my husband was, but he looked so upset that I asked Chaim what was the matter. The man said that three months ago his brother had sent him a ticket to go to America, but for business reasons he could not then leave. Now that he had decided to go, he had discovered that his ticket to America had been cancelled. He had enough money for the ticket, but he had not in addition the ten pounds which every immigrant had to possess on landing in the United States. It was a usual tale of professional beggars, and my husband said, 'No'. I took my bag, opened it, gave the man ten pounds, and off he ran.

Benjy said, 'Mother, you've been diddled'. I said, 'All right, perhaps I have been'. Benjy then suggested that the least I could have done would have been to go with the man to see whether he bought his ticket.

We said good-bye to Chaim, and in the morning when we left Southampton the ship was still there. The next day the telephone rang. It was someone from a car-hire firm who apologized because their chauffeur had 'missed' Dr. Weizmann at the Ritz! I said there must be some misunderstanding because my husband had left for America, and besides he was not staying at the Ritz. The following day the same thing happened: the car-hire firm of Packard informed me that Dr. Weizmann had hired a car in which he had gone to look for apartments, and had been dropped off at the Savoy, and their chauffeur had again missed him!

I concluded that this was either some kind of practical joke, or that the man to whom I had given ten pounds on the previous day was using Dr. Weizmann's name. A day later still, a detective from Scotland Yard called to ask if I knew who was causing all this trouble. I felt like a criminal myself, especially when I was asked for my finger-print.

I could make neither head nor tail of the whole business, but I wondered. Then I forgot all about the episode. A little later, Chaim wrote to me from America, telling me among other things that someone had come to his office saying that he had a personal debt to repay. It was the man to whom I had given ten pounds! Not only did he return this money, but he also bought a ticket for a meeting of the *Keren Hayesod* and subscribed to the funds.

I do not know whether there is a moral to this story, except to point to my instinctive behaviour and my capacity to make a fairly rapid assessment of a person's character on first meeting him. This may have been of some service both to me and to my husband.

One event did, however, cloud my husband's 1933 trip to the United States. While still at sea, he learned that Chaim Arlosoroff, one of the younger, most intelligent and brilliant of his friends, had been assassinated in Tel Aviv. Arlosoroff, who was a prominent member of the Zionist Executive and of the Jewish Agency, did not always see eye to eye with the British Administration in Palestine; but he was nevertheless 'a whole-hearted admirer of the British, of their ways and of their character'.[46]

On Chaim's return from America in 1933, he was immediately pressed to attend the meeting of the Eighteenth Zionist Congress at Prague, but he resolutely refused to go. He said that for once he wanted to breathe fresh air and did not want to go back to the stuffiness of day-to-day politics. He did not want to involve himself in all the intrigues and jealousies that prevailed at this Congress, and was extremely reluctant to give the impression that he was 'planning a return'. But I went to Prague to address the W.I.Z.O. conference which was also taking place in that city. I feel that some of the remarks I made on this occasion, especially with reference to the problem of German-Jewish settlement and the unhappy fate of Arlosoroff, deserve quoting:

> I am only sorry that, for reasons only too readily apparent to everyone here, the places that should have been filled by our friends and co-workers from Germany remain empty, and we are deprived of their valuable counsel and assistance in this critical hour. . . . The terrible situation in Germany—growing as it does more terrible from day to day and from month to month—throws upon us, as Zionists, a specially grave responsibility, over and above the responsibility which it throws upon Jewish communities outside Germany and upon every individual Jew and Jewess. As Zionists we are responsible not only for making the utmost possible contribution to the relief of suffering

and to the rehabilitation of the victims. Ours also is the task of facilitating the complete and effective re-orientation of the lives and aims of what will almost certainly prove to be the large majority of Jewish emigrants from Germany—certainly the largest and most significant single group among them.

I added that the immensity and difficulty of this task was enough to make the stoutest heart fail, especially since we had been

deprived of the wise counsel and kindling inspiration of one of the most brilliant, most sagacious, of our young leaders—Dr. Chaim Arlosoroff.

The best way of paying tribute to Arlosoroff's memory was to continue and complete the work

to which he gave his life—the work of building up the Jewish National Home in Palestine, and especially of re-establishing German-Jewish refugees in Palestine, on detailed schemes for which he was actually engaged at the time of his murder.

The influx of new refugees into Palestine would throw further burdens on W.I.Z.O., not the least of which was the raising of increased funds for its manifold activities. I concluded my address,

Well, I know of only two ways of facing new and apparently crushing responsibilities: you can either stand up to them, or you can stand down. There is no middle path. And my personal experience of W.I.Z.O. leads me to think that there is very little doubt as to what it will elect to do in the present situation. A hard task, but I know of no other so well worth while.

The reaction from W.I.Z.O. groups all over the world was immediate and generous. I cannot speak too highly of the response which our appeals for material and moral support received, nor of the devotion of hundreds upon hundreds of anonymous 'collectors' who helped to make possible the extensive mother-and-child welfare work we carried out in Palestine.

Despite Chaim's refusal to attend the Eighteenth Zionist Congress, he had to deal with an incredible number of subjects and problems. These ranged from science to politics and diplomacy, from the philosophy of Zionism to the humanities. He was the unofficial prime minister, treasurer and foreign secretary of a non-existent state; he was the commercial-traveller of his people, and was in turn admired and abused in all these rôles.

In 1934, it was whispered here and there that numerous restrictions, known as 'clauses', were being imposed on Roman Catholic nuns going to Palestine, and this, for some reason, was ascribed to the World Zionist Organization. The Zionists, of course, had nothing to do with it, since all non-Jewish immigration into Palestine was entirely in the hands of the British Administration. My husband, however, decided that he would see Benito Mussolini in order to clear the matter up, and an interview was arranged between them.

The meeting took place in an enormous room in the Palazzo Venezia in Rome. Mussolini was a great artist in producing unexpected and dramatic effects. The whole room was in darkness except for a corner where, at a large table, Mussolini sat with a direct light throwing its mysterious rays on the head of the 'great' man.

In vain my husband attempted to prove the inaccuracy and absurdity of the accusation that the Zionists were responsible for any restrictions on the movements of Catholic nuns. Mussolini did not respond and simply reacted rather haughtily. Gradually the conversation veered towards Zionism, which my husband said was an established fact.

Mussolini exclaimed, 'Dr. Weizmann, not all Jews are Zionists!'

My husband, in his quiet, somewhat mystical voice, replied, 'Of course. I know it only too well, and not all Italians are Fascists!'

At that, Mussolini came down from his heights and talked to my husband as an equal. He wanted to know why he bothered with the British when the Italians could give the Zionists all they wanted. In reply Chaim reminded him of what had happened two thousand years ago. . . .

They parted. Next day, to our surprise, a large photograph of Il Duce arrived with a respectful inscription to my husband. On one side of the inscription was the date from the beginning of the Christian Era and on the other, the date from Mussolini's ascent to power.

I may say that this photograph rendered us great service on the Italian ship which took us a little later to Palestine!

When we returned to London, the maid who unpacked our luggage took the photograph of the Duce and placed it on the piano in our drawing-room in Addison Crescent. The following morning it had disappeared. I rang for the butler, Payne, and asked him where it was. He said, 'This is not a house where Mussolini's photograph should be displayed, so I put it behind the portrait of Mr. Lloyd George'. 'Bravo,' I said to our 'Admirable Crichton'.

On the three occasions on which my husband met Mussolini, there was no trace of that anti-Semitism which marked his régime after he had hitched his chariot to Hitler's malevolent star; but the photograph of Mussolini nevertheless lay buried behind the more benign Lloyd George for as long as I can remember.

II

A Tree in the Wilderness: the Institute and Weizmann House at Rehovoth, 1933-1935

THE first time I saw Rehovoth was in the late autumn of 1919, during the very first visit I paid to what was then Palestine. No distinct recollection remains in my mind of the village itself, only an impression of sandy roads and wide uncultivated expanses as my husband and I drove through on the way to Gedera. Had I then been told that we should eventually take up permanent residence in this sandy place, I am sure I should have laughed the mere suggestion to scorn.

Years passed, and it was not until April 1933, some thirteen and a half years later, that we came back to Rehovoth, this time by deliberate design. The Jewish Agency's Agricultural Experimental Station, which was directed by Dr. Isaac Wilkansky*, had been transferred the previous summer from Tel Aviv to the heart of the citrus-groves near Rehovoth railway-station. My husband decided that it would be appropriate to erect his dreamed-of chemistry and biology research laboratories on an adjoining site.

There were several factors that led to his adopting this decision. First, the proximity of the Experimental Station; secondly, his intention that the programme of research he was contemplating should be linked with the station's work for the advancement of the country's agriculture; thirdly, his deep emotional feeling for the association with the ancient site of Yavneh, not far from Rehovoth. It was to Yavneh that the centre of Jewish learning and scholarship was removed after the destruction of Jerusalem in A.D. 70. The celebrated Jewish sage Yochanan Ben Zakkai, when asked by a sympathetic Roman Commander what he would like to have in 'recompense' for the destruction of Jerusalem, replied boldly, 'Give me Yavneh and its sages!' Chaim

* He later changed his name to Alazari-Volcani.

133

Weizmann, had he been in the same position, would have demanded no less. But the last, and by no means the least, reason my husband sought this site was his wish to create a scientific refuge for the young and promising scientists recently expelled from Germany.

Our return to Rehovoth was for the laying of the foundation stone of the Daniel Sieff Research Institute on 12 April 1933. It was a modest ceremony yet, I believe, an exhilarating one, because of the significance it held for the future. The speeches were on a hopeful note. I remember particularly my husband's prophetic statement, that Palestine was a small country which would be made to flourish by scientific research—a prophecy that has proved itself valid in the fulfilment of the past thirty years. Referring to the many un-developed stretches of land in the Jordan Valley, the Vale of Beisan, and the Huleh swamps, he said that science, marching hand in hand with colonization, would turn these places into flourishing settle-ments.

Among those who delivered addresses, in addition to my husband who helped to lay the stone, were Dr. Wilkansky, who presided; Chaim Arlosoroff representing the Jewish Agency; Itzhak Ben-Zvi for the *Vaad Leumi* (Jewish National Council); Arthur Ruppin; and Shlomo Kaplansky of the Haifa *Technikum*.

As I sat there, I thought of Daniel Sieff, a charming gifted boy of seventeen, and a great friend of my son Michael. Daniel had asked to come to Palestine to study biology and Hebrew because he was too young to go to Cambridge. His death in tragic circumstances was a sad blow not only to his immediate family, but also to all those who were closely associated with the Sieffs in their varied and generous work for the Zionist cause both in England and in Palestine. When Mr. and Mrs. Sieff wanted to commemorate their son, Chaim suggested that the best memorial would be an institute of research in his name, and this idea was promptly accepted.

A year later we returned to dedicate the new Daniel Sieff Research Institute, on 3 April 1934. It was a remarkable building for those days, and I was thrilled to see my husband's delight and satisfaction at the way in which his plans for the new laboratories had been realized. Few people were aware that when my husband once started on a project, he really had no boundaries. He saw human affairs in his own projection as a series of stages or phases stretching away into the infinite, without limits. The creation and opening of the Sieff Institute marked the completion of one of those phases; what happened after was to exceed the imagination of all who took part in the original project.*

Development at the Daniel Sieff Institute became so unexpectedly rapid that the creative work outgrew the capacity of the building opened in 1934. Ten years later, on the occasion of Chaim's seventieth birthday, Meyer Weisgal together with some friends, among them Dewey D. Stone, Harry Levine, A. K. Epstein of Chicago and Lewis Ruskin, came to Chaim to ask him what he would like as a gift for his birthday. Chaim's reply was, 'I need nothing, I want nothing, and you can do nothing for me personally.' When they insisted on doing something to mark the occasion, he finally said, 'Do something by way of "enlarging" the "Sieff Institute".' Those words were recorded and written into the Deed. After they had left Chaim, the gentlemen turned to Meyer and asked whether he would undertake this project. His reply was characteristic. He said that an effort to 'enlarge' the Sieff Institute would produce no money. People would say that 'If you want to enlarge the Sieff Institute, why don't you go to Mr. Sieff, who is a very rich man.' Nevertheless, they pressed Meyer and he asked for twenty-four hours to give his answer.

On the following day he returned with his answer: it was the idea of the Weizmann Institute of Science for which he was certain he could —because of Weizmann's name—obtain a minimum of one million dollars. It was at this point that Lewis Ruskin asked: 'Don't you think that it would be an insult to the Sieff family to change the name of the Institute?' Meyer replied that he would contact Mr. Israel Sieff about his plan to raise one million dollars and to integrate the Sieff Institute into the Weizmann Institute. Mr. Sieff's response was as generous as it was immediate. 'Why only a million?' He asked. 'Why don't you make it five million?' He also undertook to enquire about the absorption of the Sieff Institute into the larger undertaking, an idea the Sieff family supported whole-heartedly.

This was how the idea and the name of the Weizmann Institute was born. The sum of five million dollars mentioned by Israel Sieff was reached in the next few years, a figure multiplied many times over since that time.

After the death of my husband in 1952, Meyer, together with the generous support of my dear old friends the late Lord Marks and the

* I am indebted to the Editor of the *Jewish Observer and Middle East Review* for permission to quote my article 'When I first came to Rehovoth', published in the issue of 27 March 1964.

late Sigmund Gestetner, with the active support of the Government of Israel and the Jewish Agency, established the Yad Chaim Weizmann.

To write about Meyer and his energy is like solving a difficult crossword puzzle or finding oneself in a maze from which one is unable to grope one's way out. Under his dynamic guidance, the larger project of the Weizmann Institute with its magic name moved forward rapidly, and funds, through Meyer's efforts, began to pour in with unprecedented alacrity. It was with growing admiration that I watched Meyer's efforts to make this memorial area and foundation an undertaking which would truly give effect to the scientific and cultural legacy which my husband had left. Meyer, as I have told him many times, has the capacity of ten men in him, and a remarkable talent for combining the uncombinable! Not that I have always agreed with Meyer. His dynamic, gigantic, expansive ideas often clashed with my liking for poise, serenity, and careful realistic planning. I feared that the rapid growth of the Institute without adequate means was like putting the cart before the horse. I sincerely hope that I am wrong and he is right. The differences have not disturbed our friendship but have, perhaps, added mutually to its attraction. My husband, I might add, who had an admiration for him and for his charming, attractive wife Shirley, once dedicated a photograph to her by inscribing on it: 'To a long-suffering woman but, dear Shirley, it's worth it!'

Meyer has a heart of gold, a quality which has brought him many friends and supporters. Strange as it may seem, generous donors to the Weizmann Institute have even been grateful to Meyer for extracting large funds from them to create and develop the multiple and important departments of the Institute. From its early beginnings in a single building, the Institute today covers a large area, with some fifty major buildings, research stations, and a thousand workers, among whom are many famous and highly reputed scientists. It has become a scientific centre acknowledged by scientists the world over. Eminent scientists from overseas visit the Weizmann Institute for highly advanced symposia; at the same time, our scientists are continually invited to lecture in the United States, Australia, the Soviet Union, Japan, Germany, France, and other countries. It has also played a notable part in helping 'under-developed countries'. When one considers the Weizmann Institute's short existence, this is a miraculous achievement.

*

But to return to the beginnings of the Institute and of my association with Rehovoth. When it was created, Chaim wanted to offer its directorship to Albert Einstein. He wrote to him saying, 'My dear old friend, all you need is paper and a pencil, and I can provide that . . . I will step down as the head of the Institute and you will take my place and I will assist you in the work'. I am myself convinced that Einstein was ready to accept this invitation, but that his wife dissuaded him. Einstein, who had gone to Princeton University in the U.S.A., was a rather sick, disappointed man in unfamiliar surroundings. He had aged very rapidly, and Palestine would have provided a balm for his wounded spirits but, alas, it was not to be.

My early life in Rehovoth was far from happy. We stayed there for the two winters of 1935-36 and 1936-37. I found my life completely changed from the busy, energetic, public and social existence which I had had in London—so much in the centre of things. I was separated from the country where I had lived for almost thirty years, separated from my two boys—Benjy had just left Cambridge and Michael was about to enter King's College in the same University. I knew many people in Palestine but few intimately, and although everyone was very kind to me, there was no one on whose shoulder I could cry when in trouble. Perhaps I exaggerate; but if one has to change one's way of life, one should do it early, when one's personality is still in process of formation. I found myself left very much on my own—just as in those early days in Manchester—because Chaim threw himself so wholeheartedly into his scientific work at the Institute.

Chaim was now fifty-nine and working as hard as he had ever done when he was a young man half that age. He left the small temporary bungalow in which we lived in Rehovoth village at about eight-thirty every morning, and returned home to lunch with guests who had to be accommodated on our small enclosed verandah because we had no dining-room. After a short break of twenty minutes for rest after lunch, Chaim went back to work, and returned at seven in the evening, and sometimes much later. I spent many an afternoon and evening sitting on the floor listening to the wireless.

One of the most serious deprivations of this time was the fact that I could never invite anyone to stay with us. We had only two small bedrooms in the bungalow, and one living-room, which also served as Chaim's study and library. The bedrooms were so tiny that they only just held a bed, a chair, and a table. The kitchen was so inadequate that my excellent Swiss cook, Miss Hepfelfinger, used to strew all her pots and pans over the floor. I never dared enter her kitchen because

I should have fainted at the sight of so much disorder! Despite her Swiss origin, Miss Hepfelfinger had lived most of her life in Russia, so we were able to talk to one another in Russian. She was a first-class cook who enjoyed entertaining people, a useful qualification since we had a constant stream of visitors not only to the bungalow but later to Weizmann House when it was completed in 1937.

*

I have often been asked about Weizmann House and how it came into being. At the time of the opening of the Daniel Sieff Institute in April 1934, I happened to look out of the window of my husband's small study there, and my eyes alighted on a hill to the south-east. I recall saying to Dr. Israel Magazannik of the Experimental Station that I should like to have our house over there. He said he thought the land was available for purchase. I expressed the hope that the land belonged to an Arab, because we preferred to buy land from them. But it so happened that the land had belonged to one of the founders of Rehovoth, Aaron Eisenberg, a former resident of the town of Pinsk, whom Chaim remembered from his younger days. Mr. Eisenberg had died and the land had passed to his son, a lawyer.

I did not tell Chaim anything about my plans to purchase the site. The price was some five thousand pounds sterling, a large sum of money in those days for a derelict overgrown citrus grove, but I was 'buying the view', as I often told my friends—and what a superb view it was, stretching towards Jerusalem and the Judean hills. Chaim, who still knew nothing of my intentions, was greatly taken with the situation when I took him up the hill in a car to show him this view.

Later, when Chaim had been allowed into my conspiracy and we had purchased the site, I entrusted the famous architect Eric Mendelsohn, who had made a great name for himself in Germany before he went to the United States, with the drawing up of plans for the house, but on one condition: it was to be my house and not his! I should never be able to live in a new house in which I had taken no part in the layout. He said, 'certainly', but that 'certainly' was no certainty at all! We had continual squabbles as to how the house should be planned. I generally won. I told him that we could not spend more than ten thousand pounds on the house; but when it came to producing the estimates, the matter dragged on so long that I began to suspect he had gone beyond his original estimate. Later, when I was in London, I received an estimate of eighteen thousand pounds, so I cabled to Mr.

Mendelsohn cancelling the project. However, he asked me to wait until I returned to Palestine, when he presented me with new estimates. The result of these 'savings' was that I had to cut out many of the electrical installations I wanted. We reduced on this and that, but Mr. Mendelsohn was something of an architectural snob: the living-rooms had to be large and magnificent and the bedrooms tiny. He had given my husband a small, poky room and provided me with a large double-boudoir. I said that I refused to have such a small bedroom for my husband, but Mendelsohn said he could not enlarge it. I insisted. I told him to put a large jutting bay-window into the room, where my husband could put his writing table, since Chaim always liked to be alone when he wrote. But the staff accommodation unfortunately remained rather small and constricted, though I made it as comfortable as I could.

When it came to the furnishing and the interior decoration of the house, I said to Mr. Mendelsohn, 'Eric, you have built a modern house. It is very lovely and livable in, but I cannot live with your interior decoration'. I then told him of my scheme. 'But you will ruin everything', he protested. 'Probably', I answered, 'but I have to live in the house, not you!'

I also arranged for indirect lighting. This created a very charming atmosphere, so that even my long-suffering architect congratulated me on my taste. And we became firm friends after that. The house had taken two years to build. There had been difficulties in securing materials, as well as the usual quota of Arab 'troubles'. During this period I begged my husband repeatedly to come and see and approve of it. He promised to do so, but the promise remained unfulfilled. His time was fully taken up with his scientific research and various political activities on behalf of the Israel to be.

While I was in London, I had sent a complete plan of Weizmann House to Rehovoth showing where each table and chair was to go. And it was only when my husband's books, the furniture, the carpets, and the pictures were in place and his pyjamas laid out on his bed, that Chaim saw the house.

There was no end to his admiration.

But I think it was Blanche Dugdale who understood best what I wanted in my 'dream house'. In an article which appeared in the *Jerusalem Post* in 1937, she recalled that when I first pointed out the site of the house to her, I told her how it should be planned—

... the library, big enough to hold all Dr. Weizmann's books, must have an open fireplace where he could arrange (or *dis*arrange) the logs after the manner of a man *chez soi*, and a loggia where he could step out in the middle of a day's work. The guest bedrooms, which must not be too few nor yet too many, and last, but not least, in her visionary picture, the garden, which in the all-too-brief glory of the Palestinian spring she would make glow with great masses of colour that can be achieved only with English flowers, grown in the English way. . . .

In a space of time which in retrospect seems incredibly short (I suppose it was about three years), all this, and more, was brought to pass. Victor Cazalet and I were the first guests to stay in Weizmann House. We arrived in that short moment between the Palestinian dusk and dark when colours have an unearthly intensity, and white walls a moonlike brightness. From the open door streamed golden light; a background for the welcoming figures of the Master and the Mistress of this lovely home. As we crossed their threshold I formed the impression, which has never changed, that here was the noblest modern house I have ever seen—perfectly harmonious with its surroundings, perfectly appropriate to its purpose, and, above all, perfectly expressive of its owners. Like them, it is a national possession, and I believe is so looked upon by all Palestinian Jewry.

Dear Baffy had, in her own inimitable way, captured both the dream and the substance of the house and its surroundings. She was indeed the very first guest who stayed in Weizmann House, and there is a guest-room which to this very day I call 'Baffy's room', in memory of this good and dear friend. But our first visitors, for lunch, came on Christmas Eve 1937. When we arrived in December 1937, we found a message from John Gunther and his wife Frances, who were in Jerusalem, saying, 'We are leaving tomorrow for the Far East. We could not go without seeing you; can we come to lunch?' We were delighted to have them, and we had a lovely time together, exchanging reminiscences.

I had sent part of the furniture from Addison Crescent to Weizmann House; but I could not strip our London house completely of all its furnishings as we were frequently called to London. In fact, we had barely moved into Weizmann House—just ten days—when we received a cable asking us to return to London. So while John Gunther went off to the Far East to write *Inside Asia*, Chaim and I had to make plans for our London trip. 'I am tired of being a commercial traveller for the Jewish people', I said. 'When our home was in London, they kept sending us to Palestine. Now that we live in Palestine, they send us to London'. So Chaim compromised: we spent a further six weeks in our lovely house before making our way back to London.

Chaim delighted especially in the garden. I had begun to lay this out even while the house was being built. Chaim, who had no sense of property at all, came to know every leaf on those trees. In place of the abandoned orange-grove, we planted new trees, so that our oranges and grapefruit came to be regarded as some of the best in the whole country, and many crates of our citrus fruit were exported. We have magnificent, tall, jacaranda trees, with their plumes of long lavender-blue flowers, mangoes, peppers, lilacs of all kinds, and every other tree which could be found or imported. When some of the gardeners said to me, 'Why plant trees?—they will take years to grow', I answered, 'All right. I may not see these trees, but someone will enjoy looking at them in—the future!' This 'Chekhovian' mood and my love of trees have persisted with me to this day, and there is nothing I enjoy more than to hear the magnificent symphony concert which the birds make each evening as they put their children to bed.

'Kibbutz Weizmann', as I jokingly call my house, has become part of the living history of Israel. It has entertained princes, potentates, kings, presidents, members of commissions, scientists and artists of great eminence as well as humbler folk; its two large visitors' books filled with illustrious names and kindly messages of appreciation are in no sense my private property—they belong ultimately to the Weizmann Memorial and the Israel nation. The few things I have recorded here about the house and its gardens will provide those who are curious about its origins with the story of how it came to be and what it has stood for.

*

An episode which stands out in my mind is the visit of the late King Albert of the Belgians and his queen to British Mandated Palestine in the early 'thirties. We had been invited to lunch with them at Government House by the then High Commissioner, Sir Arthur Wauchope. It was not the practice of the British Administration to take visitors to the Jewish Settlements, but Their Majesties had been to Tel Aviv and had returned enchanted with it.

My husband became very stern as he asked the royal visitors, 'Have you seen the kibbutzim?'

'What is that?' asked King Albert.

'Towns we have built from the Pyramids to Brooklyn, but kibbutzim, that is co-operative farm settlements, don't exist anywhere else in the world', said Chaim.

After my husband's short explanation, King Albert and Queen Elizabeth expressed a desire to see one of these settlements. They were leaving the country next day, but it was arranged that they should visit the settlement at Nahalal before their return home.

When we arrived at Nahalal at the agreed hour, to our embarrassment we found Their Majesties had arrived ahead of us and were already sitting round a table in the office of the W.I.Z.O. school, with the head of the settlement and a number of the municipal council. The royal couple, sitting there like farmers, were absorbed in a conversation on agricultural problems, droughts, profits, and all the details appertaining to farm life. We spent three hours with them in interesting and friendly talk.

Queen Elizabeth said she would like to walk through the village, and while doing so asked if she might go into one of the houses. 'Choose!' said my husband, and we entered a cottage to find that, though the farmer was there, his wife had run off to the office of the settlement to peep at the Queen, while the Queen was visiting her home! The Queen looked round the room and was overcome when she saw on the shelves books on philosophy, housekeeping and cooking, history, finance; the Bible and the Talmud.

'Where do you come from?' the Queen asked the farmer. 'What were you before?'

'I come from Russia and I was a lawyer', replied the farmer. The lawyer from Russia turned farmer was one of the few fortunate ones who had been able to emigrate before the doors of that great country were closed fast in the face of all Jews seeking to come to Palestine.

The King and Queen of the Belgians were greatly impressed by all they saw, and by the quality and energy of the people of the settlement. This was also the beginning of the long friendship which Chaim and I enjoyed with the Belgian royal family.

*

The year 1934 saw the arrival of 42,359 new immigrants into Palestine—an unprecedented number; in the following year some sixty-two thousand new immigrants arrived. But thereafter the numbers began to fall away steeply owing to the restrictions placed upon new arrivals by the Palestine Administration. I have already spoken of the problems which the influx of such a large number of persons placed on the various re-settlement organizations in Palestine. This was an era of 'middle-class immigration' and it brought to the fore 'many aspects of present-day conditions in Palestine which, compared with conditions in other countries, are contradictory and illusory', as I said in an article which I called, not perhaps surprisingly, 'A Country of Paradoxes'.*

The majority of the new immigrants were German, and in this article I pointed out that

> Palestine is the smallest country in the world and yet it has been able to absorb the largest number of Jewish refugees from Germany. The absorptive capacity of the country as measured in square miles is apparently much more elastic than we have been led to believe by White Papers and Government reports, and in spite of the acute need for workers, immigration is still being restricted by a cautious Government.

Despite the 'high' immigration figures for the years 1934-35, more workers were needed to meet the expansion of the Palestine economy. I went on,

> Acres of land are waiting to come under the plough, waiting for willing hands to sow and reap and to bring the land to the fullness of its fructification.
> It is true that the prosperity of Palestine cannot be measured in the same terms as that of England, of France, or of the America of a few years back; there are no real millionaires in Palestine; but at the same time there are no slums and the fear of the moral degradation of unemployment does not haunt the minds of the population. Palestine's prosperity consists in the fact that every human being enjoys comparative comfort and has the possibility of leading a clean and honest life.

I described how heavily engaged was the building industry—'houses, even rooms, are at a premium in Tel Aviv, while Haifa has the appearance of a town stricken with an earthquake, with its heaps of stone and concrete blocks strewn about'. The need to provide sufficient labour to meet housing requirements called for more people instead of restrictions. But at the same time, I also pointed out the inherent danger of over-urbanization resulting from middle-class immigration. I said it needed to be counteracted 'by a corresponding increase in the rural population which is the real soul of the nation'.

I had observed the enthusiasm with which the younger immigrants from Germany entered into their new life. 'With what passion do they throw themselves into the study of the Hebrew language, Jewish history and Palestine geography in their leisure hours'. I particularly noted that space for gardens had been allotted to them, in which they

---

* W.I.Z.O. *Pioneers and Helpers*, No. 12, July 1934, pp. 4-6.

learned how to handle the implements of their future calling, how to look after farm cattle, and how to milk cows. As I wrote,

> The infiltration of the German-Jewish element into agricultural life has given rise to a new type of settler and a new type of settlement. Numbers of Jewish intellectuals from Germany have emigrated to Palestine and some have brought with them a small capital with which to establish themselves on the land. Before, however, proceeding to buy land or to start a farm they go to various types of settlements or private farms to gain practical experience of farm life. With typical German thoroughness allied to Jewish pertinacity, they have devoted themselves to their training and to their complete re-orientation.

I also uttered this word of warning:

> Satisfactory as it must be from the point of view of increase of population, this year's huge immigration has produced a great strain on those who are in charge of this gigantic enterprise. The shortage of labour, the amount of work to be done, the lack of skilled and experienced workmen, and last, but not least, the insufficiency of public funds available have all left a mark on the standard of efficiency it was desired to raise and maintain for the country. It is regrettable to find that very frequently newcomers from countries where high standards of building and efficiency prevail do not, when building in Palestine, insist on the same high standard in this country. They are all too prone to fall into line with the prevalent notion that 'this is good enough for Palestine' and that 'these are Palestinian conditions to which we must submit'. The standards of Palestinian efficiency will not be helped by such an attitude.

I ended my remarks with the reminder that Spinoza's formula of life, 'Thou must thyself partake of the six days of creation', 'aptly described the life of our Jewish farmers and workers in Palestine'.

Looking back as I do now over nearly fifty years of endeavour in the building up of Israel, I can truthfully say that Spinoza's formula has been fully applied, as all those who have visited or lived in the country will attest. But the years 1934 and 1935 were still the early days of 'the six days of creation'. Much pain, travail, and bloodshed still lay ahead before the work of creation could be completed.

In 1935, my friend Ethel Hayman and her husband came to Palestine and invited me to join them in a journey to Russia. They could not speak Russian, and the prospect of re-visiting Russia, which I had not seen since 1909, attracted me. I obtained my passport and visa, and made all ticket arrangements, when I received news that my elder sister was dying and wished to see me. So I put off my Russian journey and went to Paris to see her shortly before she died. She, her husband, and her son had come as refugees from Russia in 1920, in particularly tragic and impoverished circumstances. Her death was yet another break with my own Russian 'past'. . . .

*

For Chaim, the year 1935 also brought a change. Considerable pressure had been put on him to stand for re-election to the post of president of the World Zionist Organization. In the forefront of those who pleaded with him was his old and trusted friend Berl Locker. Chaim, who knew the magnitude of the new tasks which would confront him, and the certainty that he would again be made 'the scapegoat for the sins of the British Government', insisted that he should first seek the consent of his two sons, as he had promised to do in 1931. They came from the south of France where they were on holiday, and gave their reluctant agreement to their father's return to political life, a decision which they both knew would again separate him from them. It was a difficult decision for them to make.

*

The year 1935 also saw the beginning of the slide to world war with Mussolini's invasion of Abyssinia, followed next year by his conquest of that country and the outbreak of civil war in Spain. By 1936, the general world unrest struck Palestine where violent Arab riots broke out which the British Administration seemed powerless to control.

12

Pandemonium: 1936-1937

WE were in Palestine when pandemonium broke out in mid-April 1936 with a tidal wave of Arab-led strikes accompanied by murder and the wholesale destruction of Jewish and Government property. The situation threatened not only to destroy the foundations of the British mandatory system, but also to undo the labour of more than three generations of peasant-farmers, stifling the hopes and dreams of countless Jews who looked with longing towards the Promised Land as a haven of escape from the Hitlerite terror. The casualty figures tell their own grim story. During a period of three years, some four hundred and fifty Jews were killed and 1,944 wounded; British losses were one hundred and forty killed, 476 wounded; and Arab casualties numbered 2,287 killed and about half that number wounded. A substantial number of the Arabs were killed by other Arabs whose fanaticism had been fanned by Axis propaganda and the intrigues of neighbouring Arab states and their leaders.

British efforts to bring some semblance of order into this unhappy state of affairs culminated in the appointment in May 1936 of a Royal Commission under the chairmanship of Lord Peel which was to investigate the causes of unrest and the alleged grievances of both Arabs and Jews. Its members were Sir Horace Rumbold, Sir Lucas Hammond, Sir William Carter, Sir Harold Morris, and Professor Reginald Coupland, with Mr. John Martin, of the Colonial Office, and Mr. P. G. Heathcoat-Amory, of the Palestine Administration, as secretaries, and a shorthand-writer. The history of this Commission, probably the most famous ever to visit the stricken land of Palestine, has been fully told by many commentators. I shall therefore concentrate on such aspects of the work of the Commission as I remember, reinforced by extracts from entries in my diary made at the time.

My husband was asked on 25 November 1936 to give evidence before the Commission which was sitting in Jerusalem. Chaim and I travelled there from Rehovoth for this purpose. In my diary for 27 November, I noted that for four days before he gave his evidence 'endless discussions had taken place in the Zionist Executive, both collectively and individually, as to the presentation of the Jewish case, and the selection of those who should give evidence and what fields they should cover'. The main point of contention among the members of the Executive was the composition of the Legislative Council which both the British Colonial Office and the British High Commissioner, Sir Arthur Wauchope, seemed anxious to foist on the country. The initial proposal for the Council was that it should consist of fourteen Arabs (nine elected, five appointed), seven Jews (three elected, four appointed), two appointed representatives of the commercial classes of unspecified nationality, and five British officials.

In a Council so composed, Jewish representation would be in a permanent minority, and no member of the Zionist Executive was prepared to accept such a 'solution'. The Mizrachi members of the Executive, as well as the Revisionists, my husband and some of those closest to him, would not accept this proportion of representation and threatened to resign if it were put forward. Ussishkin proposed a 'compromise'; he declared that he did not desire to see either minority or majority representation, but 'the preservation of the Crown of David', which was no compromise at all! Leonard Stein, on the other hand, put forward all the objections which the Commission might raise, purposely arguing the Arab case. 'I am sure all this has been very useful', I noted, 'but Chaim after all this ordeal looked forward to the day of evidence as a relief'. A formula was eventually agreed upon, and Chaim was instructed not to volunteer any solution before the Commission, but if he were pressed on this point, he was to state that 'we do not wish to dominate, but neither do we wish to be dominated'.

The moment of relief came at ten-thirty a.m. on 25 November when we entered the dining-room of the Palace Hotel in Jerusalem where the Commission was sitting. Chaim was very tense, fully aware, as he wrote later, that 'any misstep of mine, any error, however involuntary, would be not mine alone, but would redound to the discredit of my people. I was aware, as on few occasions before or since, of a crushing sense of responsibility'.[47]

According to my diary, Chaim's evidence was a monumental performance. It had lasted for one and a half hours when Lord Peel asked Chaim if he wished to have a short break. And after five minutes, he returned to give evidence for a further hour. . . . Chaim has surpassed himself in content, delivery, manner of speech, and dignity. The interest, attention, and respect of the members of the Commission were so obvious that one could almost feel the contact established between Chaim and his listeners. He was treated with the utmost respect, sympathy, and understanding. Chaim's speech went like a flash through the whole country, and the morale of the people went up by leaps and bounds. The Press was full of it: there were telephone calls, visits, flowers, and telegrams of congratulation afterwards. Chaim was happy and relieved.

On the following day, Chaim's mood changed abruptly. He was asked to give evidence in camera before the Commission in a sitting which lasted nearly three hours. I noted:

What a difference from his feelings of the previous day! On his return home, he looked pale, sad, and worn out. His first words were, 'I feel the Commission has made up its mind; we shall have to make concessions. They are convinced that our case is a good one, but *imperial* interests are their first consideration; they cannot afford to quarrel with the Arabs. We have come to an impasse. The British cannot afford to establish peace by force; public opinion would not tolerate it. If they were sure of peace in Europe for the next three years, they might act differently. They will therefore have to go slowly for the next few years and see and leave the remote future to look after itself.

My husband expressed his main fear to me: it was that the Commission would try to 'crystallize' the Jewish National Home, a scientific expression of which he was particularly fond. He was afraid that the Commission would recommend freezing Jewish immigration into Palestine at a figure not exceeding the annual Arab birth-rate, thus leaving the Jews in a permanent minority.

Chaim told me that Lord Peel had asked him, 'Can you and we take upon ourselves the responsibility of bringing thousands of Jews into Palestine without being able to give them proper protection?' Chaim answered, 'We think in different terms, my Lord. The Jews, who are "protected" in Poland, would prefer to live unprotected in Palestine'. At this remark of my husband's, my diary says, 'Sir Lucas Hammond's eyes were filled with tears. They [the members of the Commission] were all most kind and understanding with the exception of Rumbold. He asked, "When will the Jewish National Home be finished?"—"Never", said Chaim, "England is never finished"'. By this, of course, Chaim

Vera Weizmann: a photograph taken during World War II.

Isaiah and Feodosia Chatzman, Vera Weizmann's parents.

Vera Weizmann (*standing*)
at the age of 19,
with a friend.

An early photograph (1904) of Chaim and Vera Weizmann.

Dr. and Mrs. Weizmann's two sons—(*above*) Benjamin, the elder, and (*below*) the late Flight Lieutenant Michael Weizmann.

The photograph of himself which Albert Einstein gave to Mrs. Weizmann.

A painting of Dr. Weizmann by the late Sir Oswald Birley.

A garden view of Weizmann House, Rehovoth, Israel;
(*below*) Dr. Weizmann's bedroom in his house at Rehovoth.

Weizmann with President Harry S. Truman and Mr. Abba Eban, Washington, (below) Mrs. Weizmann with Mrs. Eleanor Roosevelt at Ayanot in March, 1955.

Mrs. Weizmann and the then Prime Minister of Israel, Mr. David Ben-Gurion, with Mr. Meyer W. Weisgal, Chairman of the Executive Council of the Weizmann Institute of Science, November, 1958.

meant that the process of growth of any nation could never be said to 'finish'. Lord Peel then said that my husband would be called upon to give evidence again.

That same evening of 26 November, Chaim gave his impression of the Commission to his colleagues 'who had all flocked into our flat' in Jerusalem. 'There was great gloom over all of them and I had to shake them up. I told them that "We must not give the impression to the Jews, to the Administration, or to the Arabs, that we have any misgivings"'.

I do not know how far I was able to conceal my own feelings; but I was considerably cheered by a letter we received from our younger son Michael, dated 27 November and written from King's College, Cambridge, where he was studying science. Michael said to his father, 'Yesterday, I saw a report of your speech before the commission. It's the first time I ever heard you talk about a "Jewish State". Getting strong all of a sudden, aren't you?' He was pulling Chaim's leg; then he added, 'I think it was really very good indeed'.

Michael had obviously read press reports of the speech his father had made before the Commission on the 25th, but through some strange prescience, he had interpreted Chaim's remarks about a National Home in Palestine into a 'Jewish State'. In this speech, my husband had referred to the Balfour Declaration, which had mentioned a National Home for the Jews in Palestine. He explained that this meant a National Home, in the sense that we should be able to live like a nation in Palestine, at home there in contradistinction to living on sufferance elsewhere. Talk of a 'Jewish State' did not, in fact, arise until a much later meeting, on 8 January 1937. Michael's lively letter continued,

> I see that the situation in the western Mediterranean is becoming tricky. I wonder what will happen? There seem to have been a number of German submarines in Spanish waters, torpedoing Government ships. As for Madrid itself, it still continues to hold out. I really think it is magnificent, don't you?

He went on to say that he looked forward to coming to Palestine at Passover. 'It's so bloody foggy and dull here—and bitterly cold. Not like Macedonia!' (recalling an earlier holiday in the Balkans). The remainder of his letter was devoted to college gossip:

> I had tea with Professor Rutherford on Sunday. It was terribly funny. There was a huge tea party—about ten people, and typically English: everyone terribly shy, and wondering if they dared to sit down before someone else had! We all solemnly went into the dining-room for tea, and Rutherford

and I started talking about Spain, and he tends to shout when he talks so I had to shout, so everyone listened to us in awe! ! !

Michael knew what pleasure it would give his father to hear about his old friend Ernest Rutherford (who had been created a baron in 1931); Chaim had worked with Rutherford in Manchester, and had been on terms of intimacy with the great British physicist, a New Zealander by origin. Although he greatly enjoyed pulling Chaim's leg, Rutherford later became friendly to Zionism and the Hebrew University.

Michael's letter ended:

On Monday week I have an invitation to King's College Founder's feast. It should be quite a good do. All the best wine is brought out, and good food. By the way, you'll be pleased to hear that I am eating less and getting thinner! There's very little to tell you. I'm afraid my letters must be awfully uninteresting, because nothing interesting happens. I only hope they still bring you joy. Good-bye now, children. Very much love, Michael. . . .

Michael's letters, interspersed as they were with amusing commentaries on people and events, did bring us much joy, as did also the excellent progress he was making in his scientific studies at Cambridge (they included physics and mathematics). There was a great difference between Michael and Benjy. Benjy was economical and thrifty; Michael was extravagant, with a great love of life. When he first went to Cambridge, we wanted him to learn how to deal with money, so we gave him a year's allowance. After the first term he said he hadn't a single penny left! We asked him how he could be so extravagant. His reply overpowered me: 'If I knew you couldn't afford it, I would not have done it. The times we are living through . . . who knows what will happen tomorrow?' Michael was right and I was wrong. There was not much time left for him to enjoy himself. When Chamberlain came back from Munich in 1938 with his bland assurance that it was 'peace in our time', Michael, who was twenty-one, and some of his Cambridge friends said, 'We are sold!' and, like the Oxford Union, declared 'We are not going to fight for King and Country'. But when war threatened they all joined up! Michael went into the R.A.F., and when war was declared the following year, he had already gained his wings.

*

From 27-29 November we stayed in Rehovoth, returning to Jerusalem on the 30th when Moshe Shertok (later Sharett) gave evidence before the Peel Commission. Sharett was an important member of the Jewish

Agency. Devoted and able, he later became Foreign Minister and, for a time, Prime Minister of the Jewish State; but his appearance before the Peel Commission was not altogether successful. He was to speak about immigration, industry, and the labour schedule.

> He did not altogether come up to my expectations. He was too quick, too clever, too long-winded. But the anti-climax came when he was asked by Rumbold about illegal immigration. He fell straight into the trap which I do not believe had been set for him.

Sharett stated that all illegal Jewish immigrants had been absorbed into the country's economic life, thus proving that Government policy had greatly under-estimated the 'absorptive capacity' of the country, and had, in effect, encouraged illegal immigration. Lord Peel immediately reminded Sharett that, as a member of the Jewish Agency, he was supposed to advise and co-operate with the Government in preventing illegal immigration. At this, Sharett retorted that no Jew could be expected to surrender another Jew, or words to that effect. He then began to speak about the sad condition of Jews in Poland, but was interrupted by Peel, who told him that he was making a grave suggestion by admitting that he would not assist the Government in upholding the law of the land. The other members of the Commission shook their heads in dismay. On this incident, the Commission ended its session.

*

Our spirits were buoyed up, however, by a visit which Chaim and I made to Tel Aviv on 3 December to attend the opening of the new jetty constructed there by Jewish labour and capital (some sixty thousand pounds had been raised). With this new jetty, Tel Aviv became a port, obviating the necessity of using nearby Jaffa, an Arab town, as a port of disembarkation and embarkation of goods and produce coming to and going from Palestine. According to the mayor and the municipal council, the idea of the jetty had originated with them; but Sharett, who was present with us at the opening, insisted that the idea had originated with the Jewish Agency. It hardly mattered, as I noted at the time, since the concept was a magnificent one:

> We were taken to a large shed, where they are actually building boats. Why, Tel Aviv, may become another 'Hull'—who knows? The whole thing is stupendous, fantastically mad. On the first day of construction, the young men worked for nothing, handing over their pay as a contribution to

the Youth Aliyah Fund. Some of them can be seen in photos carrying a double load—as a symbol. By today, already ten thousand boxes of oranges have been loaded from the jetty. If that is so, why not a Jewish navy one day? But all said and done, I believe a good word must be said for H. E. [the British High Commissioner Sir Arthur Wauchope] for letting it go so far. Now there is no turning back.

But on 5 December I was a little more critical of Sir Arthur. I had given a ball at Rehovoth for the British officers stationed in the garrison there, and it had been a great success. 'The officers appeared to be very indignant at the inaction of H. E.'. They had been told before coming out to Palestine that the military would take over the administration and were 'confident that they could restore law and order in no time', but Sir Arthur had been reluctant to proclaim martial law.

Two days later, on the 7th, members of the Peel Commission visited the Daniel Sieff Institute at Rehovoth, but they stayed for only a short while. They 'seemed tired', I noted in my diary. It was on this occasion that Lord Peel came upon my husband working in his laboratory. When Peel asked Chaim what he was doing, he answered, '*I am creating absorptive capacity*'. I do not think the remark was lost on the charming, hard-pressed chairman of the Commission which was to bear his name.

Later in the afternoon of the same day we returned to Jerusalem and attended a further meeting of the Commission. At this hearing Sir John Harthorne Hall, Chief Secretary of the Mandate Administration, gave evidence. From my diary I take the following passage:

> When asked by the Commission what, in his opinion were the causes of the recent troubles, Hall replied, 'I cannot say'. Asked to elucidate this, Hall answered that 'it would be against Government policy', but when pressed by the Commission, he made the following points:
> 1. Federation of Arab States, including Palestine;
> 2. The Arab Agency to include representatives of the Arab Kings;
> 3. Restriction of Jewish immigration; the Jewish National Home to be kept in its present form;
> 4. The Near East was in ferment and ready to rise;
> 5. All Arabs were armed.

When the Commission asked the witness how Jews could be protected, he made no reply.

The next witness, Geoffrey Spicer, Inspector-General of Police, made a more favourable impression on me. He stated quite openly that no reliance could be placed on the police (he was referring to the Arab police who were reluctant to fire on their fellow Arabs). Spicer also stated, according to my diary, that the Jews were armed 'but they NEVER used their arms to attack'. This tribute to the policy of *Havlagah*, or self-restraint, which was initiated by the Jewish Agency and supported by the whole Jewish community, has been confirmed many times.[48] Chaim himself considered this self-imposed restraint one of the great moral political acts of modern times.

*

While we in Palestine were subject to these tensions, we were also receiving press stories and rumours about the abdication crisis in London. Most readers will be familiar with the circumstances which arose over King Edward VIII's decision to marry Mrs. Simpson and to abdicate from the throne, as well as with the part played by the then British Prime Minister Stanley Baldwin in these events. Baldwin was generally thought to have been responsible for persuading the popular King Edward to resolve both his personal problems and the constitutional crisis by abdicating. This King Edward did on 11 December 1936. When 'Baffy' Dugdale came to stay with us at Rehovoth some time later, she told us a charming story about the two young princesses Elizabeth and Margaret, which had been recounted to her by a lady-in-waiting. Elizabeth, who was ten years of age, and Margaret, who was six, were discussing their 'Uncle David's' departure. Princess Margaret asked her sister, the future Queen of England, 'Do you think Uncle David will come home for Christmas?' 'Don't be silly', answered Elizabeth, 'Don't you know . . .?' 'Know what?'—'Uncle David has run away with Mrs. Baldwin!'

On the 13 and 14 December we stayed with Sir Arthur Wauchope at Government House. Chaim had a two-and-a-half hour conversation with Sir Arthur, in which he was most outspoken, as my diary records:

> H. E. assured him that it had never entered his head to crystallize the National Home in its present state, nor to reduce the Jews to a permanent minority. He also assured Chaim that the Royal Commission's recommendations will be enforced. He himself could not take more definite steps because neither the Government nor public opinion at home would tolerate such measures. That is why he was in favour of the Royal Commission. To this Chaim said, 'Your Administration thinks otherwise'. The High Commissioner did not reply.

On 18 December, Chaim was called to give further evidence in camera before the Commission. Two days later, on the 20th, I went to

Lydda airport to meet Arturo Toscanini and his wife. This was Toscanini's first visit to Palestine, where he conducted numerous concerts. He was a remarkable and powerful personality to whom we all became very attached. When he and his wife lunched with us at Weizmann House, I noticed there were tears in his eyes when he beheld the Biblical landscape from our dining-room verandah.

At about this time, my husband and I made the acquaintance of Orde Wingate and his lovely wife Lorna. We met at a large party given by the High Commissioner. After dinner the men remained in the dining-room, the ladies retired. I picked out a most beautiful young woman of about twenty-two. She was not only beautiful, but extremely intelligent and brilliant. Afterwards, I used to tease her by telling her that she spoke like a leader in *The Times*! I did not know who she was. When the men joined the ladies, I said to my husband, 'For the first time I have met the wife of a member of the staff who is intelligent in her own right!' To which Chaim replied, 'Curiously enough, I also met a very intelligent man to whom I have taken a great liking'. The intelligent man was Orde Wingate, the intelligent woman was his wife.

The day after our first meeting, Orde expressed a desire to attend a Toscanini concert, but all seats had been sold. Chaim immediately gave up his seat to Lorna, a chair was provided for Orde, and we three attended the concert. Afterwards the Wingates invited me to have a drink with them in their hotel, but I said, 'I don't drink, not on principle—I just don't drink. You had better come round to our flat and have a chat'.

Our 'chat' lasted well into the night. Orde told us about his family background (he was a Plymouth Brother), his difficulties at school, and his early sympathy for Zionism. He remained a constant and unswerving friend of the Zionist cause which he did much to further in the darkest days of the years of pandemonium, and our personal friendship with him ended only with the ending of his life.

*

Meanwhile, momentous things were happening in Palestine in early 1937. During the closed session of the Peel Commission on 8 January, Professor Coupland, of All Souls College, Oxford, suddenly brought up the suggestion of the partition of Palestine and the creation of an independent Jewish State. His actual words, which represent the first official voicing of such a concept, were:

If there were no other way-out to peace, might it not be a final and peaceful settlement—to terminate the Mandate by agreement and split Palestine into two halves: the plain being an Independent Jewish State, as independent as Belgium, with treaty relations with Great Britain, whatever arrangements you like with us, and the rest of Palestine, plus Trans-Jordania, being an Independent Arab State, as independent as Arabia. That is the ultimate idea.

My husband heard these words with considerable excitement and trepidation. He felt that the suggestion held out great possibilities and hopes, but he could not give an answer to such a proposal without first consulting his colleagues. The practical details of the frontiers of this 'Independent Jewish State', as well as numerous other problems, had still to be worked out by the well-intentioned Coupland and those who thought like him. The idea of a minute Belgium of the Near East would have no appeal to many Jews; but, as Chaim said to his colleagues, 'I know God promised Palestine to the Children of Israel, but I do not know what boundaries He set'. It was round this issue that my husband had many consultations and arguments not only with his friends but also with the indefatigable Coupland.

Michael had been following events in Palestine closely during his winter vacations in London. On 9 January 1937 he wrote,

It looks rather serious about the price of £2,000 for daddy's head, but I saw Lewis Namier yesterday, and he said that the one certain protection that you have is that the Arabs know that if Daddy is touched, the Mufti will be killed the same day!

There had been rumours that such a price had been put on Chaim's head. Happily, however, nothing came of these threats. The Mufti Haj Amin and nine of his colleagues of the Arab Higher Committee finally agreed to appear on 12 January before the Commission, which they had boycotted up to then. Whatever the merits of their case, my husband immediately saw

in the establishment of a Jewish State a real possibility of coming to terms with the Arabs. As long as the Mandatory policy prevails, the Arabs are afraid that we shall absorb the whole of Palestine. Say what we will about the preservation of their rights, they are dominated by fear and will not listen to reason. A Jewish State with definite boundaries internationally guaranteed would be something final. . . . [49]

Chaim was never much concerned for his life; but he was not allowed to take foolish risks, and was provided with a bodyguard. Michael, who took these things rather seriously out of a genuine concern for his father, wrote later in the year (30 November), 'How is Rehovoth? A hotbed of Arab insurrection, I suppose? I think you ought to possess a revolver because I would not put very much trust in old Sach!' (Sacharov, secretary and 'security' man.) At about this time, when our house at Rehovoth was finished and we had moved in, a new body-guard-chauffeur appeared in our lives in the person of Joshua Harlap, a formidable and attractive man. My husband took a great liking to Joshua, who symbolized for him the entire Jewish people. Joshua is a fourth or fifth-generation Sabra (a native-born Israeli). He was, and is, certainly the best driver we ever had. I dare hardly call him 'courageous' because, like Orde Wingate, Joshua, who had served under Wingate for some time, did not know the meaning of the word 'fear'.

He has many other sterling qualities. He has 'golden hands' and at-tends to small repairs in Weizmann House; but if he cannot do some-thing, he promptly declares that it cannot be done. I then summon an expert from the Weizmann Institute!

Joshua also has a great fund of stories and anecdotes about my husband from whose side he was rarely separated, especially in Chaim's last years, but, like all good storytellers, Joshua also has a streak of fantasy. His affection for and loyalty to Chaim were boundless and he was al-ways a great favourite with my two sons. Joshua, who is still with me, lives in a pleasant, well-appointed house at the entrance of the orchard of Weizmann House.

*

Five weeks before the publication of the Peel Commission's report I urged Chaim to return from Merano where he had gone for a brief rest. I had heard from Jerusalem that the Commission proposed to cut off north Galilee in its partition plan for a rump Jewish State, and that the frontier was to stop at Acre and not on the Syrian border. I rang Chaim up twice in Merano; but he seemed reluctant to return, feeling that there was nothing more he could do to influence the Commission. However, on 27 May he arrived in Paris and saw the French Premier Léon Blum, who told him that the Arabs were insisting on the coastal frontier which had been turned down in the Franco-Syrian treaty earlier. Blum promised to make representations to the British Foreign Office and to Pope Pius XI. Professor Coupland also wrote to Chaim saying that he would like to consult with him again 'at the eleventh hour'.

On 30 May Chaim returned from Paris and was closeted with

Baffy Dugdale, Arthur Lourie, the Political Secretary, Dov Joseph, and Ben-Gurion. They were unanimous in rejecting the Commission's partition plan. At nine o'clock that same evening, Professor Coupland called to tell Chaim that some rectifications had been proposed, but that north Galilee had been excluded. He asked Chaim to think over these new proposals.

That night, according to my diary, Chaim dreamt that 'he came into a large synagogue filled with Jews all crying and singing the Kol Nidrei'. The Kol Nidrei is a prayer said on the eve of the Day of Atonement. This dream or nightmare made a profound impression on Chaim. Despite further representations from Professor Coupland, the Commission's partition proposals were rejected both in form and in substance. In the form put forward in the report of the Peel Commission published on 7 July 1937, the 'Jewish State' would have been bereft not only of Haifa (despite certain facilities), but also of Acre, Tiberias, and Safed. To the south, Jewish territory was to stop just south of Tel Aviv, and further south, the whole of the Negev would have been included in Arab territory. There would indeed have been 'no room to swing a cat in', as Lord Passfield had said earlier in another context. Severe limitations were also to be placed on Jewish immigration.

The *Evening Standard* came out with a cartoon by the brilliant cartoonist David Low, in which he depicted a *chalutz* (pioneer) standing on a tiny platform and holding in his hand a hammer and scythe. The inscription underneath read, 'Standing room only!'

My husband, who had previously been inclined to support the idea of partition as a talking point which could be developed on a higher level until most Jewish objections had been met, again found himself in the middle of a storm at the Twentieth Zionist Congress, where he was opposed not only by American representatives but also by the Mizrachi and by the Jewish State Party, a revisionist section, which had not left the World Zionist Organization. But a resolution was passed empowering the Executive 'to enter into negotiations with a view to ascertaining the precise terms of His Majesty's Government for the proposed establishment of a Jewish State'. The resolution did not empower the Executive to enter into any commitmants without further reference to Congress.

All in all, despite a wealth of good intentions, very little had been achieved by the Peel Commission; but the idea of a Jewish State had been firmly enunciated. In the next two years of appeasement, Chaim had many misgivings that the British Government of the day would in the end surrender Mandated Palestine to the Arabs, with terrible consequences to the Jewish community. Riots and violence continued as the Arabs, inflamed by Axis propaganda and the promises of their leaders, made repeated onslaughts on scattered Jewish homesteads and farms, bringing death to the innocent. Pandemonium could not be quelled by any Commission; but Jewish patience never broke under even the most intolerable strain.

*

The year 1937 ended for me on a more personal note. Benjy, now thirty, married a young medical student, Maidie Pomeranz, and this was a matter of rejoicing to us. I took a great liking to Maidie from the beginning: she was small and plump, lively and intelligent. After four years they had a son, David. Some years of great happiness followed, but later tensions arose between Benjy and Maidie owing to the incompatibility of their temperaments. Benjy was an introvert, Maidie an extrovert. My son found it difficult to adapt himself to circumstances; Maidie, on the other hand, when meeting difficulties in life, would exclaim, 'Well, it can't be helped!', and would dismiss the problem. To my great distress, their incompatibility ended in separation and divorce. Maidie, having finished her studies, became a Medical Officer in Dagenham while my son went to Ireland to farm. We have all remained great friends and visit each other in England and in Israel.

13

Prologue to Another War: 1938-1939

BY the end of 1937 whatever hopes anyone might have entertained that the Peel Commission's findings and recommendations would bring some semblance of peace and order to
Palestine were dissipated through the renewal of Arab violence. Not
content with attacking Jewish homes and settlements, they struck at
the British District Commissioner of Galilee, Lewis Andrews, who was
killed with his adjutant outside the Anglican Church in Nazareth.
Shortly afterwards Sir Arthur Wauchope asked to be relieved from
his post as High Commissioner, and was succeeded by Sir Harold
MacMichael.

The British Government's response to all these troubles and changes
was to appoint yet another Commission, this time under the chairmanship of Sir John Woodhead of the Indian Civil Service. The Woodhead
Commission virtually torpedoed most of the earlier Commission's proposals for partition and brought in an era of appeasement of the Arabs.

The two years which I shall now attempt to describe are some of the
darkest and most hopeless in the history of the British Mandate in
Palestine and were illuminated only by our firmly established friendship
with Orde Wingate and the handful of sympathetic friends of the
Zionist cause to be found in the Palestine Administration. Chaim himself never ceased to believe, despite every evidence to the contrary,
that the spirit of the Balfour Declaration would once more lead the
British Government to create a true National Home for the Jewish
people. Commissions might come and commissions might go, but, as
he had reminded the Peel Commission, 'it was from Judea and from
Greece, not from Carthage or Babylonia, that the great ideas which
form the most precious possessions of mankind emerged'.

We were in London when the Woodhead Commission was appointed in February 1938. We had reluctantly left our recently completed house in Rehovoth and spent a few weeks at Addison Crescent

before we again set out for Palestine in March 1938, a week or so before the new Commission began its sessions that April.

Despite the measures taken by the new High Commissioner to control Arab malcontents and the deportation of five members of the Arab Higher Committee which followed the assassination of Lewis Andrews, the Mufti and his cousin managed to escape to the Lebanon where they continued to foment further unrest and attacks on Jewish homesteads, British officials, and their own Arab rivals. The growth of the *Haganah* (the Jewish defence army) was particularly marked in this period. The emphasis, as always, was on self-defence, discipline, and restraint, qualities abundantly demonstrated in the most trying times.

We reached Haifa and were driven in a bullet-proof car to a new Jewish settlement at Hanita. The drive took approximately an hour. Here is my description of it:

> A few hundred metres from Ras el Nakura (Rosh ha Nikra), one turns off the main road to the new frontier road leading to the Huleh. The road is narrow and not metalled, rather wild, with lovely wild flowers and carob and olive trees. Suddenly in the hills we saw a white line which we took to be a village, but it was in reality a cluster of tents belonging to the settlers. We soon came to a turning and Sharett stopped and gave us an explanation. He told us that when the settlers had taken possession of the land there had been no road. The land leading to the spot belonged to Arabs. To get their consent to build a road was out of the question, as it would take ages. So the settlers took the law into their own hands and built some kind of road in four days.

When the Arabs complained, the *Keren Kayemeth* paid them in full. As we slowly progressed up the winding pass, we saw young, wiry, weather-beaten men working on the road:

> Our procession consisted of half a dozen cars loaded with armed men and a lorry filled with supernumeraries. At last we arrived. The settlement was like a military camp with dug-outs, sandbags, telephones, signals, and the skeleton of a building which will be a dining-room.

We also came across a solitary grave near a bay-tree. On the day of their arrival, the settlers had been attacked by an Arab band and a man had been shot dead going to the assistance of one of his wounded companions. I placed on the grave two white flowers which I had picked in the hills. 'It is a simple, touching, earnest, and courageous frontier life', I put down in my diary. Among the seventy or so settlers were a few kibbutz girls 'who cook, wash, and have already planted vegetables for their use. The view is wonderful, towards the sea to the west and the mountains to the east. I think it is the most impressive sight I have seen in Palestine'. The impression of that embattled settlement has remained with me to this day.

The same day that we visited Hanita we went back to Haifa, and then to Rehovoth. 'It is good to be home', I confided to my diary, but added,

> wireless reports state that two more persons were killed on Mount Scopus and four were attacked and killed on the Safed-Acre road and *so killing and creating goes hand in hand*.

Meanwhile, I received another of Michael's jocular letters, written on 17 April, from Cauterets. He told us that he and Benjy had gone to the Italian ski-resort at Sestrière to look for snow, but not finding any decided to return to London. They had made

> a fantastic row in the Italian tourist bureau and wrote to Rome demanding that they should refund us our rail fare in the name of the president of the Zionist Organization! Who knows? It might work.

Michael had perhaps not realized that the Italian Fascists had now solidified their Axis with the Nazis and would be in no mood to grant favours to the sons of the president of the World Zionist Organization! But Michael was in a gay, irrepressible mood. He was anxious to get back to London,

> to start some work and do some more flying! My flying is going very well now. I've done landings and take-offs on my own and also some spins! . . . When I am proficient I must fly you to Rehovoth one day!

He ended his letter, 'Benjy now wants my pen to write a letter, so I shall finish here. Merry Passover to you'.

But the Passover was far from merry. Chaim was in a particularly low state of mind, as a letter he wrote in May to Baffy Dugdale shows:

> I am distressed that Jews don't understand the apocalyptic nature of the times. The Austrian Jews had a warning and did not take it. . . . Our own friends in London and elsewhere will go on fiddling about in the good old way, not realizing that every minute may bring about either annihilation or redemption or both. Part of us will be destroyed, and on their bones New Judea may arise! It is all so terrible, but it is so—I feel it all the time and can think of nothing else.

Then he added in an even more despondent vein:

> A new leader should arise in Israel now who should sound the call; we are already old and used up, I'm afraid. . . .

Chaim was far from 'used up' and no new leader had appeared on the horizon. The main burden was still on my husband's shoulders.

From my diary, 14 May 1938:

> Chaim goes to Jerusalem to see the Partition Commission* on 16 May. The purpose of this meeting is to decide on procedure. Meanwhile, Sir Douglas Gordon Harris, member of the Executive Council of Palestine, presented his memorandum on partition to the Commission: everything north of Haifa is to be Arab, also all to the south of Tel Aviv—a preposterous suggestion. [In other words, this memorandum confirmed the partition plan already set out by the Peel Commission.] Chaim is full of plans and schemes, but I think he is very preoccupied and reticent. He is not too happy with our own people: the Zionist Labour Party is most productive in Palestine, but dogmatic, theoretic, and not elastic . . ., Peter [or Pinchas] Rutenberg is full of complaints without any positive plans; Ussishkin is obstinate and so he stands alone.

I may have been rather harsh in my strictures, but the divisions and suspicions in the inner councils of the Agency and the Executive cannot be glossed over. Even inside the Zionist Labour Party, which generally supported Chaim, there had been flutters of alarm.

I myself returned from Jerusalem, where I had spent two days with my friend Hadassah Samuel. I had also seen Agronsky who told me that Battershill† had summoned him and informed him that troops were being moved in to occupy the country, and that a barbed wire fence was being erected by Sir Charles Tegart around all major Arab centres.

> In this way Arab bands will be encircled in a flanking movement, or will have to escape as quickly as they can. At last the Government is moving!

On 17 May Chaim returned from Jerusalem where he, Ben-Gurion, Sharett, and Dov Joseph had met the Commission on the previous day. The three salient points under discussion were:

(1) The terms of reference;

(2) Would the Commission consult with the Jewish Agency as they went along or consult with it once they had reached their conclusions?

(3) Would the Government's memorandum presented to the Commission be disclosed to the Jewish Agency?

* As the Woodhead Commission was sometimes called.
† Sir William Denis Battershill, Chief Secretary, 1937-39.

The Commission replied that only the nature of the partition plan would be discussed. On the other points, the Commission's attitude was negative. Chaim allowed this to pass in silence but later said that he did not feel happy about the Commission's attitude. The Palestine Administration was one party to the scheme and the Jewish Agency was the other party and was therefore entitled to know the views of the first party. The members of the Commission were clearly discomfited. Mr. Percival Waterfield, one of the Commission's ablest members, then told my husband that the statistical and economic recommendations would be made available to the Agency but not the Administration's political views. According to my diary, Chaim replied:

> What business has the Administration to have political views? They have to implement Government policy. Of course the Administration has had experience of twenty years, but so have we, and now that the fate of the Jews and the fate of the Mediterranean is being decided, I have heard that the Administration has a partition scheme of its own, and we are entitled to know what it is.

When Chaim discussed with his Agency colleagues his interview with the Commission, Ussishkin was furious over what amounted to a *fait accompli*. Since the Commission refused to consult with the Agency, he said, 'I therefore need not give evidence'. 'Obviously not', remarked Chaim. On the same day, Chaim went to see Qwilliam to ask him whether the military would give their views on the proposed frontiers under the partition scheme, and added that an expert should be consulted. 'Whom would you consult?' asked Qwilliam. 'Liddell Hart of *The Times*', answered Chaim. Qwilliam promised to make an appointment for Chaim with General Sir Robert Hadden Haining who had taken over from General Wavell as commander of British forces in Palestine.

Next day, a letter arrived from General Haining inviting Chaim to lunch, and saying, 'I have a solution'. But Chaim's lunch with General Haining, on the 18th, was inconclusive—the only record in my diary is that the British commander-in-chief assured him he need not worry about the frontiers.

On 17 May Orde Wingate came to lunch with us at Rehovoth. He told us that he had just arrived from the north where he had been busy training his 'special night squads'. These squads consisted of motor cyclists and lorry-borne troops armed with automatic weapons, manned by predominantly Jewish personnel under the command of British and Jewish officers, and were responsible for guarding the Haifa-Mosul pipe-line which was under constant attack by Arab guerrillas. Wingate had a natural flair for this kind of warfare, and had as high a regard for the few hundred men under his command as they had for him. Orde repeatedly told all and sundry that the Jews made excellent fighting men.

On 19 May the members of the Woodhead Commission visited the Institute and the Agricultural Station and then came to our house for tea. They made a very favourable impression. I noted in my diary, 'Chaim thinks that Waterfield is the cleverest of the lot and is interested in all economic questions. He asked Chaim, "What will you do with the minorities? I'm worried. . . ." Chaim answered, "I am burning to show the world how minorities should be treated"'.

Orde came to lunch again on the 21st when he told us that he had been thoroughly quizzed by Haining. He had come back from Hanita expecting to be reprimanded because of his long absence; but Haining merely asked what he had been doing there. He said he had been (illegally) 'training the supernumeraries: the human material is excellent; they could easily defend themselves, and the sooner the better'. Haining knew that Wavell had given tacit approval to some of Wingate's 'illegal' activities, and cross-examined him closely. He also asked Orde to give evidence before the Commission. Loyal as ever to the Zionist cause, Wingate told the Commission that Galilee should be given to the Jews, and when Mr. Thomas Reid, a member of the Commission, asked whether the Jews would be able to defend themselves against Arab attack, Orde 'disposed of their misgivings'.

Our personal relations with individual members of the British forces remained agreeable. The young and attractive Captain Crossley came one morning at nine-forty-five and spent a pleasant day swimming in our pool and chatting; the Tegarts also came to tea, bringing two of their friends. 'They are in full sympathy with us', I jotted down; 'they stayed for the night'. On the following day, Hadassah Samuel and Eric Mills of the Palestine Administration visited us. In the course of conversation, Mills remarked that the creation of a Jewish settlement at Hanita 'was a tactical move' designed to give us a foothold in Galilee. 'You'll be able to grow a cabbage a year there', he observed sourly; but Chaim managed to shake him out of his pessimism.

On 24 May we returned to Jerusalem, where Chaim was to give further evidence before the Commission.

From my diary, 24 May.

Great excitement; early in the morning there had been firing in various parts of the city—a Revisionist stunt. Arabs retaliated by killing one Jew and wounding a few others; six Arabs were wounded. Curfew proclaimed at seven in the evening. I got a permit and went to the Tegarts' cocktail party where we met all the members of the Commission and had a talk with Reid on socialism. He is a friend of Bentwich's. Dined with Sharett. He is a wonderful talker.

Although I recorded on the 25th that Chaim had been sick most of the night, he again gave evidence before the Woodhead Commission that day. During a half-hour's discourse, he spoke so movingly that Ben-Gurion, Sharett, and Dov Joseph, who were with him, 'were moved to tears'. The questions which followed my husband's speech were something of an anti-climax, however. They went over well-trodden ground: What will happen to the Arabs? What will the Jewish attitude be to minorities? How shall we govern in a democratic state if we have a minority in parliament? Would we agree to accept Arabs in the Government?

According to the three colleagues who were with Chaim, he disposed of these questions 'brilliantly', although by this time he was 'simply worn out'. Later that evening, Captain Antony Simonds, Orde Wingate's friend, came to dinner:

> He looks like a detective. He is very intelligent, a keen Zionist, frank and very optimistic. He believes that we shall have the whole of Palestine before long through economic expansion whatever partition there may be. 'Your main object must be to occupy as many points as possible: more Hanitas. They won't evict you'.

I must have caught something of Captain Simonds's enthusiasm because my diary entry concludes, 'Definitely we have more friends and sympathizers now: Orde, Simonds, Haining, Tegart, and even the new High Commissioner'. On 27 May General Haining came to lunch with Captain Crossley. About Crossley I wrote, 'What a cultured, charming, lovable man. We certainly have a friend in him. He is anxious for Tegart to stay longer. His last words to me were: "There are wheels within wheels!"'.

There certainly were 'wheels within wheels'. On 28 May we made preparations for our return to London. Our well-informed friend Sharett came to dinner to tell us that he had heard that both General Dill and General Wavell had spoken to Captain Liddell Hart of *The*

Times, expressing themselves very favourably about Jewish development of Palestine and Jewish fighting qualities. Sharett added that he had received news that

> the French have at last made it difficult for the Mufti and asked him to leave the Lebanon and go to Baghdad. The Mufti will use the pretext of going to the Arab Conference there. Abdullah has sent him the copy of the memorandum he sent to the Commission. In this he proposed that Transjordan and Palestine should be one state: the Jews were to be allowed some immigration into the Jewish part, and, by consent, into the Arab part. But in reality Abdullah is for partition, though he must not admit it.

My diaries covering the Woodhead Commission come to an abrupt end here. Despite the optimism which they showed, an optimism encouraged by such good friends as Orde Wingate, Chaim and I prepared ourselves for the disillusionment which was to follow when we got back to London. Meinertzhagen wrote in his diary:

> *27 June 1938.* Dined with the Weizmanns this evening. They are just back from Palestine and not so depressed as I expected. He accepts partition of Palestine in principle but makes conditions insisting on a much larger area for the Jews, the whole of Galilee and a wedge right up and including the western outskirts of Jerusalem. Except on these conditions, he is not prepared to accept independence. Should the present commission return and find that partition is unpractical, then it means a return to the Mandate and Weizmann hinted that with a continuance of restricted immigration, trouble and bloodshed would follow. Up to today the Jews have been wonderfully patient, but that would soon be exhausted.[50]

The Woodhead Commission published its report on 9 November 1938; it proved to be a shattering disappointment. Christopher Sykes described it as 'a curious document, manifestly the product of puzzled and divided minds'.[51] It had no practical plan of partition to offer and simply recommended further restrictions on Jewish immigration into Palestine. A month previously Hitler had occupied the Sudetenland of Czechoslovakia as a consequence of the Munich Agreement made by Chamberlain for Britain, and Daladier for France, with Hitler and Mussolini, over the heads of President Benes and his government. 'What chance had the Jewish National Home with such a Government [of Britain], and what likelihood was there that commissions and conferences would deflect it from its appeasement course?' Chaim asked.[52]

On 27 November my husband and I, accompanied by Moshe

Sharett, arrived in Istanbul. Our purpose in going to Turkey was three-fold: Chaim was to try to detach the Turks from their pro-German orientation; to discuss the possibility of raising a loan to assist the Turks with their economic plans; and, thirdly, to persuade the Turkish Government to use its good offices as an intermediary between the Jews and the Arabs. Our visit to Turkey was, on the whole, a dis-appointing and dispiriting experience. The cross-currents, intrigues, and misunderstandings which prevailed during our visit nullified most of Chaim's efforts to find a basis for negotiation with the Turks.

It was a cold dull day when we landed in Istanbul. We were met by a Mr. Ginsberg and two or three German-Jewish professors who had taken refuge in Turkey. Ginsberg was a 'short, broad-shouldered man with a ginger moustache who looked, under his bowler hat, like a cross between a European and a Levantine'. Ginsberg was to be one of the intermediaries between the Turkish Prime Minister Jellal Bayard and my husband; another was Mr. Schwartz.

The city itself, which appeared so impressive from the narrow straits with its sprinkling of towers and minarets, struck me as 'very clean but terribly poor and dilapidated'. Even more depressing was the appearance of Mr. Ginsberg's flat where we were taken to lunch. This was crowded with 'German and Oriental junk, with hundreds of photo-graphs, dominated by photographs of Atatürk in every corner, on every table, on the walls, and in albums'. A manuscript of Atatürk's first Latin alphabet in his own handwriting and with his signature was also proudly displayed. 'The whole conversation turned around him; whether we talked of Turkey, Europe, the Jews, before we knew where we were, we were back with Atatürk!'

After lunch, the men retired to consider their plan of action and I was left with Mr. Ginsberg's two sisters and Mrs. Schwartz. From my conversation with them I gathered that German Nazi propaganda had deeply penetrated the country and that anti-Semitism was spreading, so much so that Mrs. Schwartz had taken her children from school—'despite their Turkish patriotism'. The position of Jews had already grown more insecure in the country since the death of Atatürk on 10 November, less than three weeks before our arrival.

When Chaim returned after his conversation with Ginsberg and Schwartz, he looked considerably put out. He told me afterwards that Ginsberg had said Schwartz had told him that Chaim had 'practically secured from the British Government the promise of a Turkish loan to the tune of fifty million pounds'. Ginsberg had promptly taken this information to the Turkish Prime Minister. Chaim, of course, had secured no promise of any sort: he had approached a number of Jewish bankers who said they might be interested in participating in a loan to the Turks, if proper terms could be negotiated. According to my diary notes, Schwartz himself did not believe that Ginsberg had committed himself to the Prime Minister.

We spent the evening with Mr. Schwartz and his family and met a number of German-Jewish professors and their wives. They appeared to be extraordinarily courageous and brave despite the difficulties facing them. They had no sort of security since their contracts could be abrogated at any time, and their children had no right to earn a living in Turkey. 'But they do not despair. "We have already been expelled once. We went through all that. Well, we can't do more than die!" said the wife of a professor of mathematics. I was so depressed and so forlorn I could not sleep that night', I wrote in my diary.

On the following morning one of the Ginsberg sisters and I visited the Hagia Sophia which I found 'superb in its dignity and conception'. I was particularly struck by the mosaics of this Christian Byzantine church which had been discovered under the whitewash and plaster used to cover them up when the Turks converted it into a mosque. As I noted at the time, this process of conversion was the reverse of what had happened in Spain where, for instance, the mosque built in Cordova had been turned into a cathedral. I was quick to notice that on these sight-seeing tours a team of some six Turkish detectives followed us closely wherever we went.

Next day, we got up about eight in the morning and drove to Ankara, the capital, where Chaim was to meet the Turkish Prime Minister. The flatness of the countryside soon gave way to hills, with a few scattered villages which reminded me of Nahalal in Palestine. The approach to Ankara was

> truly impressive. All of a sudden one emerges out of a desert into a lovely city of large boulevards, planted with trees, built on the plan of Washington, with neat modern houses, not altogether beautiful, but somewhat more solid than the houses in Tel Aviv.

My husband, with Schwartz and Ginsberg, was due to meet the Prime Minister at five o'clock that afternoon. But before this meeting Ginsberg began to hedge. He asked Chaim if there was anything which the British Government wished to convey to the Turks without its going through Embassy channels. Chaim assured him that there was about his mission no secret which could not be shared with the British Ambassador. Ginsberg then advised that Chaim should discuss the question of the loan before making any approaches about Palestine. He also suggested, to Sharett's annoyance, that Sharett should not accompany him on this occasion.

After the interview I wrote down the gist of the conversation between Chaim and Bayard as I heard it from Chaim. In the course of this conversation, Chaim said,

'I have friends who would like to assist Turkey in accomplishing its ten-year plan. Being a British subject, I have consulted my Government and found warm support for the idea. I have come here to find in what way we may be of assistance. I am not a financier but a chemist with chemical and industrial connexions: we may be of assistance in the chemical and industrial fields as well as in armaments, and capital for such purposes might be forthcoming'.

The Prime Minister appeared to stiffen: he had evidently expected a more concrete financial proposal. He said, 'We have drawn up our programme and arranged for all the monies we need. But we need money for agricultural developments as well as to pay for the settlement of some two hundred thousand Turkish immigrants from neighbouring countries. For this purpose we need a modest sum'.

Chaim replied, 'I should like to treat this subject with all seriousness and should not like to say something which I could not fulfil. As I have said, I have financial friends in France and Switzerland who wish to assist in some concrete form with your ten-year plan, but I must tell them what the money is for'. The Prime Minister then said, 'You may ask your friends to send me a questionnaire to which I can give a reply'.

The interview, which had lasted for an hour and a half, concluded on a friendly note, although the Prime Minister's dissatisfaction was apparent. He thanked Chaim for his visit and declared that Turkey required materials and foreign exchange. He had taken the intiative in discussing these matters without consulting his colleagues, and he therefore asked Chaim that their conversation should be regarded as strictly confidential, but he had to have something definite to bring to the attention of his cabinet colleagues.

Mr. Ginsberg remained for a further half-hour to continue the conversation with the Prime Minister. From this talk it transpired that Jellal Bayard had expected the definite offer of a loan.

The whole issue was discussed at great length, and it was agreed that Chaim would seek a further interview with the Prime Minister. Ginsberg, who forwarded this request, was told by Mr. Bayard that he had been 'very much impressed by Chaim's frankness, honesty, clear exposition and reserve'. He also mentioned that he had given Walther Funk, the German Minister of Economics, an interview lasting only six minutes and then told him to discuss details with his Treasury officials, whereas Chaim had been given an hour and a half. The purpose of this remark was fairly evident. The Germans had not only wooed the Turks with concrete proposals, but had taken considerable financial initiative in the construction of various industrial plants.

From my talks with Lily Ginsberg, I gathered that Schwartz had made rash statements to the Turks in which he had hinted that fifty million pounds were available and that 'three million would arrive in due course'. Not surprisingly, the Turks thought that Chaim was 'in control of vast fortunes, and was merely putting them off'.[53]

Chaim and I had lunch with Sir Percy Lorraine, the British Ambassador in Turkey. Sir Percy had evidently been told of Chaim's visit to Turkey by Lord Halifax, the British Secretary of State for Foreign Affairs, but Halifax had not specified the purpose of the visit. The Ambassador, who himself was involved in negotiations for a loan of some sixteen million pounds to the Turks, remarked that 'half a million pounds a year in foreign exchange would be of enormous help' to them.

After lunch, when the Ambassador and I went out on to the balcony, I mentioned the German installations at Barage with some regret. His Excellency replied, 'We can't have everything'. I agreed, but said that 'having lost Czechoslovakia, it is vital to keep Turkey. Funk is rather busy here'. The Ambassador said, 'Funk is nothing; we are doing a lot here now'.

Despite Chaim's efforts, nothing came of the proposed loan to Turkey, although he and Bayard parted very cordially. Bayard warned my husband that Arab representatives had got wind of his visit and asked him to maintain the utmost discretion. Axis secret service reports may explain the very unpleasant incident which occurred when, on our return journey to England, we were wakened from our sleep at the Italian frontier station of Domodossola.

A customs official, two soldiers, a policeman, and a woman suddenly made their appearance at the door of Chaim's sleeping-compartment. I heard one of them say loudly, 'Are you a Jew?' Chaim replied that he was. I asked Chaim if I had heard right. The blood rushed to my head and I blurted out, 'What the devil has it got to do with you who we are? Your job is to see to our passports and check our luggage'.

'Are you the President of the Zionist Organization?' the customs official demanded, and there and then began searching through Chaim's luggage, looking through every trunk, under the bed, and between the window and shutters of the compartment. In the adjoining compartment, I too was rudely summoned to get out of bed. I demanded that the official should shut my door. The door shut, I got out of bed and slipped a fur coat over my négligée. A soldier then entered my compartment and began searching my luggage. He had some difficulty in opening my dressing-case, but I did not offer to assist him. When he had opened the case, he took out my pearls and passed them to the official. 'Have you declared these?' he asked. 'No', I replied, 'I was not asked to declare my jewellery, only money'. The official then asked if I had any other jewels. I then produced all I had, whereupon he told me that I should have declared all these items. 'Very well', I said, 'you can keep them and I shall get them back through our Embassy'.

At that, the customs official appeared to hesitate, but I continued to insist that he should take them. Somewhat embarrassed, he returned my jewellery. The soldier had meanwhile made a cursory check of my luggage and pretended that he had finished, but the official said, 'There is more luggage on the top rack'. I then went into Chaim's compartment. 'I don't know what to do with the protocol'*, he whispered to me in Russian, 'Is the woman watching us? Go and stand by the door'.

I went and stood at the door of the compartment, blocking the woman's view. On the pretence of taking out a box of cigarettes, Chaim took a little bag which had already been examined. He then slipped the protocol, which he carried on his own person, into this bag. At last, the examination was over and I breathed a sigh of relief, thinking I could return to bed. But a worse ordeal was to follow. The woman detective ordered me into my compartment and insisted on a bodily search. The woman, who was very dirty and greasy, passed her hands over me, which made me feel thoroughly sick. She then opened the bed and finally looked through my writing-case. If she had been more intelligent, she would have seen my diary with all its information regarding our Turkish visit; but instead, she fussily turned over the papers and left.

This finished the examination. The customs official then returned and said rather sheepishly, 'We were notified by the police that you were on the train and that we must search you'. He added, 'You're having a lot of difficulties in Palestine, aren't you?' He was obviously trying to be pleasant, but I brushed aside his overtures and told him exactly what

* The official minutes of Chaim's interview with the Turkish Prime Minister.

I thought of all of them, adding that I would write a letter of protest to the British press the moment I reached England. He shrugged his shoulders, shook hands with us and left. It was on this note that our visit to Turkey ended.

*

We reached Paris on 6 December and learned that Ribbentrop was in the city which was seething with policemen and the Garde Mobile. The presence of the German Foreign Minister in Paris produced the usual crop of rumours. In my diary for the 7th I noted that there had been some talk in French and British governmental circles of 'offering the Ukraine to the Germans for the sake of European pacification'. I discounted these rumours, adding bitterly, 'It's easy enough to give away what doesn't belong to one! But it's a dangerous game nevertheless'. On our journey Chaim had received an invitation to visit King Leopold III of the Belgians. The day after we arrived in Paris Elizabeth the Queen Mother invited me to dinner, but I was exhausted and feeling far from well, and I had regretfully to decline. So Chaim travelled to Brussels alone and had a long conversation with King Leopold lasting through the afternoon until dinner-time. His Majesty was warm and sympathetic and asked my husband how he could help to alleviate the position of the Jews. He even offered to go to America to talk things over with President Roosevelt.

During dinner, while they were still immersed in conversation, two young children dressed in pyjamas entered the dining-room and stood looking shyly at my husband. They left after having kissed their father and grandmother. The Queen Mother said to my husband, 'Do you know why they came?' Chaim said he assumed it was to say good-night. 'No', said the Queen Mother, 'they are great admirers of Lawrence of Arabia and recently they read his posthumously published letters, in one of which he referred to you. It was in answer to a letter from Dean Inge asking Lawrence to contradict a statement made by Dr. Weizmann. Lawrence had replied, "What could be the purpose of contradicting Dr. Weizmann but to discredit him? Who are you and I to try to discredit a man whose boots neither of us is fit to clean?" The children wanted to see what the man looks like whose boots Lawrence and Dean Inge were not fit to clean!'

But Chaim's visit to Brussels was a brief interlude in a year of hard effort and much disappointment. In the spring of 1939 the British Government convened a round table conference at which Jews and

Arabs were to meet to try to find some way of settling their differences. The Arabs declined a joint conference. Chaim, though most reluctant to leave me in Palestine, once more followed the call of duty and went to London. My son Michael and his closest friend, Michael Clark, whom he had known since he was nine years old and who had been at preparatory school with him, came to Palestine to spend a holiday with me at Rehovoth. After a time my son returned to England to take his final examination at the City and Guilds' Institute. Michael Clark stayed on in Rehovoth. He was a charming and intrepid youngster who had come all the way from England across Europe and Turkey on his motor-bike. He, Lorna Wingate, and I, only a few days before the issue of the 1939 White Paper, went for a brief tour to Lebanon and Syria. We returned to Rehovoth on 15 May. We were in a particularly happy mood and had been laughing most of the day. On the morning of the 16th, I told Michael I was going to the hairdresser's 'to wash the dust of Arab countries out of my hair'. He said he would accompany me. Then he decided to go to Tel Aviv on his motor-bike to buy a Russian grammar. He hoped to go on a visit to the Soviet Union and wanted me to teach him Russian. I implored him not to go on his motor-bike to Tel Aviv, saying, 'There might be shooting, and a motor-bike presents a good target. Take my little car'—our 'Tinny Lizzie' as we called it. He said he would; but in the end he changed his mind and went on his motor-bike. On my return to Rehovoth I found Lorna Wingate pacing up and down in great agitation. She told me that Michael had met with an accident and had been taken to the polyclinic.

I rushed to the polyclinic, and as I entered the grounds, a lorry full of scientists from the Daniel Sieff Institute was leaving. I stopped the lorry and asked, 'How is he?' 'But he's dead', they answered. Hardly taking it in, I hastened on to the clinic; when I saw the still warm body of my young friend, I fainted.

It seems that an Arab, a certain Abujilda, had shot Michael dead, a mile or so from our house.

Although a curfew had been proclaimed, I managed to send a cable to Chaim asking him to inform Michael's mother of his tragic end. Chaim and my son Michael—his namesake—performed this melancholy duty together.

My sorrow and indignation knew no limits. I wrote to Mr. Crossby, the Governor of Jaffa, telling him, 'The twenty-two-year-old Michael Clark, a scholar of Rugby and Oxford, and a Christian, has been shot dead in the area under your jurisdiction. Justice has not been done and no effort has been made to arrest the murderer who bragged that he could shoot three persons with one bullet'. I received a sympathetic letter from Mr. Crossby—hardly a compensation for the dreadful loss of this beloved friend of ours. Michael Clark was buried in the military cemetery at Ramleh, his coffin carried not by his countrymen, but by a party of Jewish soldiers.

*

There was a touching aftermath to all this. A fortnight or so after the death of my husband in November 1952, I received a letter from Michael Clark's brother in England. He had read in the *Evening News* that two hours after the death of my husband, I had gone to the Ramleh cemetery, as in the past, and placed flowers on Michael's grave. I also received a letter from a Mrs. Baker who had read the same story in the *Evening News*. I was extremely surprised because I had no idea how this had got into the paper. There had been no one present at the cemetery when I went there. I concluded that the cemetery keeper may have reported my presence.

Mrs. Baker asked me if, on the next occasion that I visited the Ramleh cemetery, I would stand in two minutes' silence before the grave of her son who had died in Palestine during military service. Unlike Michael Clark, he had not been killed at the hand of Arabs. I have kept this promise to Mrs. Baker and for the past twelve years I have remembered these two English lads who lie in the Holy Land far from their own homes. Mrs. Baker, a working-class woman with a great sense of humour, writes me frequent letters and cards in which she addresses me as 'dearie' or 'darling'. Some time ago she went to the B.B.C. to ask if she could transmit a personal message of thanks to me over the Hebrew Service. She went as far as to organize a church choir in Luton to sing psalms on that occasion. I was deeply moved.

*

But to return to the round table conference of 1939. This conference broke down when, through some inexplicable error, a letter intended for the Arab delegation was addressed to Chaim.[54] It submitted for Arab approval a plan for an Arab State of Palestine in five years, with limited Jewish immigration during that time, and none thereafter without Arab consent. That was the last blow to hopes for the future of the Jewish National Home! The conference broke down and our representatives declined to attend a British Government luncheon. The Mandates Commission of the League of Nations would not accept the decision of the last prewar British White Paper. The Second World War broke out shortly afterwards, and the White Paper perished in that conflagration.

There was no alternative to 'illegal' immigration into Palestine. My husband, who had consistently warned the British Government of the consequences of their restrictive policy with regard to immigration, wrote a full and self-explanatory letter to Mr. Tom Williams, a Labour Member of Parliament who opposed this policy.*

Chaim was particularly disappointed in the attitude taken by Mr. Malcolm MacDonald, then Colonial Secretary. When I met my husband in Paris shortly after the death of Michael Clark, he told me that he had gone to see Mr. MacDonald at his country home. He returned to London in a furious mood, exclaiming to his closest friends, 'It is incredible that a man who has stood with us all these years should reverse himself so totally and be so unfriendly'. It was a sad and disappointing experience; we had considered MacDonald as one of our friends ever since his opposition to the Passfield White Paper; but in politics, consistency is not always a durable virtue.

My husband also saw the Prime Minister, Neville Chamberlain. Chaim had established warm and friendly relations with such British statesmen as Balfour, Lloyd George, and Churchill, but he could strike no spark from Neville Chamberlain. According to a memorandum in the Weizmann Archives at Rehovoth, my husband told Chamberlain:

> In the past twenty years a Jewish nation has grown up in Palestine which represents a distinctive civilization. . . . There is more moral and intellectual strength to the square kilometre in the Jewish part of Palestine than in any other country of the world. Our chief concern is not about the fate of the half-million Jews who are already in Palestine. These would give a good account of themselves in any emergency. What we are concerned about are the Jews who have yet to come in.

The White Paper of 1939 proposed that only seventy-five thousand Jews should be allowed into Palestine in the course of the following five years, and, as in the letter which had come accidentally into Chaim's hands, that after that period, none should be let in without Arab consent. At a mass rally held in London to protest against the White Paper, Chaim cried out with Biblical eloquence, 'There is a legend in our ancient land that, when the Bible began to be translated into Greek,

* This letter, dated 26 April 1939, appears as Appendix F, p. 284.

175

Palestine trembled from one end to the other. Palestine trembles tonight because it is being translated into Arabic.'

The Twenty-first Zionist Congress, held in Geneva from 16-25 August 1939, not unnaturally rejected the White Paper root and branch, yet at the same time affirmed its support for Britain in the coming struggle against Hitlerite Germany which the Russo-German Pact of 22 August made inevitable. There was also the usual quota of recriminations even at this last pre-war Congress. But perhaps the most moving part of the Congress came when Chaim rose to bid goodbye to the delegates, quoting from one of our ancient prayers:

> Who shall live and who shall die, who in time and who before his time, who shall die by the sword and who shall die by hunger, we do not know, but we part hoping that we shall meet again. Whether we shall, that is no longer in our hands. . . .

He embraced Ussishkin and Ben-Gurion; and the Congress broke up with heavy hearts. Very few of the Polish delegates, many among whom were our friends, survived the ensuing holocaust.

We arrived in London shortly before war was declared. Michael was already a pilot officer in the Royal Air Force and Benjy had enlisted in an anti-aircraft battery. The war for us had begun in earnest.

14

Michael: 1939-1942

FROM the ashes of the First World War, the Balfour Declaration arose like a phoenix to haunt the conscience of statesmen and to inspire the Jewish people with the hope of a permanent Homeland; from the ashes of the Second World War, over the bodies of countless millions, the victims of Nazi venom, a new State was born to take its place in the family of nations. It was a hard price to pay in terms of the personal grief and affliction which touched many families. Our family was no exception, and in that commonwealth of sorrow we too counted our dead.

As in the First World War, my husband girded himself for battle on the two fronts where his skill as negotiator and scientist was pre-eminent; but in 1939 he had entered his sixty-fifth year, a time of retirement for most men. Although his health was far from satisfactory, he immediately offered his scientific services to the British Government despite the bitter disappointment which he felt over the 1939 White Paper.

The outbreak of war in September 1939 put an end to all futile negotiations surrounding the White Paper, but the policy of appeasing Arab nationalism was far from finished. The early reverses suffered by Britain and her Allies in the first two years of the war only encouraged continuation of the outrageous proposal in that White Paper which limited Jewish immigration into Palestine, despite the tales of horror which had seeped from Nazi concentration camps into the cloistered corridors of Whitehall, and despite the magnificent speeches against the White Paper delivered earlier by Winston Churchill, Victor Cazalet, Herbert Morrison, the Labour leader, and other British politicians.

Chaim, with his usual zeal, not only sought interviews with many British political personalities, but, within a month of the declaration of war, had travelled to Switzerland on a mission of scientific investigation. He arrived in Geneva to consult with various German refugee scientists regarding rumours of impending massive German 'gas' attacks against Allied cities, rumours which happily proved to be without any foundation. At the same time, he made preparations for a trip to America in December 1939, the first of a number of hazardous trans-Atlantic crossings which both he and I were to make during the war.

But before I touch on these journeys, I should perhaps say something about my immediate family, our two boys, and the circumstances in which we found ourselves.

Largely at my friend Flora Solomon's suggestion, I closed down our house at Addison Crescent and moved with my husband to an apartment in the Dorchester Hotel. It seemed an unnecessary expense to run two establishments, one in London and the other in Palestine; and with our two boys away on active service, our charming Addison Crescent house seemed too large and empty for our sole occupancy. We reluctantly put up a 'For Sale' notice, without anticipating any buyers during the war.

Michael, our pilot-officer younger son, was undergoing rigorous training in various R.A.F. centres scattered over the British Isles. We saw him intermittently during his infrequent leaves. Benjy, our elder son, was stationed 'somewhere in England', helping to man inadequate anti-aircraft defences of London, in a battery commanded by our friend Major Victor Cazalet. We were frequently invited to Major Cazalet's lovely country house where his batman acted as temporary butler and an A.T.S. girl as cook, with myself as her assistant. It was my privilege to be allowed to do the washing up.

I recall Victor Cazalet with particular warmth and affection. Not only was he a splendid host, and a courageous and outspoken friend of the Zionist cause, but, as a prominent Conservative Member of Parliament, he acted as a kind of liaison officer between the Parliamentary Committee on Palestine and the Jewish Agency. Shortly after his unfortunate death in 1942 in an aeroplane crash, in which General Sikorsky, the Polish commander-in-chief, also died, his sister Thelma brought me a lovely painting by Dame Laura Knight which I had often admired in Victor's house: he had left it to me in his will.

Three days before our trip to the United States started on 20 December, Chaim saw Winston Churchill at the Admiralty. Their meeting brought back memories of the First World War, when Churchill had for a time occupied the same post. After expressing his thanks to Churchill for his interest in, and the support he had given to, the Zionist cause, my husband mentioned his hope that a Jewish State of three or four million persons would arise in Palestine in the post-war settlement: a proposition with which Churchill expressed agreement. Chaim was considerably buoyed up by Churchill's friendliness, support, and the general optimism which he exuded in this early period of the 'phoney war', although there was very little Churchill could do to deflect the general line of policy on Palestine. Other issues which would become pressing a short time later, such as Chaim's project for the manufacture of synthetic rubber, were left over. Allied preparations in this field and others were slow and laborious, and in America, where Chaim hoped to encourage interest in the scheme, the response was still very luke-warm. It took Pearl Harbor to shake the Americans out of their neutrality.

It was more than two weeks before we reached New York: we had found ourselves stuck in Lisbon for ten days, waiting for suitable transport.

In a letter dated 7 January 1940, Michael said,

> I wonder what sort of trip you had. It must have been pretty cold, because I've been skating here! There was about two or three inches of ice on the ponds and flooded fields. . . . You'll be pleased to hear that our course here is being extended by a month, which postpones the day when I go off to battle, so to speak.

I must admit I breathed a sigh of relief, although I knew that Michael was anxious to complete his training and join in the battle. Nearly three months later, by which time we had returned from the States, Michael was writing again from the R.A.F. Station at Brize Norton in Oxfordshire (23 March):

> I am now beginning to get extremely confident in the handling of the machine and very, very sure of myself. Now, therefore, is the time to be most cautious and not to overstep the mark, because between one hundred and two hundred hours is recognized as a tricky period when one has ac-quired skill and confidence, but is still lacking in experience. I now have a total of a hundred and thirty hours as pilot. It is a good thing to compare this with the amount of training people got in the last war. Often they went up to fight after only nine hours' flying! ! You can't imagine how much I am getting to enjoy it, even in bad weather. The only snag about this is that we never know in advance when we are going to get leave (if any).

On 9 April Hitler invaded Norway and Denmark. The 'phoney war' was over, and Michael's elation was again reflected in a letter he wrote on 14 April:

Events seem to have moved pretty rapidly since I saw you last. I wonder what the outcome of it all will be. Wouldn't it be terrific if this was really a decisive phase on which we are entering? Why, I might even yet spend the latter half of the summer in the South of France!

He told us he had been offered the job of instructor on three separate occasions,

but now I think I have a very reasonable chance of getting into flying-boats so I am going to stick to that idea. Besides, I don't relish the idea of being an instructor for the rest of the war and run the risk of having my own neck broken for me by some silly learner!

He had received the sausage we had sent him and finished it almost 'single handed': 'it was simply delicious, quite the best I have ever had!', he wrote.

On 10 May Hitler's armies invaded the Netherlands and Belgium; and before the month was out, they had also invaded France, and the British Expeditionary Force was making its historic retreat to Dunkirk. These events touched my life in a particular way. It had been discovered when the Germans overran the Netherlands that Germans who had lived in that country for years as apparently peaceful and good citizens were, in reality, German spies. An order was therefore given in Britain for all German refugees in Britain to be 'screened' so as to separate the sheep from the goats. Some seventeen tribunals were established in London, and volunteers were called for to act as interpreters. As I spoke a number of languages, I offered my services on behalf of the refugees and was accepted.

Within a couple of days, I had established cordial relations with three men from Scotland Yard, headed by the famous 'Fabian of the Yard', and with the presiding magistrate. They showed sufficient confidence in me to exchange reports and papers in checking the history of every person we interviewed. These were placed into three categories: Good; Suspect; Bad. It was interesting work. When the work of the tribunal was over, the presiding magistrate gave me a box of chocolates, and I gave him a pencil with his name engraved upon it as a souvenir. On one occasion while I was still engaged in this work, Chaim came home and told me with considerable distress that a dreadful thing had happened: one of our prominent Zionists had been arrested as an unreliable person. He was a refugee from Germany. Neither Chaim, nor the man himself, could account for the arrest, so my husband asked me to speak to Mr. Fabian. When I spoke to Fabian, he promised to make enquiries. Later he said, 'Leave him alone, he's a bad egg.' As I knew this could not be true, I invited Fabian to meet my husband, who received him with his usual charm and conviction. 'What has this man done?' asked Chaim. 'I've known him for almost the whole of my life. . . .'

It now appeared that this man had written a postcard to my husband from Germany during the First World War, suggesting that they should keep in touch. To this Chaim had replied, 'We are on different sides and there cannot be any communication between us during the war'. The man had served as a German officer during the war, and this was his only 'crime', but his postcard had somehow appeared on his personal file! Happily, he was released shortly afterwards on our representations.

On 14 May, the day France was invaded by the Germans, Michael was writing to us again, this time from an R.A.F. station at Aldergrove near Belfast. It was a characteristic letter:

Dear Parents,

Here we are again, and a very good thing too, because on Sunday I very nearly had my neck broken! We had a regular chapter of accidents. First, seven of us got into an enormous Wellington bomber for a test flight. Just as we were taking off, another small machine on the ground taxied up behind us and the stream of air from our propellers lifted the other machine off the ground and blew it off the field, smashing it up nicely.

Well, we got off all right, but when we came in to land, something went wrong, and we were unable to reduce speed below 110 m.p.h.! We touched down about half way over the aerodrome still going at a hell of a speed, and by this time it was obvious we would never stop in time, so we all braced ourselves against the internal framework of the machine and waited for the crash! We hurtled on to the end of the field, tore through some hedges and over a deep ditch in which one wheel collapsed, then we swung round and finally came to rest up against a fence just short of some trees—and luckily we did not catch fire and no one was badly hurt! ! ! Except the machine!

But that is not all—the same evening the garage here caught fire and I had to rush in and get my car out before it also took fire. I got it out just in time, but two other cars were completely burnt out! ! What a day it was!

Well, what do you think of the war situation now? At last we really seem to have got to work, though with what results remains to be seen. . . .

The results were fairly predictable as France fell; soon German bombers began to attack London day and night. Life became thoroughly uncomfortable with lack of sleep and severe cuts in the food rations. Chaim was working in the postage-stamp size laboratory put at his service by the Ministry of Supply, at that time headed by Herbert Morrison. This laboratory was at 25 Grosvenor Crescent Mews, a few minutes away on foot from the Dorchester, across Hyde Park. Here he worked on his isoprene process for the production of synthetic rubber, and on various developments in the production of high-octane fuels. He worked doggedly without much care for the German raiders overhead, refusing to go down into the shelters. This attitude of mind may have saved his life when a direct hit from a bomb killed more than a dozen people who had taken shelter in the underground cellars of the Alexandra Hotel in Knightsbridge, which backed on to his laboratory and was the spot where he and his assistants would normally have taken shelter.[55]

At the same time as he worked on his scientific experiments, Chaim was engaged in promoting the idea of a Jewish Brigade. Although Winston Churchill himself appeared to be favourably disposed to this idea, the Colonial Office insisted on some kind of 'parity' between Jewish and Arab recruits in Palestine, and the whole idea had to wait four more years before the Jewish Brigade received official sanction.[56] But Michael, who had got wind of Chaim's talks with Churchill, wrote in an optimistic mood on 23 September 1940, 'I am so glad you've got the Jewish Army at last. Perhaps I shall get a job there in connexion with the air force! It would be fun if it were possible, wouldn't it?'

Michael also told us that he had been training to fly heavy night-bombers and looked forward to doing some night bombing. 'It is very satisfying to fly a really big machine for a change—the type of thing which might carry forty passengers in peace time!' he wrote. He also urged us to impress on 'Ossinka' Blumenfeld the necessity of moving himself and his family from the South of France 'damned quick' before the Germans occupied the whole of that country. 'I trust you are weathering the air raids successfully', he ended. 'It must be very unpleasant indeed. Do keep me informed of your continued safety and whereabouts'.

Mercifully, we passed unscathed through these raids, without taking any special precautions. As Chaim himself observed later, 'we preferred to die in our own bed rather than be cooped up in a cellar where, to the danger of immediate death from explosion, was added the danger of suffocation'.[57]

But the outlook for our young daughter-in-law Maidie was daunting. While Benjy was away manning an anti-aircraft battery in Kent,

Maidie was left on her own to cope as best she could. She was at this time expecting a child and had found a charming little house near Buckingham Palace once inhabited by some lady-in-waiting; but the house proved too difficult to run without any domestic help, so she had to give it up.

On one and only one occasion, I found Maidie crying helplessly. She said to me, 'Even a dog has a place to have her puppies, but I have nowhere to go!' Fortunately, Sigmund Gestetner, our great friend and a prominent Zionist, who had sent his wife and three children to Australia, offered Maidie the hospitality of his house at Bosham, near Bognor Regis. Our grandson David was born on 13 October 1940. Chaim and I grew particularly attached to David—'a bright spark', as my husband called him.

At this stage of the war, I myself was far from idle. In between visits to America with Chaim, I served as a doctor in a bomb shelter in the slums of London, in an enormous cellar in Spitalfields Market. I had more than two thousand 'boarders' of every nationality, some hostile, some friendly, who used to come from work, have a meal at the snack bar or bring their rations, and settle down for the night. Whenever there were air-raids—London was bombed almost without intermission for eight months—we would put on the gramophone in an attempt to drown the sound of gunfire and bombing, and people would dance.

The shelter was run by the Red Cross, and I shared a surgery with an Indian doctor. A little Jewish dwarf, Mickie, was our most efficient manager. Since I disliked travelling in the blackout, I would leave the Dorchester at about four in the afternoon and stay in the shelter until six in the morning. The condition of the shelters was unbearable: sanitary provisions were primitive, with buckets standing in all corners, leaking through the floors of the shelters. There were three-storied bunks made of unseasoned wood where lice could move more freely than human beings. The middle bunk was so close to the top and bottom bunks that many people took it out so as to be able to sit upright.

At night I used to put on my white coat and tie a thick kerchief round my head to protect myself from unwelcome insects and, thus garbed, I would go on my rounds. On one occasion, I found a drunk man and woman, dressed in rags, smoking in a bunk. I asked them politely to put out their cigarettes because of the danger of setting fire to the place. The man replied, 'Mind your own business!' I said, 'It is my business to see that people here are not put in any danger'.

The incident passed off without any further ill-feelings. On the next morning I arranged for all the middle bunks to be removed and the wood placed on the dirty stone floors, so that people had somewhere to sit. I also made a heated representation to the then Minister of Health, Malcolm MacDonald. I wrote to him saying that I had abstained from publishing the facts about the appalling conditions in the shelters, and asked him to make the necessary sanitary arrangements. MacDonald, who had been under constant attack for permitting such conditions to prevail, saw me on the following day and promised to get the work started.

I may have been somewhat overwrought. Benjy, whose anti-aircraft battery had been subjected to heavy diving attacks, was suffering from shock and was to spend several months in hospital recovering from this shattering ordeal. Moreover, the imminent threat of Hitler's boasted invasion of Britain had set everyone's nerves on edge. We had been told that the first person the Nazis would kill if they succeeded in invading the country would be Churchill, and the second would be Weizmann![58] I bought some veronal pills to meet such a contingency, and have kept one bottle of these pills to this day as a sad souvenir of those times.

Later in the year, we received a chiding letter from Michael dated 11 December:

> If you'd only make your mind up when you are going to America I could ask to get leave earlier accordingly, but as you know I did it last time and you didn't go, and it will look bad if I ask for it again now for the same reason and you still don't go. Anyway, should you have decided by the time you get this letter, send me a *telegram*. Don't write because letters take about a week to get to this hole! ! That's just to make it more cheerful for us.

My husband was being pressed to make another journey to the States, this time by the British authorities so as to counter some of the anti-British propaganda then being spread in America, where Jewish opinion was particularly bitter because of the delays in forming a Jewish Brigade. Our second trip to the States, however, did not materialize until the spring of 1941. But in Michael's letter of 11 December 1940, he warned me not to refer to any of our conversations in my letters to him 'as you, Mummy, have already done. It is foolish, tactless, and dangerous and you know that all mail is censored'. I accepted this 'reprimand' with good grace. Anyway, Michael came home for Christmas leave, and on 31 December wrote:

It was heartbreaking to leave you on Friday, and you looked so miserable when I went that I could have cried for you. Those twelve days went all too quickly, didn't they? Still, I did have a marvellous time, and it was lovely to spend that week-end in Bosham with Benjy.

Michael had been down to visit his brother, Maidie, and his little two-months-old nephew David.

Despite his stern warnings about the censor, Michael went on to say in his letter of 31 December, written from the Limavady R.A.F. Station in County Derry:

Here, there has been very little change since I left, and I think it was false optimism to expect anything to happen in the near future. It is very muddled, incompetently handled and is not in the least encouraging. Unfortunately there is absolutely nothing that I personally can do. If only I could run the whole works for just one month, I'm convinced I'd show some results!

However, he admitted that his general mood had improved because of his home leave. 'I wish I could be more explicit', he added, 'but I'm afraid I'll get into trouble with the censor if I am. It's as bad as the Gestapo!'

Michael's restless energy and natural capacities soon found an outlet. Shortly before our second trans-Atlantic trip, he wrote on the 19 February 1941:

I have an idea that in the not very remote future I shall be leaving here for a different job, probably some sort of instructing. It is a pity because I have no desire to give up this job, having got so far with it. . . . However, it seems to be the policy to 'rest' pilots after so many months of operational flying, so there seems to be no choice in the matter, and I can only hope that if I do have to leave soon I shall come back to the same work later.

Michael had, I believe, done one thousand hours of operational flying, and had now become a Communications Engineer. He not only knew his machine inside out, but also knew how to repair it. I was told that he could read his instruments as a doctor reads a cardiogram! He added:

By the way, please don't send me any more sprats yet as I have not by any means finished the last lot you sent. They really are delicious, but I usually keep them till I need to eat at some awkward time, and then open a tin.

We had kept Michael supplied with any delicacy we could lay our hands on, knowing his fondness for fish food of all sorts. A number of our friends helped to forage for these 'snacks' which Michael ate with relish after an all-night sortie over the cold Atlantic waters.

In this same letter, Michael wrote, 'Still no announcement about the army [The Jewish Brigade]? It seems to be taking a tremendous time. . . .'

★

This criticism of Michael's was re-echoed in the United States during our visit in the spring of 1941. As Chaim subsequently wrote in his autobiography:

> It was not easy for me to explain away to Jewish audiences the humiliating delays in the formation of a Jewish fighting force, the less so, in fact, as American Jewry, like English and Palestinian Jewry, was wholeheartedly with England.[59]

The war situation was still desperate as Hitler's armies made inroads into Russia and Rommel's Afrika Korps battered its way towards Alexandria; but the war as seen through Michael's eyes had taken a turn for the better in the autumn of 1941, although he could not resist a bitter comment in his letter of 17 September:

> It's good to see that at least one didn't work for nothing through those utterly bloody winter months, when we lost so many in order to provide arguments (dead men are good arguments) for making things safer for those that followed. The fact that those losses were unnecessary and quite avoidable will, of course, never cause anyone any qualms, as those who sit in offices never care.

Like all serving men, Michael had a contempt for those 'who sit in offices'. A few weeks later, he was writing to say that he had been 'playing with such things as Hurricanes and Havocs' at an R.A.F. Station at Hurn, near Bournemouth. 'No one seems to mind what you do', he wrote on 25 October, 'and if you want to practise on a new type you've not flown before, you just get into it and take off!' He had even thought of flying up to London for lunch, 'but it really wasn't worth it as the days are so short now'.

There was no Christmas home leave for Michael that year. On 31 December 1941, he wrote to say:

> I've done forty hours in the air out of the last one hundred and fifty! In fact, every second night we've been up and slept all day so, as you can imagine, I am well past the one thousand hours.

He hoped, he said, to spend a week or so with us in London before our next trip to the United States. He had found life at St. Eval, Cornwall, where he was now stationed:

a bit more exciting than it was at Limavady as we are much nearer the enemy, and some of the jobs take us into nice warm sunny weather such as I have not seen since 1939!

I could detect the note of tiredness, of physical and mental exhaustion which Michael had now reached with his thousand hours of flying. Although posted as an official instructor, Michael more often than not was going out on operational duties. He was also perfecting the 'blind-flying' device he had developed while stationed in Northern Ireland. He had been appalled, as his letter had hinted, at the number of night accidents at this R.A.F. station, especially in the mountainous area surrounding it. Having worked on his device, he claimed he could return his plane, even in foggy weather, 'to the exact spot where I left'. He personally demonstrated his claim to Professor Patrick Blackett, the British scientist, who accompanied him on one such experimental flight. Whatever the merits of this device, the British Government awarded Michael and his collaborators one thousand pounds for it. The award was posthumous as far as Michael was concerned. Dr. John Kendrew, F.R.S. (who in 1962 shared the Nobel Prize for Chemistry), also spoke warmly of Michael's many-sided gifts when I met him many years after the war.

Michael came to London for twelve days' leave in mid-January 1942, shortly before Chaim and I were due to leave for our third and most important wartime visit to the United States.[60] Michael's leave sped by very quickly. 'I really enjoyed those twelve days immensely—more than any for a very long time', he wrote to us on 29 January, 'so naturally I was very annoyed to find that I was recalled for nothing at all, as I've been quite idle here the last couple of days'. The food had deteriorated, he complained, and the 'sugar and butter always run out before I get to the table! However, it is probably only by comparison with the food I had in London that this seems bad'. He had followed the debate in the House of Commons with interest, but thought that Churchill's speech 'was very poor'. He hoped that Churchill would not fall, but that he 'has a really rough passage to shake him up'. Shipping losses due to U-boat attacks in the Atlantic were reaching catastrophic proportions, and Michael, with all the impatience of youth but with all the experience of an operational pilot officer, saw nothing but muddle and frustration all around him. (The turning point of Alamein and Stalingrad was to come much later in the year, and the U-boat menace itself was not broken until well past the middle of 1943.)

Michael's last letter to us, dated 7 February 1942, should therefore
be read in the context of the situation at the time:

Dear Parents,

Thanks for your letters. I appreciate your sentiment about there being a
better world, etc., etc., after Germany is beaten, but I don't share your blind
conviction that we'll get it, because I see, at present, no foundation for it.

However, don't worry that I shall be depressed about it, because my main
feeling is not depression, but great anger and resentment against all those
whose laziness, ignorance, incompetence, and senile stubbornness have
brought about this state of affairs. . . .

This apocalyptic mood was new to Michael whose natural liveliness
and joy of living had been shaken by the severe losses sustained in
fighting the Germans, with half-prepared defences and armaments,
legacies from the Baldwin and Chamberlain eras. But Michael was
critical of himself, too:

I had a very long trip, over ten hours, on Thursday night, and botched an
attack on a U-boat because it was so dark. So now the silly old men are
asking why I didn't do this, that, and the other, so I am taking great delight
in writing rude reports to them!

I hope you do get away on Monday. Probably as soon as you're away, the
Government will decide it wants your process! I should then stick the price
up ten times and hold a pistol to their head if I were you—they need teaching
a lesson.

I'll ring you up tomorrow night to say good-bye.

Lots of love to you now, and bon voyage,

Mike.

Three days before we were due to leave for the U.S.A. where
Chaim was going on Zionist political work and to develop his various
scientific interests, Michael rang up from a secret R.A.F. base in Norfolk
to which his squadron had been transferred, to say good-bye. We had
a short conversation. He sounded rather sad. I asked him what was
wrong, because he was always so cheerful.

'Nothing wrong', he said, 'but I feel rather weary from all the
exhausting night-flights'.

This must have been on Tuesday, 10 February, judging from this
letter which I wrote to him immediately after the telephone call:

My dearest, we just spoke on the telephone and I feel like finishing the
conversation with you. You know parting on the 'phone is like parting at
the station just before the train leaves. One has so much to say and at the

last moment you feel completely empty of every thought and just wave your hand with an inane smile on your face. Well, thank God, you could not see that face through the 'phone! It was lovely of you to call us up. Dearest, we share your feelings of anger and resentment against apathy, incompetence, and all that goes with it. Common working people realize it, and their anger begins to rise. I feel very sure that before long there will be many changes for the better and we shall win this bloody war. The climax of indolence evidently has not been reached, but it is not too far off. All to whom we talk are dissatisfied and upset, and grumble. I think Cripps's speech was admirable, moderate, clever, and wise and won him great sympathy and support. I shall send you the electric iron and your laundry on Thursday. Please let Miss May know if you want anything. Chocolates you will get regularly. We leave on Thursday for Bristol at four-fifteen. God bless, Michael; courage, patience, and good luck above all. Your loving Mother.

On the following day—I discovered later—Michael went to his bank and changed his will, leaving some three thousand pounds which stood in his account to his brother Benjy. On Thursday, 12 February, we reached Bristol where we spent the night before our flight next morning to New York.

It was at about seven a.m. while we were waiting in the hotel lobby for a car to take us to the aerodrome that Chaim was suddenly called to the telephone. Instinctively I knew there must be bad news of our pilot son. In a few minutes I saw Chaim coming downstairs very slowly as if he were not in any great hurry to tell me the news. I asked only, 'Missing or dead?'

'Missing', he said in a low voice. 'Simon Marks rang up to say that there was a message from the Air Force to be transmitted to Dr. Weizmann'.

The text of the telegram was as follows:

Regret to inform you that your son Flight Lieutenant Michael Oser Weizmann is missing as the result of air operations on the 12th February 1942 stop Letter follows stop Any further information received will be immediately communicated to you 502 Squadron.

We took the first train back to London. We were met by Benjy and his wife and our close friend Miriam Marks. No one pronounced a word as we drove to the Dorchester Hotel. At the reception desk our faithful friend from the First World War days, Colonel Richard Meinertzhagen, was waiting to be with us in our hour of sorrow.

Friends, one after another, dropped in, if only to shake hands in silence.

I could not cry. I could hardly speak.

Meanwhile letters* of condolence flowed in. Sir Archibald Sinclair, the Minister of Air, wrote an appreciative letter; it was followed by letters from Air Marshal Sir Philip Joubert and Air Chief Marshal Sir John Slessor. From our friend Archibald Sinclair's letter, we gathered that Michael went out in his Whitley bomber at five-thirty-six p.m. on the evening of 11 February. Other details were filled in by Michael's station commander, Wing-Commander F. E. Richardson, 502 Squadron, R.A.F. Station, Docking, Norfolk. In this letter, the Wing-Commander told us that Michael was the captain of an aircraft on an anti-U-boat patrol in the Bay of Biscay. He reported engine trouble when about one hundred miles south-east of St. Nazaire. Twenty minutes later, he reported that he was alighting in the sea and that at that time he was still within a hundred miles of the shores of the Bay. Wing-Commander Richardson went on,

> A search was immediately organized, but owing to operations against the escape of the *Scharnhorst, Gneisenau*, etc., it had very reluctantly to be cancelled. However, the Bay in this particular area is usually thick with fishing-vessels, and the winds there have been light and would have taken them towards land. It is therefore not at all impossible for the crew in their rubber dinghy to be picked up and taken to France, whence the chances of escape are reasonably good. . . .
>
> 'Wizzy', as he was affectionately called, was one of the stalwarts of 502 Squadron, and his name has become widely known for his interest in the scientific development of the R.A.F., and for his exceptionally high all-round abilities. . . .

We continued to hope day after day that Michael and his crew had indeed landed in France, or some other place. But we heard nothing further.

I could not remain idle. I felt I had to be occupied every minute of the day so as not to think of the catastrophe. I thought my knowledge of German and other languages might be useful in censoring letters from prisoners-of-war of enemy countries in England to their families abroad. I went for an interview with the censorship department. I was asked many questions, as to my qualifications, my profession, and whether I was British-born. I was told that I should hear from them in writing. Next day I received a letter saying that my qualifications were too high for the job!

* See Appendix E., p. 288.

My husband, who knew the head of the Red Cross whose organization was sending food parcels to British prisoners-of-war in Germany, asked him to accept me in the packing department.

Next day I went and met the charming woman in charge. She asked me my profession and many other questions. Just as she was about to inscribe my name, she said, 'Are you British-born?' I was a British subject, although I was not British-born, I told her.

'In that case, I'm afraid, we can't accept you'.

Hardly able to get the words out I said, 'Not even if one of my sons is missing and the other is in hospital with shell shock?'

She shook her head.

Quietly I said good-bye, and walking through Hyde Park I kept repeating to myself, 'I'm not British-born. I'm not British-born'.

I told the story to my husband and a few friends. They were very indignant. Chaim got in touch with the head of the Red Cross and described what had happened. He immediately gave orders that I was to be received at work next day.

And so I started to learn to pack in accordance with a sample pattern laid down by the authorities. I do not think I ever put so much love into anything as I did into that packing.

15

More like a Wounded Bird . . .

THE passage of time left undimmed the heartbreak which my husband and I felt at the loss of Michael, a pain we shared with so many bereaved parents whose children died in the struggle against Hitlerism. Bob Boothby, our good friend over many decades, characterized this loss as 'a crippling blow', adding with his customary grace and affection that I was doing my best to support my husband.[61] Bob's warm friendship towards us helped to sustain us in those dark days.

Many good friends rallied to us when we were torn between hope and despair that Michael would somehow, at some time, return to us. It was, as my husband put it, a vain hope that pursued us for many years, and died completely only with the ending of the war. Dr. David Bergmann, a brilliant young scientist who worked with Chaim in his Grosvenor Crescent Mews Laboratory, did much to console and comfort us.[62] Private grief is not something which one can easily describe, but in writing to Baffy Dugdale (7 July 1942), Chaim had this to say about me: '. . . Vera is keeping as well as she can in the circumstances, more like a wounded bird trying to fly'. Chaim, as always, could find words for the inexpressible.

In mid-March 1942 we left for our third visit to the United States. Some time before our departure Chaim invited Simon Marks, Ernest Bevin, and another member of the Cabinet, whose name I cannot recall, to luncheon and urged them to free Britain from her dependence on natural rubber resources and to concentrate on synthetic rubber production based on starches which could be grown in abundance in the jungles of Africa. But the Minister's advisers told him that starches did not grow in jungles—in fact, nothing grew in jungles! My husband then went to the Colonial Secretary, Lord Lloyd, and developed his theory regarding the production of high-octane aviation fuel from the same resources. The Minister listened intently and was highly impressed.

He was not a friend of Zionism—he thought all Zionists were Bolsheviks; but when he realized that my husband's scientific experiments were successful in this direction, he said, 'Dr. Weizmann, if you can do that, I shall become a Zionist!'

But it was largely on Winston Churchill's initiative that Chaim and I went for the third time to America to consult with President Roosevelt on the pressing matters of synthetic rubber and high-octane fuel. Despite pressure from various powerful oil interests, Chaim's method was in the end adopted by a committee under the chairmanship of Mr. Bernard Baruch, and two parallel schemes were put into operation, one of which was Chaim's.[63]

Much has been written about the so-called 'Biltmore Conference' which took place from 9 to 11 May 1942 in the Biltmore Hotel in New York. Some six hundred American Zionist representatives and sixty-seven visiting Zionists, among them Chaim and I, attended, together with Ben-Gurion and other leading Palestinians. The programme hammered out at this conference called for the establishment of a Jewish Commonwealth in Palestine; it was supported by Chaim and by all sections of Zionist opinion, but divergences, as usual, arose as to the best methods to be adopted. Ben-Gurion, as one authority has stated, 'wanted to excite Americans into supporting a swift and revolutionary change of Palestine policy in which the British would be forced to acquiesce'. My husband, on the other hand, 'thought, with justice, that it was folly to risk a breach with England while he was negotiating for a Jewish Army'....[64]

The 'rift' which appeared between Ben-Gurion and my husband may, on the surface of things, appear to be somewhat academic and 'semantic', but it did reveal the difference in their personalities.

Ben-Gurion was a very vigorous and forceful personality in his own right, and his friendship and co-operation with my husband went back many years. They had a great and understandable regard for each other; but while Ben-Gurion was immersed in the problems of political leadership in Palestine, Chaim because of the nature of his work, background, and experience, concentrated on the complexities of diplomacy, foreign representation, and immigration into Palestine. He did not always invite B-G. to take part in the complex negotiations which went on 'behind closed doors' with world statesmen such as President Roosevelt and, later, President Truman. Chaim could talk more freely to these various statesmen in the absence of other Zionists. B-G. resented this, without understanding Chaim's motives. He also may have had some kind of 'complex' because of Chaim's pre-eminence as a scientist who had made a notable contribution to the Allied cause in two world wars: B-G., on the other hand, studied Greek and Latin, subjects with which my husband was barely acquainted. This 'rivalry' did not disturb Chaim, who always had a great regard for B-G.'s qualities and capacities, but he was often irritated at his obstinacy and the way in which this manifested itself.

These remarks should not be construed into any criticism of Ben-Gurion, for whom I have always had the greatest respect. I have listened to his oratory with admiration; but for some reason I have felt some element of human contact lacking in him: there has been 'something' missing in our relationship, despite his great personal courtesy to me and our friendly correspondence. He is one of the few people with whom I have never been able to feel at home, a quirk of personalities for which I take a full share of the blame.

As far as the 'Biltmore Conference' is concerned, I have little more to say except to quote from a letter Chaim wrote to Rabbi Dr. Stephen Wise in which he said:

> I hope you will forgive me for saying this: it is obviously nothing but demagogy continually to play the rôle of the Maximalist in the confines of a small room and, conversely, when meeting with Government or even with non-Zionist Jews, to speak in whispering timidity. I have always preferred the reverse.

*

In the autumn of 1944 we returned to Palestine after a wartime absence of more than five years, because Chaim did not want to celebrate his 70th birthday in any other place. I must now take up again the melancholy story of the restrictions on Jewish immigration into that country. According to official statistics[65], only some thirty-two thousand persons were granted permission to enter the country during 1940-1944, and this at a time when well over half of European Jewry had already been wiped out in Hitler's concentration camps. Most of the remainder under Nazi rule were to perish before the end of the war.

I can add little to the poignancy with which Chaim and I heard of the immolation of some one hundred and ninety-eight illegal immigrants who were drowned in Haifa harbour when the S.S. *Patria* went down after an explosion set off by the immigrants on that ship in November 1940.[66] These men, women, and children perished in a vain endeavour to stir the conscience of mankind to allow the helpless victims of Nazi terror to enter the Homeland. Chaim, who was beside himself with fury, turned to every British Cabinet minister he knew in an appeal for permission for the survivors to land in Palestine instead of being taken to 'exile' on the island of Mauritius. Lord Lloyd, then Colonial Secretary, tried to block every approach of Chaim's. In the end, Chaim managed to see Lord Halifax, then Secretary of State for Foreign Affairs, to whom he said, 'Lord Halifax, I thought the difference between the Jews and the Christians is that we Jews are supposed to adhere to the letter of the law, whereas you Christians are supposed to temper the letter of the law with a sense of mercy'. Chaim's words stung Halifax sufficiently to persuade him to permit the landing of the refugees. But many 'coffin ships', such as the *Struma* and the *Salvador* (ironic name, this!), were doomed to wander helplessly on the high seas until they were capsized by storms with terrible loss of lives. There were some outcries, of course, and at the British Labour Party Conference of 1943 re-affirmation was made of the Labour Party's traditional support for a Jewish Homeland.

But when we returned to Palestine in the autumn of 1944 the former British High Commissioner, Sir Harold MacMichael, had been succeeded by Field-Marshal Lord Gort, who gained considerable sympathy by allowing Jews, particularly Jewish children who had been sent to Mauritius, to enter Palestine. Our arrival in Palestine, however, was preceded by a political assassination of a particularly brutal kind. Lord Moyne, the Deputy Minister of State in Cairo, was killed by members of the terrorist 'Stern Group'. Chaim wrote to the Prime Minister, Winston Churchill, assuring him of his deep moral indignation and horror at this outrage, feelings which were shared by a majority of World Jewry. New acts of violence, terror, and counter-terror, continued to divide the unhappy land of Palestine. Opening my diary at 15 November 1944, I read:

We arrived in Palestine. . . . I fear to enter the house. It is so full of sweet memories never to return. What a dreadful word is 'never'. I do not know another word more distressing. Like a ghost, I move from one room to another and feel as dead as those who have gone for ever. I am frightened of myself. Chaim watches me. I pull myself together. Automatically I see people and talk to them. I wonder if they notice that I am dead? I suppose they do, but does it matter? Chaim makes me consult Professor Sondek. My heart is affected; I don't care. I want only to work and to forget. Professor Sondek gives me injections and pills, and I become completely free of any emotion—joy or sorrow alike leaves me cold. I can think quietly about my dear Michael. I am not sure if I think of him as living or dead. It frightens me, but it gives me time to regain my strength and balance; to attend to my public duties and to free Chaim from undue anxieties. Poor darling, he worries so much about me. He deserves a better old age.

We have not seen the country as yet, but have spent most of our time listening to all sorts of people who were happy to see us, to talk to us, to be listened to, and to ventilate their grievances after our years of absence doing political and war-work in England and the United States. Everyone seems very happy to see Chaim, to hear him, to lean on him and to be sheltered by him. They are so engrossed in their troubles that they often forget that we are at war. It is eerie. One person actually said, 'When there was a war. . . .' People on the whole look well, work hard, worry about future political policy more than future planning and economy. It is a lovely and lovable country, often absurd and incongruous. It is a land without twilight and a people without poise. The English will never understand it and I don't wonder.

On 4 December according to the Hebrew calendar Chaim celebrated his seventieth birthday. A week of festivities followed, in which he was greeted as if he were already Head of State. An armed Jewish detachment paraded before him, and a reception for six hundred people was held in his honour in Jerusalem. He was extremely touched by the warmth and affection which was showered on him on all sides. Visits were exchanged between us and the new High Commissioner, Lord Gort, whom I found 'charming, friendly and not at all "blimpy"'. He had done his best to see as much as he could of the country, and I expressed the hope that 'his mind won't be insidiously poisoned by our enemies'. Moshe Sharett was also present at the luncheon at Government House, as well as the political secretary of the Jewish Agency, Ivor Linton, and Eliezer Kaplan, a member of the Jewish Agency.

Between 12 and 20 December, we made an extensive tour of northern Galilee. We came across many well-planned agricultural settlements, with outcrops of industry such as canning factories, a factory for the production of agricultural equipment, and even a precision instrument factory. 'But people look tired, especially the women', I noted. 'They smile with their lips and never with their eyes. It makes one feel so unhappy. I may be over-sensitive. There are still too many speeches everywhere. So obsolete. I dislike politicians'. Even now, as I write these words, my mind goes back to the visit we paid to the Athlit camp on 13 December 1944. There had been nine hundred new arrivals the previous day, two hundred and fifty of whom were children, most of them victims of concentration camps who had managed to escape.

From my diary, 22 December 1944

They all crowd behind the rails to see us. So reminiscent of animals at the zoo. Children surround me and I talk to them in all languages at the same time. It is surprising how well some of them look after all they have gone through. But wait until you ask their ages. They are all alarmingly under-grown. Small bodies, large heads, old looks, and eyes that have seen too much. Nearly all have been in Transdniestria for a few years; *sixty per cent* of them are orphans. I talk for a few minutes to a girl with deep black eyes like pools that reflect too many images. The same old story. She looks about ten, talks like a woman of thirty, dainty, and fair; prompted no doubt by jealousy because no attention is being paid to her, she bursts out suddenly, 'I want to go to my aunt! Why can't I go?' I calm her. She, I assure her, will go to her aunt in a day or two. 'How old are you?' I ask. 'I don't know', says the child. She can neither read nor write. She was born grown up. I have to move away, or I shall burst into tears. I think they are just as anxious to see me as I am to see them. Why? I ask myself. And I answer myself: they have found someone to take an interest in them after so much neglect, humiliation, and insult. They all want to go to school. They are worried because they have missed so many years of schooling. . . .

In a large room, a committee of ten or twelve persons, seated at a long table, sat deliberating on the fate of a child. All shades of political and religious opinion were represented on the committee. Everyone was anxious to do the best by the child. 'I meekly suggest that the inclusion of a couple of mothers on the committee might be useful', I commented in my diary.

In the sick bay of the transit camp, we came upon two men lying in bed, naked: they had no underclothes, shirts or pyjamas. Kaplan promised to see that the men's needs were met. I spoke to the doctor in attendance: he told me that there was a high incidence of venereal disease among the children, the legacy of the concentration camps. How shall we tackle all these problems, without governmental powers of taxation and social reform? I asked myself.

In the field kitchen preparing food for the immigrants, I was invited to taste their diet. I found it simple but satisfying. The huge dining-room in the barracks was terribly crowded:

but great order prevails. People look sad, tired, weary, but terribly dignified. Their manners are perfect. Where did they get this nobility? It must be inherent in them. I want to cry, but I must not. I have so much to ask them. There is an old woman of seventy-four. Her chiselled face is white as marble; her hair is like shining silver. She is one of the fortunate ones. She has three sons in Palestine already, and she has arrived with the fourth. He speaks French; he is a secretary-bookkeeper. There is a lovely girl with golden locks and a wistful smile, from Budapest; and there is a little boy of eight or nine; he jumps to open the door for me, takes off his cap. I shake hands with him. With an elegant gesture he lifts my hand to his lips—he is from a little place in Austria. I don't know geography well enough to know where all these people come from, but I remember all the nine hundred and fifty faces. . . .

I could extract from my diaries a hundred other random impressions such as these. I remember particularly a blue-eyed little girl from Bialystok, who told us, with calm dignity born of valour, her experiences as a fighter in the Jewish underground movement. Her first remark was, 'It is easier for me to lay a mine under the heart of the enemy than to make a speech'. It was then that I began to understand the meaning of the phrase which my husband used so often, *Netzach Israel Loh Yeshaker*—'the eternity of Israel shall not be denied'. It was also then that I drew inspiration from the wonderful, life-saving work of the Youth Aliyah movement and its initiator Recha Freier, with whom I was closely associated for decades. This movement faced a terrible choice in the dark days of the war. As I wrote in an article, 'The Great Choice', published shortly after the war ended:

> In the face of the destroyer, the Zionist movement was compelled to portion out life and death according to the best interests of the people and its tradition. For what were the special certificates reserved for children, and therefore by bitter, necessary implication withheld from adults, if not an apportionment of life and death? What a terrible choice! And yet the choice had to be made.

★

On 18 December 1944, I noted in my diary a visit to Ein Gev, a small fishing-village on Lake Tiberias which made me think of the early Christians, Peter, and Paul. The settlement was beautiful and tidy, the people young and vigorous with a style of their own. Then my mind went back to another occasion, and I added,

> I can't help thinking of April 1939 when Michael, Michael Clark, Baffy Dugdale, Hadassah Samuel, and I made a tour of Palestine. The 'hamsin' prevented me from going with them to visit Ein Gev. On their return, I

join them and my dear Michael takes his seaplane from Tiberias. Did he know that this was his last visit to Palestine? He loved Palestine so; I am desperately sad.

As I copy out these words, a curious fact assails me: ever since my husband's death in November 1952, I dream of him almost every night, but of Michael I have dreamt only once in twenty years. . . . The processes of dreams are strange. I think that for a mother a son is never dead.

In March 1945 we returned to England, and my diary relapsed into silence. Barely a month before victory in Europe, Chaim was struck down with glaucoma, an affliction of the eyes which called for many complicated and painful operations; but his spirit remained unbroken as always. As the clouds of war receded, hopes rose high of a just settlement in Palestine. But the troubles of a world beset by vast problems of frontiers, re-settlement of populations, lack of food and of transport, bedevilled the unhappy land of Palestine, and justice for the Jewish people was lost somewhere in the agendas laid before statesmen. My narrative concerns events in which I was in some personal measure involved, and cannot take in the broad and remorseless sweep of history of those times.

The Jewish hopes engendered by Labour's victory at the polls in Britain in July 1945 proved vain, and the arrival on the world scene of Ernest Bevin as Britain's Secretary of State for Foreign Affairs, beneficial as it may have been in other aspects, boded ill for Palestine. My husband's encounters with Bevin, so warm and friendly in the first years of the war when Bevin required his scientific services, became acrimonious and harsh. The issuing of an inadequate number of immigration certificates for the surviving thousands who had escaped the gas chambers of Auschwitz and Treblinka was rejected with contumely by my husband.

Meanwhile, tension in Palestine mounted: an increasing number of illegal immigrants began to filter into the country, and the self-imposed restraint shown by the *Haganah* began to break down. Isolated attacks were made on installations and fuel depots. President Truman, who appealed in August 1945 to the British Prime Minister Attlee to allow one hundred thousand immigrants to enter the country, had a cordial first meeting with Chaim on 4 December the same year. The centre of Zionist political activity now moved to the United States. At the same time an Anglo-American Commission of Enquiry was appointed, and in February 1946, Chaim and I returned to Palestine. The forces of pandemonium which I described in an earlier chapter were again released as the Jewish people went into the final phase of their struggle for national independence. For Chaim who had always been an advocate of moderation and prudence and whose 'pro-British' sentiments had been under constant attack by extremist opinion, the road leading from the Balfour Declaration still seemed unending. Standing among the retorts and test-tubes of the laboratories of the Institute at Rehovoth which would shortly bear his name, he meditated on the fact that during the darkest days of the war the Institute had turned its resources to the production of pain-killing drugs, sedatives, and anti-malarial preparations. These had saved the lives of countless thousands of Allied soldiers in all the theatres of war. Our son had perished in the struggle against Hitlerism, as had many Palestinian Jews. The eternity of Israel shall not be denied, he had said, and now, stricken with illness and partially blind, he cried out with Biblical ferocity, 'Let my people go!'

There was one bright moment in his day when in June 1946, in the presence of a delegation of scientists from America and other parts of the world, Chaim laid the cornerstone of the Weizmann Institute of Science.

16

Pandemonium: Phase Two, 1946

LIKE other commissions before it, the Anglo-American Committee of Enquiry of 1946 worked hard but unavailingly to produce a solution to the thorny problem of Palestine. Richard Crossman, M.P., who was a member of this Anglo-American Committee and who became one of our closest and dearest friends, set out the dilemma facing him in these words:

> 'I arrived in Jerusalem straight from a visit to Dachau, quite overwhelmed by the need of European Jewry to return home. After travelling across Germany and Austria in the winter of 1945, I did not need to be taught the Jewish case. I knew it *by* heart and *from* the heart. And yet, directly I arrived in Jerusalem, I was forced into an agonizing reappraisal. What stuck in my gullet was the idea that British troops should be used to hold the Arabs down while the Jews were given time to create an artificial Jewish majority. Sure enough, I did at last come to the conclusion that the injustice done to the Arabs by dividing the country and permitting the Jews to achieve a majority in their portion would be less than the injustice done to the Jews by implementing the 1938 White Paper. But this was a complicated, terribly difficult decision to reach'.[67]

Dick Crossman's honesty and fairness stand out in glowing contrast to the attitude of the officials in the Palestine Administration who, in the death-pangs of the Mandate, lost not only their reason but also their humanity in dealing with persons and property. That time and charity will have tempered some of my strictures will become apparent: truth and justice are never one-sided, and I had lived too long in England to believe that such wrongs as I myself was to witness were anything but a temporary aberration provoked by the stresses and strains of those times. The generosity and wisdom which raised India and Pakistan to independent nationhood in 1947 were sadly lacking in Palestine. The corps d'élite of the British Indian Civil Service had not been reproduced in Mandated Palestine, although some capable and fair-minded officials were sent to Palestine. The Jewish people, Chaim and myself among them, knew that bayonets were a poor substitute for policy, and so it proved. A nation of seventeen million, scattered all over the globe, which had just lost six million of its sons, would fight for its survival and identity as it had done in its three thousand years of history. It was an uncomfortable fact, but a fact nevertheless.

That Chaim's chosen 'battleground' had always been in the field of human reason need hardly be elaborated upon. He had won a singular victory in the Balfour Declaration: the seed had been sown and now the fruit had to be garnered, with all its thorns and tares.

In his appearance before the Anglo-American Committee in March 1946, he reminded his listeners that the Jewish people had made a great contribution to Western civilization, citing such names as those of Ehrlich, Einstein, Bergson, and Freud. He went on:

> Now the cradle out of which these men came has been destroyed. We hope to rebuild it to some extent here in this country. . . . I need not go into the merits of others—I do not know how many Einsteins, how many Freuds, have been destroyed in the furnaces of Auschwitz and Maidanek. There is one thing I know: if we can prevent it, it will never happen again. That is what the Jewish people have set out to do, and if you help us the blessing of God will be on you and your governments.

But it was too early to pronounce our 'blessings'. The Anglo-American Committee's findings were published towards the end of April 1946; they recommended the admission of a hundred thousand immigrants immediately, the removal of land restrictions, and other minor improvements, but made no recommendation for partition. Chaim was stunned. The Committee's report, he wrote later, 'produced no effect, except to prove that the British Government had never intended to take affirmative action. The whole device had been nothing but a stall'. Dick Crossman, who thought that the increase in Jewish immigration would, if adopted by the Government, be 'useful, indeed a necessary step to an ultimate partition', was equally stunned when Mr. Attlee rejected the Report, saying to him, 'I'm disappointed in you, Dick. The Report you have produced is grossly unfair'. Dick Crossman was 'genuinely puzzled' and asked, 'Unfair to the Jews or to the Arabs?' To this Attlee replied crossly, 'No, unfair to Britain, of course. You've let us down by giving way to the Jews and Americans'.[68]

I will not touch on the political aspects of Crossman's attitude or conduct while he served on the Anglo-American Committee in

Palestine. He has expressed his feelings and views more than adequately on the subject, but he did come to Rehovoth to dinner and stayed talking with Chaim until two o'clock in the morning. He was undoubtedly a great asset to our cause. Conversation with Dick, I might add, was always stimulating and controversial no matter what subject we touched on. He reminded me of my student days when every Russian politician of whatever party promised his listeners 'the earth', ignoring realities. I asked Dick one day, 'Have you any Russian blood?' 'No', he answered, 'I believe I have every kind of blood except Russian'.

Chaim and I became very intimate with him and his first wife Zita, who died a few years ago. They often stayed with us in Weizmann House. Later on, he re-married, and he and his very pretty charming young wife came to stay with us in our home. He once said, 'Weizmann never seeks publicity and frequently goes out of his way to chastise his people'. On the last occasion he saw Chaim, my husband's health was fast deteriorating, but they enjoyed a long conversation together.

But to return to the reactions of the British Government to the Anglo-American Committee's report. Although this Committee had rejected by a majority of eight to four the proposal to disarm the 'illegal' Jewish defence force, Ernest Bevin insisted on this course of action before he would consider allowing a hundred thousand immigrants into Palestine. The reaction to such 'conditions' was immediate, as resistance sharpened and extremist forces such as the Stern Group began a shooting-match with British troops who retaliated by taking the law into their own hands and 'brutally maltreating numbers of Jews'.[69]

By mid-June the *Haganah* itself was involved in sabotage: nine bridges were destroyed, among them the Allenby bridge across the Jordan, on 16 June. On 19 June, the Palestine Administration arrested leading members of the Jewish Agency in Palestine.

We were beside ourselves with fury and indignation at this pointless arrest of Agency members, many of them our close friends, advocates of moderation who, with my husband, had done their best to restrain their followers. I immediately sat down and wrote an article entitled 'This is the Army' for the world press. Read in conjunction with my diary, the article exemplified a mood of bitterness of which I hardly imagined myself capable. The notes for this article which I jotted down on 1 July 1946 read as follows:

In the early hours of Sabbath, 29 June, the 'blitz' Army plan was put into operation. Four members of the Jewish Agency Executive, without warning or warrant, were pounced upon in their beds by the military and removed to the Latrun detention camp. One of the members was not even allowed to put on his clothes and was removed to the camp in his pyjamas. The acting Chairman of the Executive, the seventy-three-year-old Rabbi Fishman, a sick and deeply pious man, refused to break the law of God by travelling on a Sabbath; he offered to walk to Latrun, which was some miles away. His offer was flatly turned down, and he was forced into a car with kicks and violence; one of the gallant officers did not even disdain to slap him in the face. The Chairman of the Zionist Executive was thus delivered to the camp in a disgraceful, bruised, and humiliated condition. His religious feelings were more bruised than his body. Having involuntarily been made to break his religious tenets, he had recourse to penance and refused to take food or water. His condition was critical and he was removed to the military hospital next door. We have been told that he took some food this morning. The other members of the Executive were herded like gangsters into one room with camp beds, without sheets or pillows, and with no chair or stool on which to put their clothes for the night. Their families were not informed of their whereabouts. Otherwise their treatment by the person in charge of the camp was civil and correct.

The 'blitz' arrests were well synchronized, and in every corner of Palestine indiscriminate mass arrests took place. In some settlements the whole of the male population was removed and no one was left to gather the harvest. This—at a time when Europe is starved and the British loaf has shrunk. Swastikas and inscriptions on the walls—'Death to the Jews'—have appeared here and there; in some settlements officers entered with a 'Heil Hitler'. In Tel Aviv Bank Hapoalim, after minute and wilful destruction, the officer in charge did not behave in the traditional gentlemanly British way, but added insult to injury by shouting, 'What you need is the gas chamber!'

W.I.Z.O. House, the administrative offices of a purely social organization without any political bias, was dynamited, although anyone could have entered the house by simply asking the caretaker who lives in a nearby shack for the key. When the caretaker heard the noise of the approaching military lorries, he came out waving the keys in his hand since he could speak no English, but he was dismissed with a contemptuous gesture. The destruction inside W.I.Z.O. House defies description: the walls of some rooms were blown up, and huge gaps appeared; windows, furniture, crockery have been smashed in malicious premeditated fashion; papers have been torn and strewn round the place; the safe has been broken into and large sums of money and cheques 'removed'; thirty-eight electric irons used for instruction in the laundry have also been carefully 'removed', just as have rugs, handwork, and embroidery used in peaceful evening classes for young women. In the upper floor rented to the *Keren Hayesod*, the gaps in the walls are even more sinister, and hundreds of pounds in cash and cheques have been removed. No receipt for any of these sums was left behind. In addition, the index cards carrying more than thirty thousand names of contributors to the social and vocational training given by W.I.Z.O., as well as the names of contributors to our colonization fund, have been removed, paralysing peaceful social work in the land.

Was this 'blitz' ordered so as to discover the terrorists and to restrain them in lawful fashion, or was it a punitive expedition? Who are these Britishers who have perpetrated these unlawful acts? I have never met them in England, nor in other parts of the British Empire which I have visited. As a Jew I am indignant, as a British subject I am ashamed. Thus has 'Law and Order' been established. . . .

I should explain that the moment Chaim and I heard of the arrest of our friends of the Jewish Agency, we motored to Jerusalem. Chaim was determined to intervene with the High Commissioner, although he was suffering from a chill and running a high temperature. I insisted that Professor Sondek, our doctor, should accompany us on the journey. Joshua Harlap, as usual, was our driver-bodyguard.

I recall that we passed roads 'stiff with troops, armoured cars, barbed-wire barricades', our car itself being accompanied by two jeeps filled with red-caps—military police. (Diary entry, 29 June 1946.) When we reached Government House, Chaim pointedly refused to accept the outstretched hand of the High Commissioner's A.D.C., but marched head erect for his interview with the new High Commissioner, Sir Alan Cunningham, who had replaced Lord Gort some months earlier. For my part, I insisted on waiting for Chaim's return in the car, despite the midsummer heat and the oppressive thirst which soon made itself felt. I also deliberately turned down the A.D.C.'s suggestion that I might rest in the cool of Government House, and when a servant brought out a tray of cold drinks, I politely refused them.

My diary does not record the stormy interview which Chaim had with Sir Alan, but from conversation with my husband later, I learnt that he had invited the High Commissioner to arrest him also! But Sir Alan was reluctant to comply with this request. He did, however, give us permission to visit the detainees at Latrun on the following day. Chaim by this time was far from well and was confined to his bed; so Maidie, my daughter-in-law, and I went to the detention camp, taking such items as shaving-soap and tooth paste with us, together with a food parcel. The four arrested Jewish Agency men, Moshe Sharett, Dov Joseph, Rabbi J. L. Fishman, and I. Gruenbaum, had now been joined by David Remez and others. They were naturally highly indignant at their treatment, but remained remarkably cheerful in the circumstances, and were greatly cheered by our visit.

On the next day, 1 July, I attended the meeting of the Executive, bringing a message from Chaim. In this verbal message, he urged the Executive to continue its work but to 'abstain from violence'. Meanwhile, the Executive had received a telephonic communication from Haifa, stating that a number of detainees at Yagour had been tortured by British soldiers. I was extremely shocked—my 'pro-British' sentiments could never quite reconcile themselves to such behaviour—and immediately went to the King David Hotel to see Colonel Martin Charteris (later Sir Martin) of Army Intelligence. He promised to investigate the Yagour incident personally. I also pleaded with him to release Fishman and send him home. To this Martin Charteris—an old acquaintance of ours—said that Fishman could go where he pleased.

On 2 July, I visited W.I.Z.O. House at the invitation of that organization to inspect the damage which had been done. 'When I complained to the O.C., Colonel Kappy, and told him what I thought of his officers and men—Hitler's behaviour—he wriggled', I noted in my diary. He also refused to confirm our lawyer's report on the extensive damage which had been done. I sent copies of the report to Lt.-General Sir Evelyn Barker, commander-in-chief of British forces in Palestine, to Martin Charteris, to the High Commissioner, and to his chief secretary.

On this same date, I also learned that the Censor had refused to pass my article 'This is the Army' for publication! Agronsky, Editor of the *Palestine Post*, promptly issued it to the international press, and it was published.

On 4 July, I received a letter from Martin Charteris, dated the previous day, which I think deserves quotation since it puts a certain corrective on the information we had received about the 'torture' at Yagour. Colonel Charteris wrote:

> I have done what I can to look into the matters you spoke to me about yesterday, and have been fairly successful. I visited YAGOUR and talked to the soldiers there. I can give you an absolute assurance that there was NO brutality, and that only sufficient force was used to gain entry into the settlement and to remove members of the settlement for further investigation.
>
> The shouting and cries were from those who were being arrested, and the reason was their arrest and not because of brutality. Naturally they object

to being arrested and naturally they resist: the soldiers have to do it, and I promise you they do it with the least possible force. The women and children at YAGOUR, though naturally disliking the whole business, and unhappy, seemed in good health.

You spoke too of money and valuables removed from TEL AVIV. This was done, but a careful inventory was kept, and they will be returned as soon as possible. Considerable efforts were made by the officers to ensure against looting, and any cases discovered will be dealt with.

The British Army are NOT all angels; sometimes things are done thoughtlessly for which everyone is sorry, but I sincerely believe they are the best behaved Army in the world. They do NOT hate. They are NOT making war upon the Jewish people.

Will you allow me to say again how deeply distressed I am for you and for Professor WEIZMANN? During the last two months, I have valued your friendship very highly.

I was impressed with the expeditious way in which Colonel Charteris had dealt with my complaints, although I was to take issue with him again. There had been unconfirmed rumours of torture used against detainees at Rafah and these I duly reported to him. On 4 July he wrote to me again, telling me he had asked Rabbi Goldman, an American chaplain, to visit Rafah so as to report on conditions there to me personally. 'He is a most excellent man. I personally will believe anything he says', Colonel Charteris told me, adding, 'I will be grateful for anything you can tell me about the W.I.Z.O. building'. He ended his letter in friendly fashion, 'I will not say any more now. I hope Professor Weizmann is improving in health. He said that in PALESTINE it is Black or White. Just now I am afraid it is Black. I can only express my belief that one day it will be White again'.

Rabbi Goldman did confirm that no torture had been used at Rafah, and that the military had behaved correctly, but that there had been isolated cases of ill-treatment at Athlit. A number of men who had refused to give their names were taken by the C.I.D. and military into a room where they had been beaten up. One of these detainees, a Mr. Shattner, had purposely refused to give his name 'in order to find out what is being done', I wrote in my diary of 4 July. 'He was taken by four men by the feet and hair and dropped on to the floor. This they repeated three times until he fainted. Then he told his name and his reason for refusing it at first. This case and a few more are being investigated'.

I asked Rabbi Goldman and another American chaplain, Rabbi Goldfall who accompanied him on this tour of inspection, to report to

Colonel Charteris 'that I am not satisfied that people were not tortured, unless our notions of torture differ'.

On 9 July Chaim attended the Zionist Actions Committee meeting in Jerusalem, and later released to the press the statement he made to that committee. Part of it ran:

> When I am asked these days to use my 'restraining influence', my mind goes back some forty years or more to the day when a poor Jewish tailor shot the Governor-General at Vilna. We were called by Plehve [the Russian Minister of the Interior] and commanded to 'restrain' our young men, lest worse things befall us. And we told Plehve that, much as we deplored such acts of violence, they were the inevitable result of the impossible conditions which Russia herself created for her Jewish population and which deprived the leaders of the community of any influence they might otherwise have possessed. Looking back now, I see that the single shot fired by a little Jewish tailor was the first shot of the 'Great Revolution'. Nothing could be further from my mind than to suggest comparisons between the Czarist regime and the British Government today—but one's memory is sometimes irrational....
> I appeal to the British people, and its Government: Stay your hand! There is still time to undo the wrong you have done us. You are keeping behind bars, in Latrun and Buchenwald, those who, in the hour of your greatest need, when you stood alone, helped you in the great struggle for survival. Ours is no less a struggle. Let my people go!

Perhaps, in the heat of the moment, my husband can be forgiven for linking Latrun and Buchenwald—that notorious concentration camp where Hitler's former victims still languished waiting for 'permits' to enter Palestine.

On 12 July, Martin Charteris came to tea. It was not a very happy social occasion, although Chaim and I were very fond of Martin. My husband told him that he had made every effort to prevent further sabotage, but that indignation was rising and that but for his efforts 'the British would shoot thousands of Jews which would not be good for either party'. He also told Charteris that he would not be able to continue as president of the World Zionist Organization unless he could call an Executive meeting either in London or in Paris, and for this, his colleagues of the Jewish Agency would have to be released. Charteris promised to do what he could. He told us he himself was going on two weeks' leave to England.

On 14 July, against his better judgement, Chaim visited the High Commissioner, Sir Alan Cunningham. He had been persuaded that

Sir Alan might agree to release the detainees at the Latrun camp. The meeting proved abortive since the High Commissioner refused Chaim's plea, and he returned to Rehovoth saying that he had gone on 'a fool's errand'. While in Jerusalem, he had been told that General Barker had said aloud at a dinner party given by a Mrs. Pollock that he would 'like to see every Jew uprooted', a remark which was promptly challenged by another British officer who was present.

*

On 17 July Chaim and I left for London, where pressing political matters awaited him. We were met not only by a host of photographers but by Maidie, Benjy, and our grandson David, now six years old, together with Baffy Dugdale and many others of our friends. Next day Isaiah Berlin came to lunch, bringing with him the draft of a letter he proposed to send to *The Times*. Chaim made a number of suggestions which Isaiah incorporated into his letter.

The next few days were spent in deciding where to hold a meeting of the Agency Executive. Paris was suggested as a possible meeting place because B-G. did not dare to come to London at this time of upheavals and Chaim could not travel to Paris because he had undergone a serious operation on his eyes and was confined to bed in the home of Victor Rothschild at Tring. He appointed Meyer Weisgal as his representative at the Paris meeting. But delegations came every few days to consult with Chaim. One delegation consisted of Dr. Nahum Goldmann, Eliezer Kaplan, Golda Myerson and Meyer W. Weisgal. They made three separate trips during the meeting of the Executive in Paris in order to ascertain Chaim's views on a variety of important questions.

*

At four-fifteen p.m. on 17 July, the United Press rang up to say that terrorists had blown up the Military and Administrative offices in the King David Hotel in Jerusalem. There were many dead, wounded, and missing. We were both desperately upset.[70]

At eleven-forty-five p.m. Teddy Kollek of the Political Department of the Jewish Agency, came in to say that the Agency and the Va'ad Leumi (the Jewish national council) had passed a strong resolution condemning acts of terror and appealing to all Jews 'to help to stamp out the desperadoes'.

The next few days were given over to intensive political activity. The press was constantly on the telephone asking Chaim when he would be meeting the Prime Minister, but no meeting with Mr. Attlee was arranged. Instead, on 24 July Chaim lunched with Israel Sieff (now Lord Sieff) and the Minister of Health, Aneurin Bevan. To Bevan Chaim outlined his proposals which I summarized briefly in my diary as: Partition on the lines of the Peel Commission's proposals, with some improvements, plus the Negev; if a Federal State were established, this should not last for more than five years; Jewish control of immigration and of internal taxation.

I believe Bevan proved a sympathetic listener; but there was little he could do to sway his colleagues in the British Cabinet, who produced a White Paper on the next day (25 July) claiming that the Agency, not excluding Chaim, knew of the terrorists' plans in Palestine. This was naturally denied on our side.

Meanwhile there were ugly rumours that the egregious General Barker had circulated a 'non-fraternization' order to his men, telling his troops to act with 'hatred and contempt' towards all members of the Jewish 'race', adding to these remarks the observation that his object was to punish the Jews by striking at their pockets.

General Barker's circular was published in the world press on 29 July, after it had been seized by the Agency, causing a furore not only in Palestine but in Britain as well.

The Government dissociated itself from these remarks, but the damage had been done. Politics were clearly something that could not be safely left to generals, and circulars such as General Barker's merely increased the terrorists' activities.

Chaim himself made this very clear at a meeting he had with Ernest Bevin on 1 October when he said, 'I do not want to waste any words on a man like General Barker. Terrorism will not be stopped so long as the Army and General Barker do the things that are being done in Palestine. A solution can be arrived at. The solution I have in mind is partition.'[71] To this Bevin answered, 'The Arabs won't accept partition. Am I to force it with British bayonets?'

The Arabs had shown no inclination to find a solution, short of condemning the Jews to permanent minority status in Palestine; but it was pointless for Chaim to argue the issue further. The sympathetic but not very effective Colonial Secretary Creech Jones then proposed that there should be a 'conference' between Agency representatives and the British Government in January of the following year, and it was on this issue that an artificial 'rift' appeared in Zionist ranks. Ben-Gurion had written to my husband on 10 October expressing his view that the Agency should boycott such a conference:

> Our line should be the Mandate—or a State. For as long as Britain rules Palestine she must carry out the Mandate as the League of Nations intended. . . . If Britain is unable or unwilling to carry out the Mandate, she should agree to the establishment of a Jewish State, even if not in the whole of Palestine, but at once. . . .

Chaim wrote back on 11 December:

> I am in cordial agreement with the main lines of your policy, though I think it would be wrong to abstain from the conference, even if our point of view is not accepted beforehand. I believe the others will eventually come round to it.[72]

These letters were couched in the friendliest, in even affectionate terms, but the rift which had been growing between them could not be disguised. A new generation is ever impatient with the old, and Chaim, with nearly half a century of Zionist service behind him, had become something of a 'father figure', something to be revered but not followed. This has been the fate of most politicians and statesmen, as Ben-Gurion was to discover when he himself surrendered the reins of power.

So far as Chaim was concerned, the situation was not without its ironies. On the two occasions on which he suffered 'political assassination' at the hands of the Zionist Congress and at the hands of some of his closest friends, he had the galling experience of hearing his policies rejected by the most vocal sections of the Movement, only to find that those selfsame policies were implemented later! When the shouting died down, Chaim's wisdom, maturity, tenacity, and superlative gifts of diplomacy and statesmanship were again called on by the bitterest of his self-appointed critics. When the house was on fire, it was to him they turned to put out the flames; when the holy land of Israel was to be bereft of the Negev and the tiny outlet to the Red Sea, it was to him they appealed. It was he who parted the waters to allow the children of Israel to take possession of the desert.

On 5 November the members of the Agency Executive who had been detained since June without any charges being preferred against them were released, and steps were taken to elect delegates to the Twenty-second Zionist Congress at Basle, the first to be held after the Second World War. Of the 396 delegates who attended this Congress in December 1946, 386 were elected by 2,158,920 Zionists, the others were present in an advisory capacity.[73] Without going into too much detail, the Palestinian delegates numbered some 79, elected by 196,189 votes, 28 of whom belonged to the Mapai (Palestine Labour Party), 11 were Revisionists, 2 Mizrachi delegates, and the rest were divided among other allegiances.[74]

Chaim and I noted with deep anguish the absence of many of our friends among the Polish, German, and Central European delegates who had attended so many pre-war Congresses. The American group, led by Dr. Abba Hillel Silver, was, as my husband remarked, 'from the outset the strongest, not so much because of enlarged numbers, or by virtue of the inherent strength of the delegates, but because of the weakness of the rest'. The difference between this Congress and others was marked by 'the absence—among very many delegates—of faith, or even hope, in the British Government, and a tendency to rely on methods never known or encouraged among Zionists before the war'.[75] The resentment against Britain was, as usual, turned against Chaim, especially when he reminded the Congress that, difficult as it was 'to retain a belief in the victory of peaceful ideals', it was imperative to retain this belief. The Jewish people had come to Palestine to build and not to destroy. 'Masada,* for all its heroism, was a disaster in our history. Zionism was to mark the end of our glorious deaths and the beginning of a new path whose watchword is—Life!'

It was when he was excoriating the futility of blind 'activism' that one American delegate, Emanuel Neumann, for reasons which were never clear, cried out, 'Demagogue!' The Congress was abashed into deathly silence. My husband paused, removed his glasses, and with a voice of thunder said,

> Somebody has called me a demagogue. I do not know who. I hope that I never learn the man's name. I—a demagogue! I who have borne all the ills and travail of this movement! [Loud applause at this point, according to the official report of the Congress.] The person who flung that word in my face ought to know that in every house and stable in Nahalal, in every little workshop in Tel Aviv or Haifa, there is a drop of my blood. [More tempestuous applause: all delegates except for the Revisionists and Mizrachi rose to their feet.] You know I am telling you the truth. Some people do not like

---

* A Jewish stronghold, near the Dead Sea, which held out against the Romans.

to hear it—but you *will* hear me. I warn you against bogus palliatives, against short cuts, against false prophets, against facile generalizations, against distortion of historic facts. . . . If you think of bringing the redemption nearer by un-Jewish methods, if you lose faith in hard work and better days, then you commit idolatry and endanger what we have built. Would that I had a tongue of flame, the strength of prophets, to warn you against the paths of Babylon and Egypt. 'Zion shall be redeemed in Judgement'—and not by any other means.

He walked out of the Congress amidst rows of applauding delegates. The applause came even from those who had reason to feel ashamed. I watched his progress as he moved slowly, gropingly into the street. He was half-blind, old, and heavy of heart: he was also part of the history of his people. I embraced him tenderly, without words of comfort. He required none.

A few days later, when the vote was taken whether the Zionist Executive should attend the London conference in January 1947, a small majority voted against such a motion. Chaim regarded this as a vote of no-confidence in him, and stood down as president. No president was elected in his place.

In the last words he addressed to the Congress, he challenged the Religious Zionists, the Mizrachi, who had always clamoured for a Jewish State 'immediately', with these words (I quote from memory): 'I can't understand you, Mizrachi. I don't believe in the Messiah and therefore can afford to wait for the propitious moment. But you who believe in the coming of the Messiah, why are you in such a hurry?' To the others, he addressed words of greater gentleness, 'If I have said harsh things to anyone, I did not intend to hurt. The Jewish people, especially those waiting in the camps, look to you to open the gates. I thank you all'.

All delegates, Revisionists and Mizrachi included, rose to their feet and sang *Hatikvah* (the Hope), the hymn which was to become the national anthem of Israel. Chaim Weizmann had left for good the arena of Congress affairs, the scene of his triumphs and setbacks. And the same 'majority' who had voted against a meeting with British Government representatives in January 'went to London by a back door'. Chaim and I arrived back at Rehovoth on 6 February 1947.

17

The Rites of Spring: 1947-1948

OUR arrival in Palestine on 6 February 1947 coincided almost to the day with the issue of the so-called 'Bevin scheme' which followed yet another abortive London conference in January attended separately by the Jewish Agency and the Arab Higher Committee.[76] Its merits or demerits need not concern us since both Jews and Arabs turned down the scheme in its entirety, thus forcing Bevin's hand and compelling him to refer the Mandate to the United Nations, which he did on 14 February. A United Nations Special Committee on Palestine (U.N.S.C.O.P.), formed from representatives of the 'smaller' uncommitted powers, was appointed to try to find some acceptable solution. It was to sit in Jerusalem from 16 June to 24 July.

My husband had meanwhile taken the opportunity of this breathing-space to immerse himself once again in his scientific work at Rehovoth. Bereft once more of his position as president of the World Zionist Organization, and reduced to the status of a private person, he nevertheless followed with close attention and with alarm the gyrations of British policy and the increasing tension brought about by Jewish and Arab extremists. But he rejoiced more particularly in the growth of the Weizmann Institute of Science whose foundation stone had been laid in 1946: by the summer of 1947, the shell of the central building had been completed. It was symbolic, perhaps, that this seat of learning and research which was to bear my husband's name, arose from the ashes of death and destruction.

On 1 March 1947, for example, the British Officers' Club in Jerusalem had been blown up by terrorists with the loss of some twelve lives. Sickened by this event, I wrote on 9 March that I was 'too distracted and worried to enter properly all the events, terrorist acts, martial law and its consequences'. I did note, however, that

> the country is more or less paralysed: raw materials cannot be brought into the Tel Aviv area; manufactured goods cannot be exported. Ten thousand

persons have been thrown out of work, so that, instead of shortage of labour, there is unemployment. And I ask myself what is all this about and how will it help to stamp out terrorism? . . .

The military try to enforce martial law with as little discomfort to the local population as possible. Food supplies are ample; schools have been re-opened and there are not as many indiscriminate searches with brutal looting and insults as in General Barker's reign. I have even heard that the military are bored and tired and see the futility of martial law, but that the civilian administration insists upon it. . . . Both General Gale and Brigadier Rodney Moore act humanely in the circumstances and look as if they are unwilling to do what they have to do.

I castigated in particular the return to the policy of the 1939 White Paper, that bedrock of folly, which successive British Governments seemed so reluctant to abandon and which had driven the peaceful and friendly Jewish population of Palestine to the brink of despair, and encouraged terrorism. 'The British have gone mad and the Jews have become desperate and despondent', I confided to my diary, 'and the Jewish Agency Executive is incoherent, clumsy and arrogant'.

General Gale and his wife, together with Brigadier Moore, came to lunch with us at Rehovoth on 10 March. I found our British guests extremely pleasant and sympathetic, in spite of Chaim's having had a recent clash with one of their subordinate officers. The private road leading to our house at Rehovoth had been declared 'out of bounds' by this officer following a raid by some Jewish youths on a British military encampment situated near our house. Joshua, our driver-bodyguard, had complained on his own initiative that my husband's car was forced to use a minor road full of potholes when he went to and from the Institute. I happened, incidentally, to mention this at lunch that day. General Gale said, 'What was that? What did you say?' I repeated it. He took out his pocket-book and made a note. Next day the direct road to the Institute was re-opened.

On 11 March a ship carrying 'illegals' was stranded on a rock outside Gaza. Bus loads of settlers arrived on the scene, and took off many of the passengers whom they dispersed among the crowds before the police could intervene. In the sweep which followed, a number of settlers were seized in mistake for these illegal immigrants and deported. Similar action was taken when the S.S. *Theodore Herzl* tried to land some two thousand four hundred immigrants. During the fracas which ensued, two young men, one of twenty-three, the other of twenty-four, were killed by the boarding party. I wrote in my diary of 16 April:

I wept bitterly as if I knew them. What have those two boys had in their lives—ten years of concentration camps, escape, a perilous, heroic journey, and finally—death in sight of their land!

Tragedy and comedy stalked hand in hand through the riven land: when one British civilian who worked in Jerusalem was asked why he had not been repatriated with other British civilians he replied, 'I have a Jewish grandmother'.

On 16 April we put off an invitation which we had made to Sir Alan Cunningham to visit us at Rehovoth: the circumstances were hardly propitious for such a visit. We had heard that the sentence of death which had been passed on the young Irgun terrorist Dov Gruner who had been implicated in the murder of a policeman earlier in January had been confirmed. Three other young terrorists, guilty of sabotage and other crimes, were also to be executed. Neither Chaim nor I had any sympathy for 'activism' of this sort, but considered that an act of clemency would have reduced the tension in the country.[77] As it was, Gruner and the other three terrorists were hanged on the night of 16 April; their parents were not informed, and they were not given the benefit of a rabbi's presence at their execution. The stark announcement of this execution was put out on the wireless at seven-fifteen on the morning of 17 April.

I received the following letter from the High Commissioner on 20 April:

> Many thanks for your note. I too was disappointed that I could not come down to Rehovoth, and trust that I may have the pleasure of doing so later in accordance with your kindly expressed wish.

Sir Alan had been 'fighting like a tiger with London to keep the remainder of the twelve hundred immigrants [who had been removed from the *Theodore Herzl*] here. Rumours of his resignation have been flatly denied by the Colonial Office'. But despite Sir Alan's efforts on behalf of the immigrants, the British Government withdrew some three hundred and fifty immigration certificates from those detained in Cyprus as a reprisal for the landing of 'illegals' at Gaza. Riots flared up in the Cyprus camp, in which one detainee was killed when troops opened fire. The British commanding officer of the camp resigned in protest against the Government. But terrorism continued on all sides. The Cairo-Haifa train was derailed on 22 April, killing five soldiers and wounding twenty-three others. On 4 May, the Irgun, in one of its most daring sallies, liberated some two hundred and fifty prisoners from Acre prison. Worse was to follow when the bodies of two British sergeants were found hanged near Tel Aviv at the end of July.

It was in this somewhat unpropitious climate that the members of the United Nations Special Committee on Palestine came to have lunch with us at Rehovoth: we entertained the first group on 23 June and the second on the 29th. Chaim was in splendid form, as usual, playing his role of 'a private person' to perfection, while catching every nuance of conversation, listening and explaining, the perfect host in every way. I, too, was able to spot the likely 'opposition' among the members of U.N.S.C.O.P. On the 29th, for example, I noted in my diary that the Indian member turned down the invitation to visit us; the Australian member, who did not pay me the courtesy of replying whether he would be present or not, turned up nevertheless; and the Iranian member, despite his diplomatic politeness, could not disguise his feelings.

On 8 July we went to Jerusalem, where Chaim received an honorary degree at the Hebrew University. In his academic gown, he looked most distinguished. The speeches were mercifully very short on this occasion since the ceremony was broadcast 'live' from the University. This was followed by lunch with the High Commissioner, which went off very pleasantly.

Next day, at nine-fifteen in the morning Chaim gave evidence before the United Nations Committee. He began by reading his notes, but soon abandoned this because of his defective eyesight, and began to improvise. 'Everyone thought that he spoke even better than he had done before the Royal [Peel] Commission. He answered frankly, aptly, and wittily. He certainly put the Indian delegate in his place, who did not dare to be as insolent as he had been to Ben-Gurion', I put in my diary.

Chaim himself has put on record what he said to the United Nations Committee, and I shall refer only to one part which impressed itself on my memory. He told the Committee that the White Paper

released certain phenomena in Jewish life which are un-Jewish, which are contrary to Jewish ethics, Jewish tradition. 'Thou shalt not kill' has been ingrained in us since Mount Sinai. It was inconceivable ten years ago that the Jews should break this commandment. Unfortunately they are breaking it today, and nobody deplores it more than the vast majority of the Jews. I hang my head in shame when I have to speak of this fact before you.[78]

He urged partition of the country, and the creation of a Jewish State which would co-operate in raising the standards of life of everyone in the Near East, Jew and Arab alike.

Chaim's speech undoubtedly made a great impression on the U.N.S.C.O.P., as did the event which occurred on 18 July when a battered American coastal vessel, the *President Warfield*, renamed *Exodus 1947*, arrived at Haifa from a French port with four thousand five hundred illegal immigrants. The *Exodus* returned to France, and later to Germany, where the refugees were distributed in various camps, *the explanation given by the British authorities being that the camps in Cyprus were too overcrowded to receive them.*

I had already anticipated some such reaction by writing a letter to the *Palestine Post* published on 13 July:

Sir,

The Government announced yesterday that five hundred orphans between the ages of six and seventeen, now detained in Cyprus, are, for humanitarian reasons, to be brought to Palestine immediately.

The first reaction of every lover of children and fighter for the cause of humanity was one of relief. But this sense of relief, however, was very short lasting. Why five hundred? Why were humanitarian reasons so parsimoniously doled out? Why is this lottery, which is so strictly forbidden in Great Britain, applied to children of the human storm? Who will be the fortunate one to regain the rare treasure of becoming a child again amongst his own people?

There are at present in Cyprus over two thousand children, most of them orphans; a hundred and forty babies from one week to a year old; a thousand unborn await their entry into a sad, hostile world. In the last war, Great Britain made every effort to save her children by evacuating them. Cannot this great Britain unstintingly rise to the occasion and save Jewish children and bring them to safety?

In the name of those who fought and fell in the war, I appeal to the traditional generosity of the British to evacuate our children from existing camps.

I must, in all humility, state that the British authorities heeded my request and evacuated all the children to Palestine. The argument that there were not sufficient places for the refugees on the *Exodus* was therefore fallacious. Refusal to allow these victims of Nazi terror a resting place a stone's throw from their homeland was a deliberate act of policy. But Bevin's 'crude blind lurchings'[79] could not save his policy from ultimate defeat. On 1 September, the U.N.S.C.O.P. published its majority decision that Palestine should be partitioned, with a large part of the Negev going to the Jewish State which should be in some kind of nebulous 'economic union' with its Arab neighbour; the dissenting minority, which included India, Iran, and Yugoslavia, advocated 'a federal state', an idea already often mooted and as often rejected. Australia, another member of the U.N.S.C.O.P., abstained from voting. The British Government, as might have been expected, refused to put into effect the U.N.S.C.O.P. plan which was to go before the United Nations towards the end of November, and announced that it would surrender its Mandate on 15 May 1948.[80]

★

In October 1947, we arrived in New York where my husband was to appear in mid-month before the Ad Hoc Committee on Palestine of the United Nations. A special text in very large letters was composed for him, which he read out with the greatest difficulty. He told the Committee that when they came to plan for the creation of a Jewish State they would be 'fulfilling a proud historic mission'. He concluded his oration, relying on his memory, with these words from the Book of Isaiah:

> The Lord shall set his hand the second time to recover the remnants of his people. And he shall set up an ensign for the nations, and shall assemble the outcasts of Israel and gather together the dispersed of Judah from the four corners of the earth.

No sooner had we arrived in Washington than an urgent message came from Sharett (then Shertok) saying that the American representative at the United Nations had made a speech in which he proposed to partition the Negev in such a way that it would cut off Jewish Palestine from the Red Sea. So my husband sent for maps of Palestine and studied them carefully in order to be able to deal with this situation when he met President Truman.

On 19 November Chaim rose from his sick-bed—he had been ill with a temperature—to make his plea to Truman about the Negev, showing him the map of Palestine. Truman took in the position at once. My husband said, 'It is the first time in my life that I have met a President who can read and understand maps'. Truman was amused at this. Then he said, 'Don't worry. Go home, and before you reach your hotel I will have put it right'. My husband, 'a private person' with no official standing in the World Zionist Organization, had wrested a concession which could be set beside the Balfour Declaration as one of the great turning points of modern Jewish history, but, like many great

219

victories, this one remained in doubt for months while the 'final' solution of the Palestine problem was not only debated in the United Nations, but also decided by force of arms in the War of Independence which shortly followed.

Nevertheless, President Truman was as good as his word.[81] When the American delegates asked Moshe Sharett to visit them in the United Nations building on the following day in order to convey to him the decision regarding the Negev, their obituary notice was interrupted by a phone call from the President himself. He told them of his decision that the Negev and its Red Sea port must be included in the Jewish State in any partition scheme before the U.N. When one of the American delegates, General Hilldring, returned from taking this telephone call from the President, he murmured that he had 'no changes to suggest'. I do not know who was the more nonplussed—Sharett or the two U.S. delegates.

The world will go on existing and fighting; history will be made and destroyed; but in my humble opinion President Harry Truman will always be remembered as one of our 'founding fathers'.

Before the drama over partition was played to a finish in the General Assembly of the U.N., Chaim, who suspected that the French delegation was wavering in its support, cabled our old friend Léon Blum, asking him, 'Does France really wish to be absent from a moment unfading in the memory of man?' On 29 November, when the vote was taken in the Assembly, thirty-three nations voted for partition, thirteen against, ten abstained, and there was one absentee, the last, somewhat unaccountably, being Siam. Among those who abstained was the United Kingdom. France, the United States, and the U.S.S.R. were among those who voted in favour. It was a rare spectacle, rarely repeated, to see the two great rival powers, the United States of America and Russia, voting together—for motives, of course, which were entirely different. I promptly left the Assembly room to be the first to inform my husband of the decision.

Chaim had decided not to attend this fateful meeting of the U.N. Assembly. He was too tired and too overwrought. Just before the Jewish Agency representatives, Sharett, Sprinzak, and Shazar, left our suite in our New York hotel for Lake Success, Chaim had broken down in a fit of uncontrolled sobbing. By the time they returned with the great news, he had recovered completely. The emotional storm which had swept through him so unexpectedly had spent itself in the moment of victory which he himself shared.

The news of the UN resolution spread like wildfire throughout New York, and tens of thousands gathered spontaneously at the St. Nicholas Skating Rink, the only place available for assembly at a few hours' notice. Chaim was prevailed upon by his friends to go to this meeting, and when he finally arrived, tired, sick and exhausted, he was carried forward on the shoulders of the masses. There had never been such pandemonium, such enthusiasm and exhilaration as at that moment when Chaim made his appearance on the shoulders of the surging crowd. The *Hatikvah* was sung with a fervour never before or since repeated.

*

We returned to our London home in the Dorchester Hotel in order to bid good-bye to our son Benjy, his wife, and our grandson before making our journey to India and Burma. We were also busy making preparations for the removal of our last personal effects to Rehovoth when, late at night in mid-January, all our careful arrangements were disturbed by an urgent telephone call which reached us across the Atlantic from Ivor Linton, my husband's former political aide.

I cannot recall the entire substance of his conversation with Chaim, but I know that, because Linton suspected that their telephones were being 'tapped', they both referred enigmatically to the 'weather'. To Chaim's query about the general state of the climate in New York, Linton replied that it was 'extremely cold, both indoors and outside!' 'What can I do about that?' asked Chaim. Linton suggested that he return to New York immediately. My husband was so furious at this intrusion on his plans that he put down the receiver. He turned to me and said, 'We have just left New York, and the idiots now want us to go back'. The prospect of facing the Atlantic gales and really bad weather was appalling indeed.

Ivor Linton, meanwhile, sat tight in his hotel room in New York, waiting for a further reaction. It came about half an hour later when Chaim rang him up and made it plain that he would return to New York only if officially invited to do so by the Jewish Agency; otherwise we should leave within the next two days, as planned, for India and Burma before making our way home to Rehovoth. He put the telephone down again, but not so abruptly this time.

Next day Weisgal strongly advised my husband not to go unless he was formally invited by the Agency.

My husband received a cable from Abba Eban in the name of the

Agency, which said, 'The most crucial phase of all now approaches here in which we sorely miss your presence, advice, activity, influence'.

Then Arthur Lourie, secretary of the Agency, rang up and told my husband that his presence was desirable. Finally Moshe Sharett, Executive member of the Jewish Agency, telephoned and asked my husband to come immediately to New York. So Chaim and I once more re-packed our bags and took passage on the *Queen Mary*.

We arrived in snow-bound New York on 4 February 1948.

18

Redeemed in Judgement: 1948

THE weeks that followed our return to the United States developed into a round of political activities of such intensity and complexity as my husband and I had never before experienced. I can only describe it as the most hectic period of our lives.

My husband had been called back to New York to deal with a complicated tangle, totally unacceptable, in which attempts were being made to substitute for partition either internationalization or a system of trusteeship. It was a most difficult situation to tackle, but he had no alternative to undertaking the mission.

When Chaim and I arrived in New York at six o'clock in the morning of 4 February 1948 a blizzard enveloped the city in a snowy mist. A less favourable atmosphere for the beginning of our visit was hardly conceivable. Meyer Weisgal, Ivor Linton, and my brother-in-law, Dr. Joseph Blumenfeld, met us at the port. One of Chaim's first tasks was to give a statement to the press.

The *New York Times* published an article attributing to the British Foreign Office a statement that a large number of Bolsheviks were being smuggled into Palestine among the so-called illegal immigrants.[82]

Shortly after our arrival, Herbert Bayard Swope came to see us. He confirmed our fears that President Truman had changed his mind on partition. There was a strong tendency in the State Department, according to Swope, to seek Arab support. As a result of this conversation, it was decided that Swope should try to get the President to receive Chaim.

The miserable weather had its effect: Chaim fell suddenly ill and his temperature rose to 101°. Next day the fever was down, but he was rather weak. One of our callers at that time was Franklin Delano Roosevelt Jnr. He was an attractive young man bearing an uncanny resemblance to his father. As he was always so friendly and charming I decided, on my own initiative, to admit him into Chaim's sick chamber for a few moments, and lively talk ensued.

Later on David Ginsburg came and was slightly more optimistic than Swope. He said that the situation was bad, but not desperate, and thought that something might come of it if Chaim wrote to President Truman laying the whole matter and our difficulties before him, and asking for an interview. Chaim suggested that Felix Frankfurter and David Ginsburg should assist him in drafting the letter.

The next afternoon Swope and George Backer came to put the final polish to the letter; but, after some discussion, they decided to hold it back until the President indicated if and when he would receive Chaim. I find a note in my diary that day stating that, because of pressure of events, some irritation had been expressed in Washington and that we had to rely on people who had access to the White House.

Welcome news came on 8 February. We were informed from a good source in Washington that neither the President nor the Secretary of State, George Marshall, had deviated in their support of partition. A day or two later someone who had seen the President confirmed this. Chaim was advised to ask the President directly for an interview, and a letter to this effect was taken by Josef Cohn to Washington for delivery to the President.

Chaim, who meanwhile was under medical orders to rest in bed for a week, was depressed, and anxious to see President Truman before the President went on holiday. David Niles, the President's administrative assistant and adviser on Jewish affairs, meanwhile informed us that the President would be glad to see Chaim on his return from holiday.

The weeks passed slowly. Chaim's temperature had come back to normal. A letter arrived from Washington stating that the President would be away and consequently unable to receive Chaim before our departure for Palestine. In some alarm my husband telephoned to Niles, who assured him that this was not so: the President would see him.

One afternoon, two weeks after our arrival, Arthur Creech Jones, the British Secretary of State for the Colonies, called on us and spent two hours with Chaim. As he was leaving he said to me, 'Dr. Weizmann and I had a very good and frank discussion'.

I asked him what would happen at the Security Council.

Creech Jones said, 'I have always upheld the idea of an International Force and urged that the United Nations Palestine Commission should take the necessary steps before they decide on partition. So many sins are attributed to us: it has been said that we have sinister motives, that I have come here to reverse the partition decision, and so forth'.

I answered, 'So we've read'.

Creech Jones went on, 'We were told by the Jews of Palestine to clear out, and now they want us to stay longer; they did not believe that we were firmly resolved to go. It all comes from the *New Statesman*'.

I interjected grimly, 'You have powerful competition in us Jews to whom all the sins of the world have always been attributed'.

'But not as much as to Great Britain', he replied.

'Think of it', I said. 'We have been perpetually accused for over two thousand years! Don't forget it was Bevin's own choice to go to the United Nations. We didn't ask him to do so'.

'I wouldn't say that. Mr. Bevin did it only after negotiations with the Jewish Agency had broken down'.

'But what is to happen now? You say you are for the International Force, but you won't let them in until a fortnight before you withdraw from Palestine on 15 May.[83] Almost three months have elapsed since the partition decision and nothing has been done; you prohibit the import of arms by Jews,[84] you do not provide the Security Council's representatives with accommodation in Jerusalem. It is only lip service. Meanwhile, the problem has ceased to be Jewish and has become international'.

At this juncture Creech Jones burst out, 'I have to look after sixty million people. I have on my desk papers on the Argentine trouble, Ceylon, Malaya, China, and others—and here is Palestine!'

I said, 'Mr. Creech Jones, I should like to exchange our worries'. And at that we parted.

Rumour succeeded rumour. One fantastic story after another was brought to our ears. We were told that the British wished to evacuate Palestine bag and baggage as soon as possible. Then came a counter-rumour that the British wanted to get together with the Jews to talk seriously about co-operation and to be invited to serve as an international trustee for Palestine or something of that sort. It seemed like a trap to detach us from reliance on the United States and the U.N., so that we might fall between the two stools. Another story went the rounds that King Abdullah of Transjordan was ready to enforce partition if he were given the Arab part of Palestine and could get British consent for his plan.[85] Sharett delivered an effective and informative speech at the Security Council. He trenchantly though politely attacked the British

Government, which he accused of being responsible for many recent events.[86]

Chaim decided that it was time for him to make a public statement. Abba Eban and Meyer Weisgal came with a draft, but Chaim was too weak and tired, and they discussed it for only a few moments, promising to bring a revised draft. The days went by. David Hacohen called and reported that the Arabs were leaving Palestine by tens of thousands: Jaffa was half empty, and fifteen thousand Arabs had left Haifa.[87] The entry in my diary on 4 March indicated the mood of those times:

> Matters hang in the balance in so far as the U.N. Security Council is concerned. With the new European situation that has arisen in Czechoslovakia and elsewhere, everyone is jittery and preoccupied, and the Palestine affair has been relegated to the back pages of the papers.
>
> Creech Jones telephoned asking to see Chaim. He explained that he wished to justify his uncompromising attack on the Jewish Agency while addressing the Security Council. 'No doubt everybody has made mistakes, but it all depends on whom, and on how and where the attack is made', he said. 'If you had spoken, Dr. Weizmann, it would have been different; oh, if only you were in office!' Chaim replied, 'If you had made concessions when I asked for them, I would still be in office'. Creech Jones had no reply to make to that.

Two or three days later, David Ginsburg came to lunch and brought 'terrifying' information. If I understood him right, some people thought that war seemed to be imminent, this time against Russia. It was no longer a question of *if*, but of *when*. All Government departments in Washington were as busy as they had been during the recent world conflict, all were strongly guarded, military production was on the increase, a hundred and fifty thousand war planes were to be built, the tonnage of new bombs was such that the conscience of politicians need not be unduly disturbed by the inhuman use of atomic bombs—the new megaton bomb would do the job.

Ginsburg had been asked to take on the economic side of the war effort and told us not to be surprised if he should soon appear in uniform. He added that he intended to impress on James Forrestal, the Defence Secretary, and others in Washington the importance of Palestinian Jewish scientific and industrial support.

The Communist take-over in Czechoslovakia had put everybody on the alert. On 10 March I find myself writing:

> Jan Masaryk is dead—reported to have jumped from a third-storey window. Press is doubtful whether it was suicide. Poor, poor Jan, so full of life, hope

and joy. The world is staggered and everyone seems to think, 'It might have been me'. The threat of another war is coming nearer and nearer.

A sombre note came in the news from Palestine. An Arab driver took an American consular car flying the Stars-and-Stripes right into the courtyard of the *Keren Hayesod* and Jewish Agency building in Jerusalem and left the vehicle, containing a load of explosives, outside the offices. The Arab driver got out and walked away. 'The resultant explosion killed nine people, including the managing director of the *Keren Hayesod*, and the poet Leib Jaffe. Ninety persons were wounded. What next?' I asked myself.

Alexandre Parodi, the French representative at the U.N., came to lunch on 13 March. He was against partition, but favoured a federal state. He felt that if there were partition the Arabs of neighbouring territories would massacre the Jewish population in ten years, but if there were a federal state there could be an immediate immigration of two hundred thousand Jews and a substantial annual quota thereafter. Chaim proved how absurd it was to reason in this way.

On that note my March 1948 diary ended. For the rest of what happened that month, I am compelled to rely on my memory and observations given to me by friends, supplemented by subsequent later diary entries.

Chaim's illness, and the constant seesawing of events, produced in him a black, even cosmic mood of despair. The letter which he wrote to Felix Frankfurter in March illustrates this mood:

In going about this somewhat shabby world of ours, very often reminiscences of my youth well up in me and I think of one great figure which always dominated my feelings in my young days, particularly in times of great stress, such as the pogroms at the end of the 'eighties and the beginning of the 'nineties.

There was a venerable old Rabbi in Berditchev near Kiev. This city was almost exclusively Jewish. The name of the Rabbi was Rabbi Levi Yitschak, a pious, saintly man, and when things went hard with his flock he used to betake himself to the great synagogue at a time when nobody was there and go to the Ark, open the doors, pull the curtain and enter into conversation with the Almighty—something of the following nature, 'God of Israel, I have come to ask you to tell me why you persecute your people so much and so often. You have done enough harm. It is about time you stopped, and if you won't I will call you to Court [Din Torah]'. I am sure the great Rabbi felt considerable relief after having spoken thus, and it is very unfortunate that even this sort of comfort is not given to us, and we have to carry the pain in us until the heart breaks and the moral force begins to ebb.

Every day some new hope is dangled before our eyes, and when the sun sets, it is nothing but a mirage. How long, oh God, how long?

On 14 March, the clouds suddenly broke. President Truman, who had so far avoided a further meeting with Chaim, all of a sudden agreed to see him. This was through the interventionof Eddie Jacobson, an old friend and one-time business partner of the President. Eddie Jacobson was in despair at the President's negative attitude in not meeting my husband. He conceived the idea of asking President Truman to grant him, Eddie, an interview. At the end of the long discussion which took place between them, Eddie impulsively burst out, 'Mr. President, your hero is President Andrew Jackson. My hero is Dr. Weizmann whom I've never even met. Won't you do me a favour and see him?'

For a moment the President was silent. He got up, went to the window, looked out for a few moments and then turned to his old friend, 'All right, you bald-headed son of a bitch, you win. Tell Matt [the appointments secretary] to invite Dr. Weizmann here'.

Four days later, on 18 March, Chaim rose from his sick bed and travelled to Washington to see President Truman, when he again repeated his plea for the Negev.

At this point I return to my diary: the entry for 13 May gives a brief report of this episode, and of other events which occurred between March and May 1948:

> Chaim's illness, my 'flu, and the most intricate intrigues, twistings, and almost daily proposals by the U.S.A. at Lake Success, have prevented me from writing systematic daily entries. I shall never forgive myself: it was real history-making.
>
> When Chaim visited the President, he pressed for three points: (a) a lifting of the arms embargo; (b) support for partition; (c) immigration. The President told Chaim that point (a) is being seriously considered by the State Department, and that he supported partition.

In President Truman's own account of the meeting, he said:

> Dr. Weizmann, by my specific instruction, was to be brought through the East Gate. There was to be no press coverage of his visit and no public announcement. . . . We talked for almost three-quarters of an hour.
>
> Dr. Weizmann was a man of remarkable achievements and personality. His life had been dedicated to two ideals, that of science and that of the Zionist movement. He was past seventy now and in ill health. He had known

many disappointments and had grown patient and wise in them. When he left my office I felt he had reached a full understanding of my policy, and that I knew what he wanted.[88]

It was all the more surprising, therefore, when next day, 19 March, twenty-four hours after Chaim's interview with the President, the American representative at the United Nations, Ambassador Warren Austin, threw a verbal bombshell into the Security Council, proposing to suspend the partition plan and substitute instead 'a temporary United Nations trusteeship'.

'Chaim is nonplussed and indignant', I wrote in my diary. Chaim himself called the blow 'bitter and, on the surface, fatal to our long-nurtured hopes'. He did add, however, that he doubted whether President Truman 'was himself aware of the extent to which his own policy and purpose had been balked by subordinates in the State Department'.[89]

My own diary entry regarding this proposal on the 'Black Friday' of Jewish diplomatic history was more emphatic, and, as it turned out, inaccurate: I wrote that Chaim believed Truman had deceived him. In actual fact—and this was something that neither Chaim nor I could know at the time—the President had summoned Clark Gifford, his administrative assistant, at the early hour of seven-thirty on the morning of Saturday 29 March, saying 'There is a story in the papers on Palestine and I don't understand what has happened'.

When Clifford entered his office, Truman said, 'How could this have happened? I assured Chaim Weizmann that we were for partition and would stick to it. He must think I am a plain liar. Find out how this could have happened.'[90]

Chaim, far from thinking that Truman had 'deceived' him, tele-phoned Eddie Jacobson telling him he was still confident that the President would stick by his promise. In a letter Chaim wrote to the President a few days later, he made the issue quite plain, 'The choice for our people, Mr. President, is between statehood and extermination. History and providence have placed this issue in your hands, and I am confident that you will yet decide it in the spirit of the moral law'.[91]

Intense diplomatic activity followed. Warren Austin would not budge from his trusteeship plan, for reasons which became apparent in a speech he made on 26 April in which he said, 'I cannot accept the contention that trusteeship is impossible of enforcement. I still hope that Great Britain will keep her forces in Palestine, and use them *to enforce trusteeship* with the co-operation of the United States and such other nations as may be willing to help'.[92] In my diary of 13 May, I called this

> another trap which would lead to an Anglo-American condominium. . . . Many veiled threats have been made that if we do not accept a truce there would be economic sanctions and a blockade of Palestine, for men, arms, and food supplies.

Once more, the fear of Soviet intervention in the Middle East, on the pattern of the Communist coup in Czechoslovakia, was uppermost in the minds of the British Foreign Office and the U.S. State Department, and the interests of Jewish Palestine were to go by the board.

The entire U.S. delegation to the U.N., Warren Austin, Professor Jessup, and Mr. Ross, came to visit Chaim on his sick-bed at the Waldorf.

> I must have astonished as well as disappointed them, for I declared bluntly that I put no stock in the legend of Arab military might, and that I considered the intention of Palestine Jewry to proclaim its independence the day the Mandate ended thoroughly justified and eminently realistic . . .

was my husband's comment on this visit in his autobiography.[93] He spoke in similar terms to M. Parodi, the French delegate, who came to dinner, bringing with him the 'veiled threat' that the U.S.A. would not send troops for the enforcement of partition, but would send cruisers to the Mediterranean to enforce the blockade.

Chaim had meanwhile decided on two courses of action. The first was to work for the appointment of Major-General J. H. Hilldring, the American alternate-delegate at the United Nations, as liaison officer to the policy-making section on Palestine in the State Department: a powerful group of persons, including Ed Kaufman, Judge Rosenman, David Ginsburg, and Ben Cohen, 'were put on the job'.

General Hilldring, although he was not a Zionist, had shown considerable sympathy for the Jewish cause; but when President Truman appeared willing to make the appointment, General Hilldring, I noted, 'was reluctant to accept it'. Chaim had to speak on the telephone to Hilldring six times in San Francisco before the General accepted the appointment.

> The announcement is made public, to the great consternation of the U.S. delegates at the U.N. and the State Department. . . . No one knew that Chaim was behind it all,

says my diary.

At the same time, Chaim invited Judge Rosenman for a lunch, which lasted two and a half hours. He asked him to press President Truman to make a statement that he would recognize the Jewish State the moment the Mandate ended on 14 May.

A few days later, Judge Rosenman having sustained a leg injury, Chaim visited him at his hotel. The Judge had seen President Truman whose first words to him were, 'I have Dr. Weizmann on my conscience'. Truman then said that he would recognize the Jewish State on 14 May, but that he would deal with only one Jewish representative—Weizmann himself! He asked that this information should be kept secret.[94]

My diary note for the time stated that the State Department and the British Delegation were waging a campaign to enforce a truce and a trusteeship proposal. Chaim was opposed to both these ideas. He called in Sharett and told him not to discuss any of these propositions. 'Cease fire—yes, but no trusteeship, and no political stand-still' Chaim said.

A little later, he asked Sharett to take a personal message to Ben-Gurion and his colleagues. 'Moshe, don't let them weaken, don't let them swerve, don't let them spoil the victory—the Jewish State, nothing less.' Chaim followed this up by telephoning to Sharett at the aerodrome before his flight telling him to repeat his message to Ben-Gurion: 'Proclaim the Jewish State, now or never!' But Sharett's flight was unaccountably diverted and he was delayed somewhere.

Meanwhile other events supervened as the Proclamation of the Jewish State moved towards its climax. Meyer Weisgal who happened at this time to be in Palestine where Chaim had sent him to report on the situation was by now anxious to return to Chaim's side.

When Meyer made preparations to leave for New York, B-G. at first insisted that he should delay his trip, but a few days later telephoned urging him to leave for New York. Communications with the United States and the outside world were particularly bad, he told him, and Moshe Sharett had been delayed somewhere. B-G. therefore wanted Meyer to contact Chaim and discover his attitude towards the Proclamation of the State. He arranged an air passage for Meyer, with a stop-over in Nice. From Nice Meyer telephoned Chaim.

He was about to launch into a lengthy explanation, telling him that B-G. had asked for his opinion, when Chaim cut him short, 'What are they waiting for?' he demanded in Yiddish. Meyer then sent a cable to B-G.: 'The answer is Yes'. Ben-Gurion immediately called a meeting of the Jewish Agency and the National Council and proclaimed the State of Israel.

*

It was then that real trouble flared up between the Arabs and the Jews. Our warriors were not professional soldiers with a long tradition of army service. They were civilians who had had some training in the *Haganah*. There were no Nelsons or Dukes of Wellington; there wasn't a Moses or a Joshua. The first Chief of Staff, Yaacov Dori, was an engineer by profession. He had been in the Jewish Legion in the First World War. When he had to resign his command of the Jewish Army on account of ill health, his place was taken by Yigal Yadin, a student of archaeology. He was followed by Mordecai Makleff who had been an officer in the Jewish settlement police and had served with the British army during the Second World War. Yigal Allon, a farmer of Ginosar, became the conqueror of the Negev. These were the men who commanded our armies. The man in the street, actuated by *ein breira* (no choice), played an important part in winning the War of Independence.

When Bartley Crum, a good friend who had been a member of the Anglo-American Commission of 1946, visited the President on 7 May, Truman promised, I wrote in my diary,

> to recognize the Jewish State on 14 May at six o'clock. The President is anxious to do so before the Russians. What a joke. Nevertheless B. Crum does not wish to be too optimistic. One never knows what influence will be brought to bear on the President by the British, the State Department, and anti-Zionists. Rosenman is being pressed by Chaim to go to see the President today—it is almost zero hour, and the President will have no credit in the Jewish State's birth if his recognition comes too late. Meanwhile, the British go on with their caretakers' proposal. I wish it was all over.

The dilemma facing world statesmen was excruciating, as excruciating as the birth-pangs of the Jewish State. The British, for all their mistakes and follies (and I shall pay tribute to them in the postscript to this chapter), knew that they were leaving Palestine to become a battlefield between Jews and Arabs, and that there was no one who would willingly step into their shoes. There were also signs that President Truman was anxious to postpone the declaration of the Jewish State until a more propitious moment. But in the titanic battles of wits and wills, Chaim, who had declared that 'Thou shalt not make of the Torah a crown to glory in, or a spade to dig with', knew that if Israel was to be redeemed in judgement—it was now or never.

At five p.m. on 13 May, the American delegation to the U.N.

proposed that a mediator should be appointed for Palestine. It was a last despairing gesture to solve an issue which could be decided only on the battlefield of ravaged Palestine.

The same day, David Ginsburg rang up advising Chaim to send a letter to the President by special messenger that very evening. Josef Cohn was deputed to take it to Washington by the night train. Meanwhile, Sharett cabled from Palestine that, despite the British public statement that the Transjordan Arab Legion would be withdrawn by 15 April, this British-officered Legion was fighting in Jerusalem and King Abdullah's invasion was imminent. He advised that someone should urge President Truman to issue a stern warning immediately to King Abdullah. Chaim immediately telephoned to David Niles.

Bartley Crum rang up to say that the situation in the White House seemed to be good. The President had seen General Marshall and Robert Lovett the day before, and during their discussion had told them, 'I'm the boss here and I'll take the decisions'. Crum urged that no criticisms or attacks on President Truman be made during the planned Jewish rally in New York on Sunday or at any subsequent time. But vigilance would have to be maintained until the last moment, he said.

The first issue of Jewish State stamps for internal circulation was pictured in the press, one of them with Chaim's head. It was a thrilling moment. And in all these exciting events, with all that was happening round us, poor Chaim was in bed, solemn and sad, issuing directions, using the telephone at his bedside, drafting letters and memoranda, holding conferences. His life's work was about to be crowned with victory; but there would be no consummation on the morrow if both friends and enemies interfered to spoil it.

'And so, for the second time in history, the Exodus begins', my diary note for 13 May ended.

Although my diary is open before me as I consider these lines, the memory of what happened the next morning will remain with me as long as I live.

At ten o'clock a.m. on 14 May came the thrilling news that the Jewish State had been proclaimed by the National Council in Tel Aviv, and called Israel. This had happened at four p.m. Palestine local time, eight hours before the ending of the British Mandate over Palestine at midnight and the end of nearly thirty years of British rule in that country. Chaim sent a moving message to the new provisional government. He himself was worn out, tired, and wearied by the strain and pressure of the past weeks.

Our joy was tempered by deep sorrow. Our very dear friend Baffy Dugdale had died at her home in Scotland that very same morning, 14 May at three o'clock. She told her children before she passed away, 'It is the happiest day of my life'. She knew that the State of Israel, for which she had yearned as long as we had, was going to be proclaimed. Her death was a grievous blow to us. She was a great woman.

Baffy Dugdale was in my mind as we scanned the headlines and newspaper stories that morning. There was not a word about Chaim in the statement by the provisional government, no whisper of the Balfour Declaration.

At six o'clock that evening Josef Cohn returned from Washington, saying that the President's recognition would come through shortly: President Truman, indeed, authorized recognition at five-sixteen p.m. on 14 May, saying, 'The old Doctor will believe me now'. Within the hour news of the recognition of the new Jewish State by the U.S. Government was broadcast.

Chaim was entertaining a number of Zionist friends for tea when Ivor Linton, his political aide, suddenly burst into the room excitedly. 'Chief—' he began, when Chaim interrupted him. 'President Truman has recognised our State,' Chaim said, decisively. Linton appeared surprised. 'How could you know, Chief?' he enquired. 'You haven't a radio in this room!' 'I saw it in your face,' Chaim answered gently, 'and I also had faith in the work we've been doing. . . .'

What a day it had been!

The President's announcement of recognition came as a bombshell at the U.N. Even the American delegation had not been previously informed. As a matter of fact, Ambassador Philip K. Jessup rang up the White House from a public call-box to get confirmation before making an official statement in the General Assembly.

The following day, 15 May, Egyptian aircraft raided Tel Aviv, killing one person and injuring five, and the Egyptian government declared that its armed forces had entered Palestine with a view to establishing 'security and order' and suppressing the 'Zionist terrorist gangs'—not to wage war on Palestine Jews! How this could be reconciled with air attacks on Jewish inhabitants was not explained. Five Arab armies moved from the north, south, and east to attack the new State.

One puzzling note in the midst of the general jubilation that had swirled in and round our Waldorf-Astoria apartment the day before had been the absence of any message or cable to Chaim from the provisional government.

The following day Ben-Gurion and four other leaders cabled:

> On the occasion of the establishment of the Jewish State, we send our
> greetings to you, who have done more than any other living man towards its
> creation. Your stand and help have strengthened all of us. We look forward
> to the day when we shall see you at the head of the State established in peace.[95]

Further Egyptian air raids on Tel Aviv as well as other Arab 'suc-
cesses' were reported the next day. That evening, we settled down in the
hotel to spend a few quiet hours. I had given Chaim his supper and
seen that he was comfortable in bed. He was still far from well. I joined
my sister Raya, my brother-in-law Dr. Blumenfeld, and a friend
in the sitting-room. The telephone rang. My friend picked up the
receiver. The news editor of an important New York daily wanted to
speak to Dr. Weizmann. My friend said that he was ill in bed. Could
she give Mrs. Weizmann the message?

'Yes, please', said the editor. 'We have just received a cable dispatch
from Tel Aviv that Dr. Weizmann has been elected President of the
Provisional State Council of Israel and we would like to know how he
feels about it'.

I went into the bedroom and said to my husband, 'Congratulations,
Chaim'chik. You are now the President!'

He looked up at me. 'What nonsense are you talking?' he asked.

I then gave him the message, and added that he would undoubtedly
receive a cable from our people in Israel the next morning confirming
his appointment as President.

The immediate effect of the news was to send him into a reflective
mood. Although Chaim tried hard to conceal his emotions, I could see
that he was deeply moved by that tremendous event. As for myself,
it is not part of my temperament to respond at once to events, whether
good or bad.

The news spread like wildfire through New York. Chaim's political
advisers—Abba Eban, Arthur Lourie, Ivor Linton—immediately
came to the hotel from a mass meeting celebrating the proclamation
of the State, and joined us in the apartment. We shared a bottle of
champagne in honour of the occasion.

It was only next morning, when the anticipated cable arrived from
Tel Aviv,[96] that I realized the full significance of what had happened.
I knew then the great honour and the even greater obligation that had
fallen on my husband.

Later, when he felt better, he told me that his first thought on hearing the news was to whisper a blessing that History had spared the remnants of the Jewish people so that it could taste the thrill and joy of having a sovereign independent State and a President of its own.

On 17 May the flag of Israel flew for the first time over our hotel. An American millionaire who occupied a permanent suite in the Waldorf-Astoria complained to the manager that the flag obscured his view. He was told by the manager that the President of Israel was staying in the hotel, and if he did not like the flag, he could leave!

*

If my comments on the actions of the British Administration in Palestine have at times appeared harsh and uncompromising, I make no apology. The major rôle which the British Government played, during three decades, in shaping the instruments by which statehood would be implemented cannot be repudiated or belittled; nay, statehood itself—the very existence of Israel—owes an immeasurable debt to the Balfour Declaration. Moreover, the British Government left a great heritage behind in Palestine: British discipline, organization, administration, public conduct, civic order—all left their mark on Israel. I am happy to say that no bitter feelings remained in Israel towards Britain, with whom our relations subsequently became increasingly friendly.

On my return home to Israel later that year, I was impressed by our policemen who reminded me of British 'Bobbies'—they were as smart and correct. I still cannot get over the fact that our public takes orders from them in Hebrew! And everywhere one goes there are traces of our true sentiments towards the British people—Allenby Street in Tel Aviv and Haifa, Balfouria village, Ramat David for Lloyd George, Princess Mary Avenue.

The memory of all that was best and just in the British way of life has never been expunged from my mind.

19

Just a Symbol: 1948-1952

FOR 'the first totally free Jew of the modern world', as Sir Isaiah Berlin characterized my husband,[97] elevation to the Presidency brought little relief. The war in Israel with her Arab neighbours saddened and wounded him. It was not a quarrel that either he or the Jewish people had sought. Throughout the years of political activity, he had shown an abhorrence of strife and bloodshed. As a scientist, he believed that science and its application would suffice to feed and clothe all the countless children of men. I need hardly labour this point, nor the fact that, as a young doctor and later in all my social endeavours, I too did all I could to alleviate human suffering, and that in hospitals and other institutions which I helped to establish Jew and Arab citizens of Israel received equality of attention. This, too, hardly deserves any comment: in the face of sickness and death, we are all equal.

On 18 May 1948, a few days after the declaration of the State of Israel, I burst out with bitterness in my diary:

> What a waste of life! The Israelis have opened the Jordan dam and drowned five hundred Arabs with their tanks and ammunition carriers. Jerusalem, the old city, is occupied by the Arab Legion. Tel Aviv bombed: forty-one dead and fifty wounded. God, where are our bombers? Eight bombers are still stuck in Mexico because of legal formalities, our people are active in Washington pressing for sanctions against the aggressor States. David Ginsburg says we have four hundred planes.

Perhaps the usually well-informed Ginsburg was mistaken. According to Ezer Weizmann[98], our nephew (who, like his cousin Michael, had served in the British R.A.F. as a pilot officer and had come to Israel with a handful of young pilots to start the Israeli Air Force), at this period, 'We flew on the ground'. Apart from a fighter squadron which comprised a few Messerschmitt 109s, the Israeli Air Force had a far smaller force than was available to the Egyptians and other Arab countries. It is not surprising therefore that Egyptian bombers were able to break through Tel Aviv defences, despite the heroic and self-sacrificing efforts made by the young Israeli pilots—'the few' who finally routed and broke the Egyptian air force, with all its British Spitfires and bombers.

On 19 May I wrote in my diary:

We are doing badly in Jerusalem, where Brigadier John Bagot Glubb, in Arab head-dress, leads the Arab Legion. Oh, God, let our bombers go through! If international formalities will not allow it, show your hand as you did in Pharaonic times!

★

On the following day, we discussed the itinerary of our return to Israel. At first we thought of visiting England, but our lawyer Mr. Robinson advised against this, pointing out that 'the President of Israel cannot arrive in England as an ordinary traveller without diplomatic privileges': Britain had not yet recognized the State of Israel, and both Chaim and I were still British subjects. We therefore decided to disembark at Cherbourg and proceed through France to spend a brief holiday in Switzerland, where Chaim was to receive an honorary degree from the University of Freiburg (Fribourg). But while we were in the midst of these preparations, David Niles, one of President Truman's secretaries, called at our hotel at ten o'clock on the morning of the 21st with an invitation to us from President Truman to stay at Blair House on the night of 24 May and to lunch with him on Tuesday the 25th. 'Chaim feels it is a great strain for him, but it is so important for the prestige of Israel and the Jews of the U.S.A. that he should accept', I noted in my diary.

At mid-day on 21 May, Mrs. Golda Myerson[99] came to our hotel in New York to report on the situation in Israel. She felt confident that with the arrival of heavier arms, Israeli forces could beat the Arabs 'hollow'. She also told Chaim and me a fantastic story of her meeting, on the previous Monday, and at the King's request, with King Abdullah of Transjordan. Abdullah, she told us, looked 'frightened and haggard: his ambition now is to annex the whole of Palestine and sit on the throne of David', I noted in my diary. The extraordinary proposal which he asked Mrs. Myerson to convey to the Jewish Agency was that the Jews should accept some kind of 'autonomy' under his kingship. Both Mrs. Myerson and the Agency turned down this incredible offer.[100] Despite certain gains made by the British-officered Arab Legion, Abdullah's soldiers generally fought badly; 'the soldiers sit in their armoured tanks and shoot from a long range, but if we get nearer and shoot at them, they run away'. In the north, Iraqi and Lebanese armies had been halted; but in the south the Egyptians had made some progress towards Jerusalem.

On 23 May, at a New York session of the B'nai B'rith (a Jewish fraternal society), I made an appeal to Britain to recognize Israel. I said that both Chaim and I had been British citizens for many years, and that we acknowledged our debt to Britain, adding:

> It is with profound sorrow in my heart that we must for the time being accept the attitude of that great power; but I am sure that the moment is not far off when Great Britain will join hands with western civilization and will abandon the people who are fighting against us. We are an old nation, and I am sure that we shall always remember our friends and will try to forget our enemies.

The Mayor of New York, William O'Dwyer, who brought the city's greetings to the two thousand delegates of B'nai B'rith said:

> I have just as much of a thrill as any one in the room to hear the First Lady of Israel. . . . It took us about a hundred and fifty years to get a First Lady to go round the country to tell us a few things. Here is Israel the very first day and—pop—they get a First Lady who does the same thing!

At three p.m. on the 24th, Chaim and I travelled from New York to stay at Blair House. Apart from ourselves, the party consisted of my husband's medical attendant Dr. Stern, a nurse, Ivor Linton, Josef Cohn, George Backer, and Abe Feinberg:

> We are accompanied, or rather preceded, by a police escort on motor bikes, who make an unholy noise, like air-raid sirens, and we go through all red traffic lights. A special railway carriage is reserved for our party, with a drawing-room for Chaim and myself. On arrival in Washington, we are met by a few members of the State Department, Mr. Woodworth, Chief of Protocol, Eliahu Epstein [now Elath], the Israeli representative, and his wife, General Klein of the Jewish Veterans, and a rabbi who pronounces a few words of blessing. The Mayor of Washington also says a few words and presents Chaim with a large, lovely key of the city. Crowds of people with Israeli banners line the streets and sing 'Hatikvah'. Pennsylvannia Avenue and Blair House are beflagged. On our arrival at the house, the housekeeper is presented to us by the Chief of Protocol, and the whole house is put at our disposal. The house is lovely and old, and is furnished in old colonial style. Guests arrive: Felix Frankfurter, David Ginsburg, David Niles, Ben Cohen, Bob Natham, Glass, and a few others. General Langham—all beribboned and

bemedalled—represents the White House. Tea, drinks, cold cuts, cakes are served, after which we retire to our respective apartments. Chaim and I are on the first floor, with two bedrooms, two bathrooms, and an enormous sitting room, all very comfortable and full of charm. As a rule, on such occasions, a reception is held in the White House, and on the following day Chaim would have had to address both houses of Congress. But, fearful of the strain on Chaim, we ask to forgo these ceremonies, and have a private dinner for our party, a few friends and General Langham, some fourteen persons altogether. The party goes off beautifully; everyone serene and in good spirits. We retire at ten p.m. The goodwill shown to us by our American hosts was truly touching: even our 'opponents' in the State Department have somewhat mellowed. The mood of euphoria continued the next day when the Chief of Protocol and General Langham came at eleven-fifteen a.m. to take Chaim to the President.

Amidst the flash of press cameras and the whirr of newsreels, the first President of Israel, on the steps of the White House, presented the Thirty-Third President of the United States with a gift of the Torah. It was a beautifully designed parchment, handwritten, in a lovely case embroidered in gold with Hebrew emblems. Then President Truman and Chaim retired for a private conversation. I later recorded in my diary that

Chaim, after thanking the President and his Government for all they had done in recognizing the State of Israel, asked for three things: (1) the immediate lifting of the arms embargo; (2) a loan of $100,000,000 for defence and reconstruction; (3) recognition of our representative in Washington. The President replied: (1) is under very serious consideration; (2) I don't see any difficulty in advancing the loan, since Jews always pay their debts; (3) will come in due course.

They then parted in a jocular mood: when Truman told Chaim that he was the President of so many millions of Americans, my husband retorted, 'But I am the President of a million presidents!'

After a luncheon party, we returned to New York at eight p.m. 'utterly exhausted'. Next day, 26 May, we left our hotel, accompanied by the ubiquitous police sirens. An army of photographers besieged us on the ship taking us to Cherbourg. 'Chaim hates it', I noted in my diary, 'but under pressure he does not behave too badly. Small, cramped cabin, packed with press and others. At five p.m. we move off at last...'

*

The first President of Israel's triumphant journey was continued in France where great crowds greeted his appearance in Paris. At an official dinner at the Presidential Palace given by Vincent Auriol, the French President, and Madame Auriol, the President told me the history of the Elysée Palace, the architectural structure of the building, and the various historical events connected with it. But one of the most touching moments in our brief stay in France came at our reunion with our old friend Léon Blum, who had survived German imprisonment during the war. In his lovely cottage home near Versailles, a group of fifty Jewish children who had passed through the anti-chambers of death in Nazi concentration camps, sang beautiful Hebrew songs. 'Blum's eyes are full of tears', I wrote in my diary on 11 June, 'Chaim is solemn as a judge'. When Blum and Chaim talked on international affairs, Blum spoke of his suspicion of Russian intentions. He had never trusted them since his youth, he said, 'Ils sont énigmatiques. . . .'

It was with some sorrow that Chaim and I had had to abandon our visit to England, where we had so many friends and so many close associations; but Benjy and his wife Maidie saw us briefly in France. Benjy, when he had heard that his father had been appointed President of Israel, had telephoned to us in New York from London, remarking that it was strange a British subject should be a foreign president! It was this 'strangeness' which we had to resolve. When we reached Geneva, Chaim wrote to the British Home Office, relinquishing his British passport, with an appreciative letter expressing his warmest feelings towards Britain whose citizen he had been for forty years. He received no acknowledgement of this letter.[101]

After a three months' holiday in Switzerland, we left Geneva, in a 'Skymaster' plane flying the Israel pennant, on 29 September, arriving in Israel at five the next morning. Members of the Government and friends from the Institute, as well as relations, met us at the aerodrome, and we were escorted to breakfast. 'Not an enjoyable party: tired to death', I noted in my diary. On our drive to Tel Aviv, where Chaim was to deliver a short address to the Provisional Council in the Dizengoff Museum, I observed with sadness the desolation in the Arab quarter in Jaffa. Most houses were in ruins, and the lands lay fallow. I felt sorry for the poor Palestinian Arabs who had fled the country because of mischievous encouragement to do so by the Arab leaders. When we passed lorry loads of soldiers moving towards the war fronts I found it hard to adjust myself to reality, and took them for British Tommies.

Indeed, it was this lack of 'adjustment' which Chaim and I felt during our first few weeks in Israel, and which left traces of bitterness in us both.

From New York Chaim had sent to Mr. Ben-Gurion the important message, 'Proclaim the State now or never!' Ben-Gurion proclaimed the State next day. Chaim was therefore particularly galled by the fact that when the Proclamation of the State of Israel was set out on parchment, to which the signature of members of the Jewish Agency and the National Council had been affixed, no room had been left for his signature! In fact, the document was never presented to my husband for his signature, although room had been left for two or three other persons who were absent at the time of the Proclamation. To this day, the historic Proclamation does not bear the signature of the first President!

Chaim was also irritated by the elaborate protocol with which his office was surrounded, and he complained to me that the government was filled with upstarts. Chaim's mood was not improved when he asked his old friend Moshe Sharett, the then Foreign Minister, what his responsibilities, duties, and privileges were. Mr. Sharett replied, 'Oh, just to be a symbol, Dr. Weizmann'. To which my husband replied, 'I do not wish to be "symbolised", Moshe'.

Chaim had no wish to be embalmed into an empty symbol, a tool of any government or party. He had not assumed that his functions as President of the State of Israel would be identical with those of the President of the United States; but, having vast experience in international politics, a fact recognized by statesmen the world over, he thought that he should be consulted on Israel's policies. That was not done. As I put it in my diary:

> The Government neither consults him, nor keeps him informed. Of course, it hurts Chaim, but instead of saying so, he constantly threatens to resign. He says he is not in the least interested in what they do. . . .

He called in the members of the government, telling them that under such conditions he would have to resign the Presidency. They pressed him hard to remain at his post, so he had no choice but to yield as otherwise the world would interpret his resignation as disapproval of the Government. When Chaim requested the minutes of cabinet meetings, Prime Minister Ben-Gurion said he would consult his colleagues, but nothing came of it. Instead, Zeev Sharef, the cabinet secretary, visited Chaim every Monday and read out cabinet decisons to him! But the stenographic record of the proceedings was denied to him. And so my husband became the Prisoner of Rehovoth.[102] Such is the way of the world.

Chaim was happiest perhaps with 'men of action' such as Yigal Allon, the conqueror of the Negev, later Minister of Labour, who kept him informed of the progress made in chasing the Egyptians out of the Negev area, which President Truman had agreed should be allotted to Israel. On one occasion, when Chaim inspected General Alon's troops at Beersheba, which had been captured on 21 October, he turned to him saying with gentle irony, 'This is the first time I have had the feeling of being Royalty'.

As I confided to my diary, I was very, very lonely:

> The final break with all my English and European associations, separation from my little family and a few dear friends, weighs on me desperately. Chaim has not found his bearings as yet and has no definite duties. I cry a lot in my bedroom. I have no occupation or function to fulfil except to entertain, which gives me no inner satisfaction. I feel useless.

This mood soon passed as I began to devote myself to the rehabilitation of the war-wounded. With the aid of Dr. Sheba, a dear and cherished friend of mine, I raised funds and support for the establishment of Tel Hashomer Hospital, of which Dr. Sheba became the devoted and brilliant head. Despite its primitive physical appearance of barrack-like sheds, it soon came to be considered one of the most up-to-date centres of healing in the country, thanks to Dr. Sheba's efforts and vision. I have a special fondness for members of the medical profession and I regard Dr. Joel, my husband's medical attendant and mine for many years, as a particular friend. I also have the highest regard and affection for Dr. Sondek, Dr. Spira, and Professor Neufeld.

It would be hypocritical to pretend that Chaim's relationship with Ben-Gurion always went smoothly. The two men had taken a proper measure of each other, and knew each other's strength and weakness. But apart from the relatively minor clash over the Presidential functions, Chaim always endeavoured to be helpful and co-operative with B-G. On one occasion when Ben-Gurion had great difficulty in getting an impressive majority in the Knesset (Israel parliament), without uniting the three main Labour parties (Mapai, Mapam, and Ahdut Avoda), Chaim called in B-G. and impressed on him the danger to the Knesset if this union was not achieved. Chaim suggested mildly to B-G. that should he fail in this task, he should ask him, Chaim, to undertake to find a solution. 'I don't belong to any party, but I am the best living friend and supporter of all of them', he said to B-G. 'It is for them that I worked and travailed. Should you fail to unite them, let me try. I shall talk to them. They will listen'. B-G. agreed to this, but later, he said, he had almost succeeded. He did not succeed, and he did not inform Chaim! The three parties were still not united at the election of 1966.

Yet Chaim was not unappreciative of the efforts made by Ben-Gurion and his administration in the successful military operations of October-December 1948 when the entire Negev was cleared of Egyptian troops. This is what my husband wrote to Simon Marks in October of that year:

> I follow closely the activity of the young Government, and though many things seem somewhat amateurish and groping, they work out quite nicely on the whole, considering the circumstances. B-G. as Prime Minister and Minister of Defence proves a great success. Whether he will prove to be the right choice in peace times as well, I am not prepared to say at this juncture. . . . But it is still too early to draw conclusions.

The conflict between B-G. and Chaim, therefore, was not always as great as many people imagined, and, with give and take on both sides, amicable relations prevailed. However, on many occasions Ben-Gurion's instability and lack of understanding of human relationships gave Chaim doubts and fears. Chaim, however, was given the right to confirm the appointment of high-ranking army officers and the selection of Israel representatives abroad.

There were moments when all 'differences' between B-G. and myself also disappeared. During the dedication ceremony of the Blanche Dugdale Memorial in the Balfour Forest at Ginegar, B-G. paid a moving tribute to Baffy, who, as I mentioned earlier, had died on the same day as the declaration of the State of Israel. In his address, B-G. extolled her as one who had 'identified herself completely with what we call Zionism. If there was a Zionist abroad who was entitled to that name and at the same time to live abroad, it was she'.

Standing in front of the simple rectangular monolith of Galilee stone, faced with black Tiberias marble, on which had been inscribed the simple words—'Blanche Dugdale—Faithful Worker for Israel—1880-1948', I spoke of her as 'our spiritual Joan of Arc, our moral Deborah', and recalled the numerous occasions in which she stayed with us at Weizmann House. . . .

Lady Ferguson, Baffy's daughter, who was deeply moved by the ceremony, said, 'Mother used to say that the Jewish people are full of the virtue of gratitude. You are showing how right she was'. Our old friend Lady Violet Bonham Carter remarked, 'I've never seen anyone more completely identified with a cause'. Among those present was Baffy's son Michael, an architect of distinction who had designed his mother's memorial, Berl Locker, Sir Robert Boothby (later Lord Boothby), and Captain (later Sir) Colin Coote, then managing editor of the London *Daily Telegraph*.

On 3 November I noted in my diary our satisfaction and joy at President Truman's re-election: 'Truman elected President against all predictions. Chaim and I were confident that he would be elected'. Since Truman's election coincided with our sweeping victories in the Negev, which were not to Mr. Bevin's liking,[103] Chaim hastened to write to Truman congratulating him on his election and reminding him of his interest in the Negev.

On 29 November—the first anniversary of the U.N. partition resolution—the President wrote back, saying:

> I remember well our conversation about the Negev, to which you referred in your letter. I agree fully with your estimate of the importance of that area to Israel, and I deplore any attempt to take it away from Israel.[104]

The year 1948 ended with the hope of an early armistice between Israel and her Arab attackers; but on 9 January 1949, an incident occurred which inflamed British-Israel relations even further. On the morning of that date, a sortie of five British Spitfires flew over Israel lines in the Negev area. One was shot down inside the Israel frontier; in a further sortie that afternoon, twelve Spitfires were engaged by four Israel Spitfires, under the command of Ezer Weizmann, and four British planes were brought down: Ezer's training and fighting with the R.A.F. had stood him in good stead. There was a great rumpus in the House of Commons; but this was smoothed over when Dick Crossman was allowed to interview the captured British pilots, who admitted they had violated the Israel frontiers. They were released shortly afterwards.

On 25 January 1949 I cast my vote in the first general election held in the independent State of Israel. A few days later, on the 29th, Bevin called in the Israel diplomatic representative in London, Ivor Linton, and told him of the *de facto* recognition of Israel by Great Britain: this was followed by recognition by Australia, New Zealand, Chile, and many other countries. In my diary for the 29th I wrote,

> Chaim ought to be happy, but is he? He looks like a man who has climbed the highest mountain, and on reaching the top is more exhausted from his efforts than elated by his achievement.

As a result of the January elections in Israel, Chaim was elected President, and Ben-Gurion confirmed as Prime Minister. On 14 February, Chaim formally opened the Knesset in Jerusalem, making one of his most moving speeches, in the course of which he said:

> All my life I have laboured to make science and research the basis of our national endeavour. But I have always known full well that there are values higher than science: the only values that offer healing for the ills of humanity, the supreme values of justice and righteousness, peace and love. This day is a great day in our lives. Let us not be thought too arrogant if we say that it is also a great day in the history of the world. At this hour a message of hope and good cheer goes forth from this place, from this sacred city, to all those throughout the world who are persecuted and oppressed, and who are struggling for freedom and equality. A just struggle is indeed of avail. If we, the people of sorrows and affliction, have been vouchsafed this event of today, then truly there is hope at the end for all who long for justice.

He was nevertheless saddened by a letter he had received from our old friend Lady Violet Bonham Carter, in which she told him that because of the general amnesty which had been proclaimed, which had embraced some forty members of the Stern Group, she could no longer feel any friendship 'for the new State of Israel'. Israel, she wrote, 'will no doubt in time be "recognized"—*de facto* and *de jure*. But it has lost the *hearts* of all its truest friends in this country'. Chaim promptly replied to this broadside by the formidable but charming Lady Violet, telling her:

> The hangman and the jailer, on whom the British Administration relied for fighting terrorism, have as you know certainly not produced results. This is not an age of humanists, but speaking for myself I still believe that there is boundless wisdom in Goethe's great dictum that if you want to change the hearts of men, treat them as though they were already what you want them to become.

On 1 March, his spirits were raised by the popular rejoicing which attended our first official visit to Tel Aviv. Some hundred and fifty thousand persons crowded streets, balconies, and roof-tops. Gaily coloured carpets hung out of most of the windows, and children fluttered little blue and white Israeli flags. An armistice had been signed with the Egyptians on 24 February, and was followed in March and April by armistices with Lebanon and Jordan; the armistice with Syria was delayed until 20 July because of internal conflicts within that State.

But in April, much to our reluctance, Chaim was again persuaded to visit the United States, to be present at a dinner for the Weizmann Institute. Our departure, which had been scheduled for January, had been delayed by another of Chaim's periodic illnesses. Our leaving on 7 April meant that the first President of Israel would miss the first anniversary celebrations of the founding of the State on 14 May. But despite this, Chaim's last visit to America was an outstanding success. Many millions of dollars were collected on behalf of the Institute. For days afterwards, Chaim's right hand had to be supported by a sling because he had shaken hands with so many people!

One of the most moving moments of our last stay together in the United States came on 14 May—our Independence Day—when a great crowd of American Jews, friends, and sympathizers gathered in the huge auditorium of Madison Square Garden. Chaim, who was expected to make an appearance, suddenly developed stage fright and refused point blank to attend. But in the end Meyer Weisgal and I prevailed on him to go to the meeting. Apart from the enormous crowd in the Garden, another far larger assembly of people, estimated at a hundred and fifty thousand, who could not hope to get in, were massed in the streets. Chaim's entrance brought the entire audience in the Garden to its feet in an outburst of frenzied cheering and clapping that lasted for many minutes. It was not only a personal tribute to Chaim, but to the country whose titular head he was, a fitting climax to the many months which both he and I had spent in hospitable America, the scene of so many triumphs and disappointments. When we left later that summer, we both knew in our heart of hearts that we should not return together.

As the autumn passed into winter, and the orange groves were heavy with their harvest, the new Institute of Physics and Physical Chemistry at Rehovoth was dedicated on 2 November 1949. An impressive assembly of Israel and foreign scientists, together with many diplomatic representatives, came to honour my husband's seventy-fifth birthday and to view the superlative 'birthday present' he had received from American friends, headed by Mr. Dewey Stone, chairman of the American Committee of the Weizmann Institute. Prime Minister Ben-Gurion made a moving and eloquent speech in which he described Chaim as 'a man to whom it has fallen to be adorned with two crowns, the crown of statesmanship and the crown of learning.' In a letter which I subsequently wrote to B-G., I expressed my warmest thanks to him for his generous sentiments.

Although wearied through age, and the incessant storms and stresses of his life, and afflicted by constant bouts of ill-health, Chaim continued to show a lively interest in all the scientific work of the Institute, much of which he himself had inaugurated.[105] Early in 1950, we made the acquaintance of Boris Guriel. Boris, who had been born in Latvia, was by training a lawyer, through his extensive knowledge a walking encyclo-paedia and historian, and through his courage a soldier. He had been a prominent member of *Haganah*, and a successful chief of counter-intelligence. During the war he had enlisted in the Jewish Brigade of the British Army. At the age of thirty-seven he was taken prisoner in Greece, and was held for almost four years. On his return home, he found that the whole of his family, his mother, brother, sister and her husband, had all been killed by the Germans in Riga.

After Chaim's death, Meyer Weisgal on Dr. 'Ossinka' Blumenfeld's recommendation, appointed Boris Guriel as the official curator of the Weizmann Archives. With my assistance, more than twenty thousand letters written by my husband have been collected, some twenty per cent of them written by my husband's hand. During Chaim's illness in 1952, Boris moved to Weizmann House where he remained until he married a few years ago.

The succeeding two years before my husband's death are poorly chronicled in my diary. I was engaged in that battle which every wife knows of trying to support and comfort Chaim through many months of illness. But I notice that on 19 March 1950 I wrote that we had received a 'phone call from Meyer Weisgal from Montreal, telling Chaim that President Truman was anxious to meet him, and that 'if it were not for protocol, he would come to see Chaim in Israel'. Much as Chaim would have liked to visit Truman, his doctors forbade any further travel.

In the following year, on 19 November 1951, Chaim received a most charming note from Winston Churchill. I had made a habit of sending Churchill a box of citrus fruits—the product of our own orange and grapefruit groves—every Christmas for the last twenty-seven years. But in November 1951 Chaim had evidently written to congratulate him on his birthday: Churchill had been born in the same year as Chaim (1874), and only three days later. Churchill answered saying:

> Thank you very much for your letter and good wishes. The wonderful exertions which Israel is making in these times of difficulty are cheering to an old Zionist like me. I trust you may work in with Jordan and the rest of the Moslem world. With true comradeship, there will be enough for all. Every good wish, my old friend.

There was nothing in these sentiments with which either Chaim or I could disagree but, despite many Israel overtures, the Arab world continued its propaganda war against our State.

My diary entries for 1951 mark the steady decline of Chaim's health. On 26 March I wrote with great alarm:

Chaim is sinking. Today, for the first time, he did not recognize me for a moment as he'd had an injection of morphia. I am broken-hearted. Chaim has been sick since last November and has never left his room. He has been sitting up in bed for an hour, but not for the last few weeks.

A few days later, on the 30th, I noted some improvement in his condition:

Thank God, he recognizes everyone again. He is so weak, but noble and kind and so inexplicably patient and charming. He has developed some kind of extra sense-telepathy, and whenever we talk about something downstairs, he refers to the subject when I come up to see him.

Four months later, on 30 July, I noted:

Chaim's health keeps changing from extreme weakness and loss of appetite to extreme excitement and insomnia. He wants to get up and dress, go away: he is extremely restless. I don't know which is worse. I hardly leave him. Yesterday Lord and Lady Mountbatten were here.

For a whole year preceding his death in November 1952, Chaim was, except for three days, confined to his bed. His heart had become enlarged, and the scar on his lung from a childhood illness re-opened every few weeks and he would cough up blood. Although he was extremely weak, his mind remained remarkably lucid. He even retained his sense of humour. Once, hearing voices downstairs after lunch, he asked the nurse, 'What's happening?' She replied, 'Mrs. Weizmann is entertaining people for lunch'. Chaim answered, 'You're wrong, nurse. People have come too early for my funeral!'

Although he had four nurses in attendance—one every eight hours and each a day off—I hardly left him. They were strenuous, nostalgic hours and days for me. I could not help realizing that this was the beginning of the end. Occasionally his brothers and sisters and closest friends used to visit him; but these meetings exhausted him so much that I reduced them to a minimum. I gave him his meals myself, and after tea I would ask him if I could go for my usual walk in the garden. His usual reply was, 'Certainly', until the last days, when he answered, 'You'd better stay'. He was conscious of his approaching end, and that

I would soon be left alone, but did not dare to say it in plain words. But on some occasions, he would turn to me, saying, 'You have been a wonderful wife to me. Continue my work'. I could hardly restrain my tears. 'Who can continue your work?' I would ask him, 'I can do so little without you'. 'You can', he would answer with great firmness.

In the year following Chaim's death, I put down in my diary on 23 May the events which preceded his passing, and some of the remarks which he made to me. He fought bravely, gallantly for life as he had fought for his principles. Whenever I noticed that he was becoming dispirited and about to give in, I would say, 'Chaim'chik, you were always such a fighter all your life; go on fighting; don't give in'. He replied, 'Verotchka, you can't fight the inevitable'. But after a while he would resume his struggle against the inevitable.

On another occasion, he said to me, 'Verotchka, are you wearing your best dress? You must always be elegant. . . .' Then he would look at me with infinite sadness, tears running down his cheeks, saying to his two doctors, Dr. Sondek and Dr. Joel, 'I cannot bear her suffering face'. At other times, he found his own struggle for life too exhausting. 'This is too long', he would say, 'the end must come. I love you, Verotchka'. And when he was given morphia to relieve his pain, he would suddenly imagine that he was travelling; must catch a 'plane or board a ship. I would assure him that there was no need for him to leave his home, and he would sigh with relief, saying, 'Oh, I am so glad not to have to go'. The Ambassador-at-Large of the Jewish people had deserved his rest.

I spent many sleepless nights in a room next to his, until I was persuaded by Dr. Joel to sleep in my own bedroom, while the kind and efficient Dr. Joel took my place. It was on such occasions as this that I would go for a brief walk in the garden, with Chaim's approval. Three days before he died, he refused my request, muttering softly. 'You had better stay'.

On one of those days, a Friday, when I entered his room I heard him singing softly to himself. 'Chaim'chik, is it Beethoven?' I asked. He replied, 'No—it's a psalm'. I knew then that he was consciously singing his own funeral service, 'burying himself', as I recorded in my diary. Then he asked me for a needle and cotton, but I could not make out for what purpose. It was to sew his own shroud. Then turning to the nurse, he said, 'I am going on a very, very long journey. Prepare everything'. On Saturday, 8 November, he again asked me to stay in. When he went to sleep, I slipped out of his room and went down to rest for a while. I returned a little later to give him his supper. He ate it very slowly: it took almost an hour to feed him. Tears were running down my cheeks. 'Chaim'chik, don't you want your food?' I asked. 'I do, Verotchka', he replied. When he had finished, I asked him if he had enjoyed his meal. 'Very much', he answered. Those were his last words to me. When I returned to his room, I found him fast asleep. He was so peacefully asleep that I did not dare to give him a kiss.

I retired to my own room, took a sleeping draught, read for a while, and dropped off to sleep. It must have been about midnight. Within a quarter of an hour I was aroused by a light in my room. Someone was holding my hand. Terrified, I sprang up. It was Dr. Joel. 'Don't be frightened', he said, 'but your husband is unconscious'.

I slipped on my dressing-gown and spent the rest of the night by Chaim's bedside. At four a.m., sensing that his end was near, I asked the nurse to waken my brother-in-law, Dr. Joseph Blumenfeld—Ossinka—who was staying with us. Chaim opened his eyes once, and I imagined that there was a sign of recognition, but he did not utter a word. At four minutes to six, he stopped breathing. I fainted and was carried into my room. The sound of my husband's difficult breathing continued in my ears, and I vaguely remember repeating to myself, 'Stop it! Stop it! Stop it!'

At six o'clock in the morning, it was announced to the world that Dr. Chaim Weizmann, Israel's first President, had passed peacefully away. The Jewish religious authorities demanded that my husband should be buried on the day of his death, 9 November, according to ancient custom, but I wished to give my son, my sister, and our lifelong friends sufficient time to arrive from abroad for the funeral. When General Yadin, the victor of the War of Liberation, came to see me, I burst into tears, telling him that I had gone against my own interests so often, and had always given in, but that now I asked that my wishes should be respected. General Yadin managed to persuade the religious authorities to accede to my wishes.

Chaim lay in state in front of Weizmann House the whole of 9 and 10 November 1952, and over three hundred thousand persons in all walks of life came to pay their respects to the First President. Members of the Israel armed forces stood at his bier set in the garden of our house at Rehovoth. On 11 November, Armistice Day, he was buried in those same grounds according to his long-expressed wish—within sight of the mountains of Judah, in the Holy Land of Israel. All members of the Knesset and government were present at his funeral, four hundred persons in all, and psalms and the Prayer for the Dead were sung by the famous cantor Wilkomirsky.

When all the pomp and circumstance was over, I went to the British military cemetery at Ramleh and placed a bunch of flowers on the monument of the Unknown Soldier and on the grave of my younger son's best friend Michael Clark, killed by an Arab bullet in 1939. And in my heart I remembered all known and unknown soldiers, my own son Michael, and now my husband, that soldier of peace and science, who had brought his people home after long wandering.

20

The Years After . . .

WHEN my husband passed away at five-fifty-five a.m. on 9
November 1952, I was not as desperate as I had feared I
would be. It was an end to his year of suffering. I saw his
image in every kibbutz, every moshav (co-operative); in every inch
of Israel's soil, acquired with such love and labour; in the Hebrew
University, the Weizmann Institute of Science, and in the face of every
wandering Jew who had settled at last in his ancient Home. But I could
never come to terms with loneliness.

In December, a few weeks after my husband's death, Meyer Weisgal,
the chairman of the Executive Council of the Weizmann Institute,
persuaded me to attend a memorial meeting in New York dedicated
to Chaim. The mood in which I accepted this invitation is described
in my diary entry of 16 December 1952:

> Left Israel on 11 Dec. by Air France. What an ordeal to leave Chaim'chik
> in his grave alone. I cannot get used to it. I have already developed a double
> personality: the Verotchka of the old days, proud and happy with her dearest
> one, and another, who is lonely, desolate and forlorn. These two should never
> be allowed to meet.

On the day before my departure from Israel, there had been a memorial
meeting in Jerusalem, which I described as 'a dull, soulless performance'.
As I was leaving, Mrs. Ben Zvi, wife of the new President, said a few
kind words to me. A voice behind her exclaimed, 'Rachel, get a move
on!' It was the Prime Minister Ben-Gurion—'like a policeman,
directing the traffic', I wrote in my diary, an unkind observation
perhaps, but 'the other me' was extremely, even morbidly sensitive.

Just before I left for the airport the Ben Zvis visited me. I took them
to my husband's grave on which they wanted to lay flowers. Mr. Ben
Zvi asked me what the inscription was on the tombstone. 'Chaim
Weizmann', I replied. 'Is that all?' he asked in amazement, 'not the
President?' 'No', I said, 'just his name'.

When we returned to the house and they signed their names in my guest book, he wrote, 'Itzhak Ben Zvi, President of Israel'.

Before they left, the Presidential standard which had flown over Weizmann House since 1948 was hauled down. I felt a stab in my heart —not at the passing of such a temporal thing as a flag—but at the thought of what it had symbolized for four long years.

Over a thousand persons attended the Memorial Meeting in New York on 17 December. It opened with the performance of Chaim's favourite symphony by Beethoven, the 'Eroica', conducted by Leonard Bernstein; many good friends were present: Simon Marks and his wife Miriam, Nahum Goldmann, Abe Feinberg, and others too many to mention. Tears continued to well up in me, though I remained coldly composed on the surface, or so I was told. But I felt unable to attend the banquet which followed, and when I was alone in my hotel suite, I broke down. 'Chaim'chik follows me like a shadow wherever I go', I wrote in my diary that day. 'Horrid as it may seem, I try to chase his image away. I cannot live on memories; they are too precious, poignant, and only underline my loss. I am not myself, *but* someone else'.

I continued for some time to be 'someone else', although I dutifully attended all the meetings and press interviews which had been arranged for me. To Margaret Parton of the *New York Herald Tribune* I said on the 19 December:

> I came here a few days ago to help enlist support for the Weizmann Institute of Science in Israel. There are the laboratories where my husband worked, there are the laboratories where scientists may continue to discover ways of making our barren lands productive. My husband used to think of the institute as a scientific state within a state—a powerful place dedicated to the welfare not only of our country, but of the entire Middle East.

★

Early in January 1953 I planned to return home via England—my other home for so many years. The pull of England remained extremely strong. Indeed, after Chaim's death many persons, tried to persuade me to resettle in England. Not everyone did so from purely altruistic motives! A first 'First Lady' can be a trial and a tribulation, especially one with such exacting standards as I had developed over my long years of service; but when Boris Guriel, the curator of the Weizmann Archives, once asked me, 'What keeps you here?' I replied, 'The grave'. The past and the living present had anchored me to Israel.

On 7 January I had received an invitation to visit President Truman. It was a bitterly cold, snowy, 'skiddy' day when I arrived in Washington. I spent an hour in the National Gallery in the morning before going to the White House with Abba Eban at three p.m. The meeting with the President and Mrs. Truman was extremely cordial and affecting. We posed together for a number of 'official' photographs and, while Mrs. Truman tactfully stood aside, the President and I immersed ourselves in conversation.

He asked me about present-day conditions in Israel, and I told about our resettlement plans for the numerous oriental Jews who were being expelled from Arab countries. He also brought up the question of the Negev and asked how our development programme was getting on. 'Slowly but surely', I replied, recalling his earlier meeting with my husband when the fate of the Negev was decided. I told President Truman that when Chaim returned home, he remarked to me that 'for the first time in my life I met a President who could read maps!' At this Truman laughed heartily, saying that he could well recall his meeting with Chaim and the orders which he subsequently gave ending the partition of the Negev. 'Your husband was a great man, a very great man, and I had looked forward to co-operating with him for many years to come', he said. To this, I answered, 'My husband not only greatly respected and admired you, but he also had deep affection for you'. At this the President turned his head away: I could see there were tears in his eyes. He was silent for quite a while. It was hardly necessary for me to express my gratitude to him for the rôle he had played in the establishment of the State of Israel. I asked him when he was contemplating a visit to Israel, and he answered that he hoped to come in the following year. I assured him that his reception would be tremendous, and asked him to honour me by staying at Weizmann House, a wish which my husband had frequently expressed. At this we parted: our meeting had lasted a full half-hour. It was my last meeting with President Truman, a remarkable man and a remarkable President who will rank high not only in the annals of his own land. Before I left I noticed that there were two portraits on his desk: one was of Andrew Jackson, the seventh President of the United States, and the other was of Chaim Weizmann, the first President of Israel. . . .

*

Another encounter with a great contemporary followed shortly afterwards while I was making my return journey on the *Queen Mary* for a brief visit to England. Mr. and Mrs. Winston Churchill were among the passengers on the ship. On 26 January, they invited me to lunch in their stateroom. When he heard of my husband's death, he had spoken of his deep grief 'to lose my old and valued friend Dr. Chaim Weizmann', adding 'Those of us who have been Zionists since the days before the Balfour Declaration know what a heavy loss Israel has sustained. He was famed and respected throughout the free world, and his son was killed fighting for us. . . .' During the Second World War, he said to Bob Boothby—I paraphrase from memory, 'I cannot always see Weizmann when he needs me. He is my conscience and the last time I saw him, I spent three sleepless nights'.

Here I should like to express my opinion of Churchill's remark that Weizmann was his conscience. I think there was more to this than meets the eye. I have the idea that, after having detached Jordan from the future State of Israel, he began to doubt the wisdom of this move. At the time, he imagined that the Arabs had a rôle to play in the Near East favourable to Great Britain. Later, he may have wondered about this when his poetic vision dwelt on the revival of the ancient Jewish State. I cannot help thinking that this mental conflict hung over him like the sword of Damocles.

It was my melancholy privilege to recall some of Churchill's remarks when I was asked to broadcast my impressions of that great statesman when he died in 1965. He and Chaim had known each other since 1906, a half-century of unbroken friendship.

But on 26 January 1953, we had an extremely lively conversation, despite Churchill's incipient deafness. I shall give this conversation in 'dramatic' form as I wrote it in my diary. Among those present at our luncheon party, apart from Winston and Mrs. Churchill, were Mr. and Mrs. Soames (Mary Churchill and her husband), another British M.P. and his wife, and Churchill's private secretary.

Winston Churchill (during lunch): I am glad you won the war with Egypt.

I: Certainly; but there is no peace, only an armistice.[106]

Winston: This war should have never taken place. It was all Bevin—an anti-Semite.

I: Why should a Socialist be an anti-Semite?

Winston (jokingly): All the Foreign Office is.

I: So is the State Department, I believe. This permanent armistice does us a great deal of harm: there are daily frontier incidents and shootings. The frontiers are precarious, with infiltrators penetrating into Israel.

Winston: I hope you welcome them.

I (refusing to see the joke): How can we? They would become another Fifth Column. We can't afford a Sudetenland in Israel. Take Mount Scopus: we hold the University and the Hadassah Hospital, but the Arabs hamper our access to these places. They refuse to discuss this problem or negotiate with us. . . .

Winston Churchill then began talking about some remarkable temple building in Israel. A moment later, while we were drinking coffee, an R.A.F. plane began circling low and signalling over the *Queen Mary*; we were near Newfoundland. Everyone thought that the plane was in some kind of distress, but I felt sure that Winston was being welcomed home. He then went on to the Captain's bridge and shortly afterwards came back to say that the plane had signalled a 'welcome home' message to him. A little later we parted.

'The rest of the journey was uneventful', I wrote in my diary.

My contact with Winston Churchill continued right up to a year before his death.

When Randolph Churchill visited me at Weizmann House, a few years ago, I remember he asked me to obtain an interview for him with Ben-Gurion. My secretary telephoned to the Prime Minister's office and the request was refused. Astonished at this negative reply, I telephoned again, saying that I was not asking for an appointment for Randolph Churchill but for the son of Sir Winston Churchill, and it was arranged!

★

My return to London after my long absence was a nostalgic moment for me. My mind flew back over all those forty years of promise and struggle which Chaim and I had lived in England: our early life together in Manchester, our various London homes, our children, friends, pets and servants: the great day of the Balfour Declaration, the London 'blitz'. We had played our part in the drama of those days. The dove-grey twilight falling on the London parks, the carefully tended flower-beds, a troop from the Guards trotting sedately through Hyde Park to their Knightsbridge barracks: these were all part of the memories which seemed to deepen my solitude. But when I arrived in London in February of 1953, so many friends came to keep me company and to comfort me that it would be difficult to mention them all by name. But I remember how happy I was to see my old friends gathered at a reception arranged for me by Eliahu Elath, the Israel Ambassador in

London: among a host of others were Colonel Meinertzhagen, Dick Crossman, Clement Davies (then leader of the Liberal Party), the Samuels, Irene Ravensdale, Sir Charles and Lady Webster. Isaiah Berlin, too, came up from Oxford to visit me. He urged me to set down my memoirs—a task I have almost completed as I write. We recalled an episode in New York in 1948 when I met him in his hotel room where he was convalescing from influenza. The sight was awe-inspiring. There was Isaiah standing in front of a mirror with an electric shaver in one hand, casting an eye on the *New York Times*—and at the same time 'conducting' a symphony purring over the radio with the other hand! No wonder Winston Churchill described Isaiah Berlin as one of the most brilliant men he had ever met!

*

On my return to Israel in the spring of 1953, I found that my two 'separate selves' were beginning to merge into one person again as I devoted myself to charitable and social work in Youth Aliyah, the rehabilitation of war-wounded soldiers, and in the Magen David Adom (our Red Cross) of which I am president.

Youth Aliyah has become a living proof of the vision which inspired its founders, supported by such patrons as Eleanor Roosevelt, Field-Marshal Smuts, and Elizabeth, late Queen Mother of the Belgians. At Youth Aliyah's twentieth anniversary celebrations in 1953, I recalled that over sixty-four thousand orphaned children had found a home and 'a mother' in Israel through the devoted work of the organization. Today, the number of its charges is over a hundred thousand. 'Of such is the Kingdom of Heaven', said the great-hearted Field-Marshal Smuts in a message he once sent to Youth Aliyah, 'Let this remnant be planted in the soil drenched with blood and tears, and hallowed by the prayers of their ancestors'. To every Jew and Gentile, I record my thanks and admiration for the work which has been done in this mighty rescue operation.

Perhaps I may be allowed to say a few words about myself in this concluding chapter. Unlike Anglo-Saxons, very few Israelis enjoy hobbies, or even know how to relax. I myself caught this refreshing habit from the British, but my hobbies take second place to my other activities. I have little time to be an active patron of the plastic arts, but I enjoy both music and literature. I ought, perhaps, to get 'used' to modern music, but I have not been able to devote sufficient attention to it. Nor am I a great admirer of the modern novel. I do not like or understand poetry, except the poetry of Pushkin, Lermontov, and Nekrassov, on which I was brought up. On the whole I prefer essays and biographies.

Like other people in the public eye, I have received my quota of preposterous requests, appeals, and begging letters. Some ask me for a 'potted history' of my husband; others enquire whether their name of *Weissmann* would indicate some family affinity despite the difference in the spelling of the names; I cannot count the letters I have had from fond parents telling me that their child was named after my husband! And all these 'Chaims' invariably invite me not only to remember their birthday but also to attend their *barmitzvah*—their coming of age at thirteen. I can understand the motives of affection which prompt many of these letters, but cannot, alas, answer every one personally, let alone attend all these ceremonies.

*

My 1953 diary records events pleasant and unpleasant, and some which bring a smile to my lips even as I recall them. I do not refer to the mortality rate among dictators in March of the same year: Stalin, the iron man of the Soviet Union, died on 6 March, and Gottwald, his Czechoslovakian imitator, passed away shortly afterwards; neither was universally regretted, but at the Mapam (left-wing socialist) and Communist headquarters here, the flags flew at half-mast.

On 16 April Jascha Heifetz, the celebrated violinist, gave a concert in Jerusalem: he and other violinists, Yehudi Menuhin, Isaac Stern, Milstein, Vitya Vronsky, and Victor Babin—all my beloved friends— have given their artistic services at concerts organized in aid of the Tel Hashomer Hospital for the rehabilitation of soldiers wounded in the War of Liberation.

On 8 June the greatly loved Adlai Stevenson, twice a candidate for the American presidency and later a noble and impassioned pleader of his country's cause at the United Nations, came to visit me at Weizmann House. He greatly admired the portrait of Chaim painted by Sir Oswald Birley which hangs in the library. I asked him if he had ever met my husband, and, to my great embarrassment, Stevenson reminded me that he had once had dinner with us at the Dorchester in 1944. It was a rare slip of memory on my part. He was gentle and charming, and visited Chaim's grave on which he placed flowers. 'I wonder to whom I owe the honour of his visit', I wrote in my diary. I was subsequently informed that he had told our Foreign Office that it would have been inconceivable that he should not visit Mrs. Weizmann. This visit was not included in his itinerary.

On 7 January 1954, I had a brisk passage of arms with Aneurin Bevan, prominent Labour Party politician and stormy petrel of British politics, over the Suez Canal Zone which the Egyptians had asked the British to evacuate. Becky Sieff had given a party for Bevan in her Tel Mond House to which I had been invited. Bevan was very much the lion of the evening, full of charm, dialectics, and sophism, a man who could not easily tolerate contradiction. 'I went for him politely, but ruthlessly', I wrote in my diary.

Bevan began his conversation with me by declaring that the British had no business to remain in Egypt, adding, 'I can't grant Israel something I would deny to Egypt. People must decide their own fate'. He was referring to the ferment of unrest in Egypt which would shortly topple General Neguib and replace him with the more implacable Nasser.

I demurred firmly, telling Bevan that 'the people' in Egypt could hardly decide anything, since it was still a feudal country, where the average *fellah* earned a bare thirty pounds a year, and was both physically and politically too weak to express his will, let alone take part in a revolution.

'We were starving when millionaires were stuffing their pockets in England', Bevan replied, in a temper.

'At least, those millionaires paid taxes', I riposted. 'Well, if the United States give the Egyptians funds for education, instead of for arms—' Bevan said when I interrupted, saying 'I would give them neither!' He nearly jumped out of his skin. 'Wouldn't you?' he demanded. I was being deliberately provocative, of course.

'We have no business in Egypt, and should clear out', Bevan then declared. 'Our people won't have their sons killed—for what?' He delivered this last remark with emphatic finality, but I continued, 'By evacuating the Suez Canal you will create a vacuum, and a vacuum cannot exist. Either the Americans or the Russians will come in. What you propose to do is to liquidate the British Empire and create a Moslem Empire in the Middle East instead. If you have no right in Egypt, what right has Egypt to occupy the Gaza strip, and the Lebanon to prevent our work in the Huleh,[107] which will benefit tens of thousands of people?' Bevan did not answer. At this, our conversation ended. As we got up, Bevan said loudly, 'Mrs. Weizmann has been pulling me to pieces'.

He repeated this remark to other persons, so he evidently enjoyed being 'pulled to pieces'.

'There were many things I could have told him if we had been on neutral ground', I put in my diary.

Three weeks later my great friend Lola Beer brought me an interesting piece of diplomatic gossip. She had been told by the Turkish Minister that the Russian Government had invited me to Russia; he had received a cable to this effect from Ankara. 'How on earth did they get this information?' I wrote in my diary entry of 30 January. Lola Beer, I should add, is not only a very talented dress-designer—perhaps the best we have in Israel—but she is also very gay, pretty, and graceful, with a great deal of vitality and very strong political views. I invariably tease her about these just to see her sparkle.

I ought to explain, perhaps, that I was on extremely cordial terms with the then Russian Minister Abramov and his wife. Mr. Abramov was busy negotiating a visit for me to Russia at this time, in the brief period of 'relaxation' which followed the death of Stalin. They were charming, easy, intelligent people and the conversation flowed easily round the table until Ossinka (Dr. Blumenfeld) could not resist telling them that Trotsky had lived in the same house as he—Blumenfeld—in Paris on the Rue Oudry, and that he had often seen Lenin visit Trotsky! 'Dead silence', I noted in my diary.

On 12 February, I put down in my diary:

> Twelve years since my youngest son Michael was missing. Am so sad, nervy, and tense. All the old sweet memories surge upon me. How I loved him. I went this morning to put flowers on Michael Clark's grave, as I always do on this day. Now I wait for eleven-twenty p.m. when my Michael's last signal was given.

In the same entry I noted that there had been a great to-do in the Hebrew Press about the alleged correspondence between Mrs. Molotov and myself (which never took place—in fact I never even met her) concerning the immigration of former German or Polish prisoners-of-war from Russia:

> West Germany strongly supports this move despite the denial by our Information Agency in West Germany. I hope this won't get Mrs. Molotov into trouble. Who is behind it? I fear it is someone who wishes to discredit the Molotovs.

A few days later Moshe Sharett came to have tea with me. I found that he was a changed man. 'Although he talks well, he now listens more', I wrote in my diary. 'The responsibility of the Prime Minister's office weighs on him and he is subdued and makes a good impression'. We talked about the proposed abolition of capital punishment in Israel: the majority of the Knesset supported such a move against the majority opinion in the cabinet, he told me. Israel abolished capital punishment, one of the first countries and I believe the only one in the Middle East, to take such a step.

On 1 March I was invited by Ben-Gurion and his wife to lunch at the Sde Boker kibbutz near Beersheba where B-G. had gone into brief retirement. He appeared 'sunburnt but too fat', I wrote in my diary— and Mrs. Ben-Gurion did not look too prepossessing wearing her husband's trousers. Their bungalow was 'bright and comfortable but overcrowded with odds and ends. B-G. seemed happy but rather dull and has little to say. . . .' But Mrs. Ben-Gurion confided in me that the government could not do without her husband, and that he had been called in for consultations especially on problems concerning Arab countries. Shortly afterwards, B-G. rejoined the government in his former rôle as Prime Minister. But I saw Moshe Sharett on a number of occasions during his brief tenure of office as Prime Minister. On 15 March (according to my diary) we spoke about my forthcoming trip to Russia. There had been a cabinet meeting to discuss this question, he told me. Moshe Sharett appeared to be worried. I jotted his remarks in my diary:

> What would the Russians think? The Jews are so clever. Mrs. Weizmann is not a member of the government, but she was the former President's wife, so unofficially she will act officially and will negotiate about Jews in Russia— what will the United States say? Won't they assume that unofficially she will try to make contact with Russia to counteract American support for the Arabs? Mrs. Weizmann will never be able to go to the United States again!

Zeev Sharef, the secretary of the cabinet, said, 'It is a very good idea. Let them think and guess.' I think both of them were pulling my leg.

During the months of March and April 1954, fierce frontier incidents on the Israeli-Jordan border continued, despite the pacification efforts of the U.N. Armistice Commission. I was happy to welcome A. J. Balfour's nephew, the third Lord Balfour, who came as head of the British delegation to Israel.

On 1 April I received a letter from Dr. Sheba telling me that Mr. and Mrs. Abe Kay of Washington, would, with great generosity, subscribe $100,000 to the Disabled Veterans project, if their name was attached to the building. I thanked them warmly, but I had to decline this wonderful offer as the estimate from the architect for this rest-house was in the region of half a million dollars. My correspondence with Mr. Kay went on for nearly two years. In the end I suggested that he come to see me in Israel when we could definitely settle the question between us. He came immediately; fell in love with the country and with Naharia where the proposed Disabled Veterans' rest-house was to be situated; and accepted the full financial responsibility for the building. I gave up my name for the building in exchange for his.

It was about this time that I learnt that my projected trip to South America had been arranged. Before leaving, I had the melancholy duty of going to Haifa to await the arrival of a ship bringing the bodies of Baron and Baroness Edmond de Rothschild, Mr. James de Rothschild's parents, for re-interment in Israel. It was during this ceremony that Ben-Gurion said to me, 'Why don't you settle in Sde Boker?' 'Can you imagine me on a kibbutz?' I answered, 'We don't go together'.

On 15 April I wrote:

> Hurrah! Sharett rang up at lunch time to inform me that Russia has granted me a visa. My head is in a whirl—to see Russia. What will they let me see? Whom shall I meet? Will they ignore me? Perhaps I shall be able to do something or merely flop?

The answer to all these questions was to come later. Meanwhile, I travelled to South America at the end of April 1954, visiting Argentina, Chile, and Brazil to address meetings on behalf of the Israel bond drive and the Weizmann Institute, in particular to raise funds for the auditorium named after the famous Argentinian liberator, San Martin. I was received when I arrived in each of these countries by their respective Presidents, including Peron.

Peron invited me to meet him at eight o'clock in the morning, but as I had arrived in Argentina at two a.m. that same day, I apologetically asked for an appointment for the next day. During the course of our three-quarters of an hour's conversation, we spoke of Jewish immigration into Argentina, and touched on the question of anti-Semitism. 'Einstein', I told him, 'is regarded as Swiss, Karl Marx is German, but Trotsky is a —Jew!' He laughed heartily at this remark.

Of more interest, perhaps, was the decoration bestowed on me by the President of Brazil. I had an enjoyable if strenuous time in South America, followed almost immediately by my journey to Russia, where I travelled accompanied by my secretary.

After an absence of forty years, the visit to Russia was a memorable event in my life, although I did not record it in my diary. My fears that I might be prevented from seeing anything I wanted to see were soon dispelled. I made the usual routine tourist visit to crêches and collective farms, the opera and the theatre, and attended a number of concerts. But my request to visit my native town of Rostov-on-Don was discouraged. It was explained to me that Rostov had changed hands some five times during the war and had been so thoroughly destroyed that I would see nothing of my old home. And since all my relatives and childhood friends were dead, I saw little reason to press the point. Shortly after my return from Russia, I wrote to President Voroshilov asking him to grant a visa to my sister-in-law Masha, a physician, who had been arrested during the notorious 'doctors' trial' in Moscow which had preceded Stalin's death in 1953.

After my husband's death on 9 November 1952, a small notice had appeared in *Pravda*. That was how Masha first learned of her brother's death. She lit a small candle in the privacy of her home, and this was reported to the authorities by some busybody. At her arrest she was interrogated about the candle. She told the truth, but 'they' knew better. You did not light a candle in memory of your brother, she was told, but in memory of the Zionist leader—Chaim Weizmann! In 1955, Masha and her Russian husband (a non-Jew) were allowed to leave the Soviet Union. Her husband, who had endured some years in a Stalin concentration camp, passed away three years after his arrival in Israel.

In 1955 Soviet technicians, arms, and aid began to flow into Egypt and other Arab states. Early in the same year, a number of young Jews were apprehended in Egypt, accused of being involved in a sabotage mission. Since their lives were in jeopardy, I took the initiative into my own hands and appealed to Sir Winston Churchill to intervene on their behalf. On 5 January 1955 I cabled to Sir Winston:

> Though deeply reluctant to intervene political affairs feel compelled and am encouraged by your friendship to appeal for your personal intercession behalf ten young Jews now awaiting sentence before Cairo military court stop Sentence is about to be passed and wont be made public until after its confirmation by Prime Minister stop Greatly fear that in the highly inflamed atmosphere surrounding trial and prevailing Egypt generally death sentences originally demanded by prosecution may be passed stop Remembering your profound saying that grass grows over battlefields but never over gallows I beg you use your influence to prevent executions as these would arouse grave bitterness in Israel and irretrievably poison relations between

two countries stop Only your universal personality can tip the scales stop Matter is extremely urgent stop Implore you to do what you can gratefully Vera Weizmann.

Shortly afterwards the British Ambassador, Sir John Nicolls, called on me to convey the British Prime Minister's personal message. As the burden of most of it was confidential, I can only say that representations were made to Nasser by the British. The number of executed victims was limited to two while the remainder of the young Jews were sentenced to long terms of imprisonment. The generous humanitarian response Sir Winston made to my appeal has remained indelibly fixed in my mind.

A year later, almost to the day, on 9 January 1956, as relations between Egypt and Israel worsened still further, I wrote to Ben-Gurion who was again our Prime Minister, suggesting that he should meet Nasser privately to discuss outstanding differences between the two countries.* The advantages of such a dialogue were obvious, I told Ben-Gurion. If Nasser turned down such a meeting the world would know where the fault lay. On the next day, I received a most courteous letter from B-G. saying:

> I was very pleased to receive your note, and deeply appreciate the interest you take in the government's political problems. I doubt whether there will be any use in sending a personal note to Colonel Nasser—at any rate, not at this particular time when our friends in the United States are trying to bring about joint talks. However, I shall certainly bear in mind your suggestion, since an opportune time for its execution may well arise.

However, our friends in the United States did not bring about such a confrontation between Nasser and Ben-Gurion, and my suggestion was lost in the crash of guns as war broke out between Egypt and Israel in the second Sinai campaign in October 1956, which ended with the total defeat of Nasser's forces. This was followed closely by the so-called Suez Crisis in which Britain and France were involved as well as Israel. American and United Nations intervention brought this operation to a halt, and Israeli forces again retreated within their frontiers. Since that time, a further uneasy truce has prevailed, while Nasser continues to make Hitlerian speeches about the coming annihilation of Israel. I, who have seen two world wars carry away two generations and six millions of my own people, cannot easily forget. The long-suffering Egyptian people will, I hope, throw off the bondage of this

* *See* Appendix F. p. 290.

so-called 'socialist' and learn to dwell in peace and amity with their Jewish neighbour.

So the years passed with their measured tread. There were many blessings to count, and lost friendships to retrieve. I recall with particular happiness the visit Lady Violet Bonham Carter paid me at Weizmann House early in 1957. In the gracious letter which she wrote to me afterwards, she said of her visit:

> What memories it brought back! Of those agonizing years before the war, the hopes and fears we shared, the dream which is now realized, the impact of the personality of your great husband. I count myself *blessed* to have known him. *Il y a des absences qui sont des présences.* I felt his presence with us when you showed me the room in which he worked, in which he walked —his books—his writing-table—his picture—the bust* which I remember so vividly in your London house. His is 'a presence not to be put by'—in the State which he created. What a triumphant achievement! A great experiment in internationalism—combined with a burning sense of nationhood, a dynamic, progressive State with every scientific resource and device which yet holds fast to the tradition and faith of two thousand years, an unbroken thread, a vision intact.

She also asked for a copy of Chaim's letter in which he quoted Goethe's famous dictum—'If you want to change the hearts of men, treat them as though they were already what you want them to become'.

*

All the Belgian royal family have always shown the utmost sympathy with Israel. I have described earlier the visit paid to mandated Palestine in the 'thirties by King Albert and Queen Elizabeth. In 1959 Queen Elizabeth, then Queen Mother, lunched at my house in Rehovoth. It was difficult for Her Majesty to climb the stairs to rest after lunch, so we prepared the couch in my husband's study for her to lie down on. That couch thus became historical! As a memento of that visit, I have a photograph signed by her: 'To Mrs. Chaim Weizmann, incomparable companion of a great President. A souvenir of my visit to Rehovoth in April 1959.' Some five years later, in 1964, King Baudouin and his consort Queen Fabiola visited Israel. I met them at a dinner given by President Shazar at the King David Hotel in Jerusalem. His Majesty's first words to me on our introduction were, ' I bring you my grandmother's love. . . .' He must have known how fond I was of that very lovely lady.

*

* By Jacob Epstein.

Sir Charles Webster, the historian, in whose work on diplomacy is to be found such a moving tribute to my husband's statesmanship, spent long hours with me, allowing me to regale him with stories, many of which now appear in this volume. In a letter he wrote to me later, he said, 'What exclusively fascinating stories; what a book they would make'. I must leave the reader to judge how exclusive or fascinating these have been. Robert Graves, the novelist and poet, also had some kind words to say about me in an interview he gave to the *Jerusalem Post*. He said that the most impressive person he had met in Israel was myself: 'She is like a great Queen Mother of the country; happy and dignified; not a ghost of the past, but a living present in full possession of her faculties, without being a touching old lady'. I treasure this remark. It is a constant joke in my family that my great ambition is to be 'the housekeeper of the government'. This is because of my meticulous attention to detail, my dislike of anything slovenly or untidy, either in clothes or manners; but I doubt very much whether the Israel government would ever honour me with such an elevated title as its housekeeper!

*

My own relations with my domestic staff have always been friendly and sympathetic to their needs and requirements. Although I myself took lessons at the Cordon Bleu Cookery School in Paris, I had little opportunity to practise the culinary art. But I passed on many useful tips to my cook Batya, who has been with me for many years. She is a perfect cook and an excellent manager. My Russian-born maid Zipora ('little bird' in Hebrew) speaks three languages fluently. She has slept in the house ever since my husband's illness, so that I should not be alone. Elsa, the head parlour-maid, came originally from Hungary, but worked as a secretary in Rumania for some years. Her devotion to me is boundless. She can foretell my wishes in advance, and looks after my guests as if they were hers. There is also Esther; she came from Morocco, so her background and language are French. She is kind, efficient, and affectionate. And finally there is Clara, a woman of great refinement, gentleness, and tact.

Joshua, still my chauffeur, is almost the master of the house, gently bullying everybody. He is extremely devoted and undertakes all sorts of jobs for me.

I rely a great deal on my present secretary, Retty Kreisberg, who has been with me for eight years. She is an excellent secretary in every

267

way, speaks five languages fluently, and her devotion is remarkable—a feeling which I fully reciprocate, for I am very fond of her.

Thus my narrative draws to its close.

I am, as Robert Graves said, far from being 'a touching old lady'. I have grieved over the departure of my son and husband, and the passing of many good friends. Yet I have tried constantly to look to the future. Although I have spent much of my life abroad, I have a profound affection for the native-born 'sabras' of Israel. They are, I think, a reversion to type. They are physically tall, slender, of good proportions, with long legs and a graceful carriage. In them lies the hope of the future of Israel. Like all sons of pioneers, the sabras have been accused of being ill-mannered and rude. It is not a trait which I have observed. They express their thoughts freely and with few inhibitions.

Because of rapid immigration, our schools have become overcrowded, and our education is sometimes old-fashioned and inadequate, a complaint shared with many other countries. Apartments are small and crowded and there are not enough youth clubs. Such things will be remedied in time, no doubt, and aesthetics, cleanliness, and orderliness will play their part in the ordinary school curriculum.

People of my generation are getting tired, weary, and out-of-date. Many of them, with few exceptions perhaps, must make way for the new rising generation of leaders, for a new way of life altogether. Yet I cannot help thinking of my own early life in Russia with the story of which I began my narrative—our large house, our closely-knit family, our evenings together, the balance between youth and age, and the respect and affection we all felt for each other. The conflict between 'fathers' and 'sons' depicted so graphically by Turgenev returns in every generation, but today it is also Nation against Nation.

As I look back over a life which has bridged part of two centuries, my thoughts, behaviour, and reactions seem to belong to another personality altogether.

Today, I am confused and bewildered, distressed and sad. The situation confronting Israel grows more serious. There are daily attacks, firing, abductions along our frontiers: even the waters of the Jordan which flow between Israel and our neighbour have been menaced. How long can we remain spectators of this attempt to shatter our very existence?

Yet I am not without hope as I think of the future. I firmly believe that the moral values which my husband upheld will once more prevail. It was in this hope that I was prompted to write the following letter to the *New York Times* which was published on 6 June 1963. With it I shall conclude my narrative:

> Current developments in the Middle East, coupled with the ambiguous American, British, and Soviet policies towards them, have created a confused and confusing situation not only for the Israelis, who feel their security gravely jeopardized, but also for people of goodwill everywhere who cannot fathom big power attitudes.
>
> Indeed, one wonders whether the so-called guardians of world peace are actually interested in maintaining pacific relations among Middle East countries, as they solemnly profess at the U.N., or regard this region solely as a manoeuvring area for power conflicts.
>
> Fifteen years have passed since Israel was established and recognized by the U.N. Nearly one and a half million refugees have settled in it, to be productive in agriculture, industry, science; to develop its raw materials, establish its educational and welfare systems, and provide for the immigrants, the aged, the feeble, and the sick.
>
> For fifteen years we have been reminded of the half-million Arabs in neighbouring countries who left of their own free will. Yet more Jewish refugees left Arab countries than Arabs left Palestine. Nevertheless, the vicious assertion that there are a million—not half a million—Arab refugees is Egypt's greatest political asset, even greater than its MIG jet fighters.
>
> Today Egypt poses the State of Israel with the same threat that Hitler, 25 years ago, posed the House of Israel. Intoxicated by success with two great rival powers, Nasser fails to realize that even Rameses lost in the end, and that the inquisition, pogroms, and gas chambers could not annihilate the Jewish people. The valiant inmates of the Warsaw ghetto did not fight in vain. Today is no longer yesterday. History will not repeat itself. If the Nassers of the world recognize this, it will be the first step towards peace.
>
> As for myself, I believe, as my husband did, in the ultimate triumph of moral values—although people must get a little push now and then so as to see them more clearly. I believe in the spirit of George Washington who fought for freedom over Boston's 5 o'clock tea; in the spirit of Lafayette, who left his own country to help another people fighting for their human rights; in the spirit of Cromwell who invited Jews to settle in England; and in the authors of the Balfour Declaration and those who made the State of Israel a miraculous reality. Their spirit will prevail again.
>
> And I believe that no power on earth can balance the oil and political rivalries of the Middle East against the fate of two million and more Israelis. For it is said in I Samuel, xv, 29—'And also the Strength of Israel will not lie nor repent: for he is not a man, that he should repent'.

APPENDIX A

From Sir Charles Webster's *The Art and Practice of Diplomacy* (Chatto & Windus, London, 1961), pp. 5-6.

One of the best examples of such successful diplomacy is that by which Dr. Weizmann brought into existence the Jewish National Home, which I was able to observe closely in the later stages of the First World War. When that war began, his cause was hardly known to the principal statesmen of the victors and its administrative centre was in Germany. It had many enemies and some of the most formidable were amongst the most highly placed of his own people. The task which Dr. Weizmann set himself of transferring the centre of Zionism to London and obtaining the co-operation of Britain in Palestine was more difficult than that of any other statesman of the smaller powers, not excepting Masaryk or Venizelos. He once told me that 2,000 interviews had gone to the making of the Balfour Declaration. With unerring skill he adapted his arguments to the special circumstances of each statesman. To the British and Americans he could use Biblical language and awake a deep emotional undertone; to other nationalities he more often talked in terms of interest. Mr. Lloyd George was told that Palestine was a little mountainous country not unlike Wales; with Lord Balfour the philosophical background of Zionism could be surveyed; for Lord Cecil the problem was placed in the setting of a new world organization; while to Lord Milner the extension of imperial power could be vividly portrayed. To me who dealt with these matters as a junior officer of the General Staff, he brought from many sources all the evidence that could be obtained of the importance of a Jewish National Home to the strategical position of the British Empire, but he always indicated by a hundred shades and inflexions of the voice that he believed that I could also appreciate better than my superiors other more subtle and recondite arguments. The skilful presentation of facts would, however, have been useless, unless he had convinced all with whom he came into contact of the probity of his conduct and the reality of his trust in the will and strength of Britain. He was so careful never to give a handle to his enemies that I had a copy of every letter and telegram which he sent out of this country, and when he went to Palestine in 1918 even his wife sent me her letters to him unsealed, until I told her not to. He was of course assisted by many ardent helpers, Jews and non-Jews. But some of these had also to be handled with delicate diplomacy lest they should say or do unwise things. It is often the tragedy of the diplomat to be most thwarted by those who most wish him to succeed, and the cause Dr. Weizmann had at heart often went so deep that it sometimes overcame the prudence or even the good manners of those that held it. These enthusiasms were muted, reconciled, diverted or transformed so that each could make its contribution to the final objective, a Jewish Home in Palestine under British protection. By the time the Peace Conference had begun, his cause had become so much a part of British policy that it was only a question of how it could be best translated into practice with the consent and goodwill of the Arabs and the French.

See also Chapter 7 (pp. 113-132), 'The Founder of the National Home': The Chaim Weizmann Memorial lecture which Sir Charles gave in 1955.

APPENDIX B

From the *Jerusalem Post*, 4 April 1958:

ZIONIST COMMISSION: WEIZMANN'S LETTER TO BALFOUR
Unpublished Correspondence Recalls First Appeasement of Arabs

The arrival of the 'Zionist Commission' in Palestine exactly 40 years ago today in response to a request from the British Government was the first practical outcome of the Balfour Declaration.

The principal objects of the Commission were to form a link between the local Jewish population and the British Authorities, to co-ordinate relief activities, to help in the organization of Palestinian Jewry, to prepare the establishment of the Hebrew University and above all to draw up plans for the future development of the Jewish National Home.

The Commission were to include Zionist representatives from all Allied countries. However, American Zionists were prevented from sending delegates by their Government, since the U.S. was not at war with Turkey and the delegates from Russia could not leave in time. Thus, in addition to Dr Chaim Weizmann, the Chairman, the Commission at first included Josef Cowen and Leon Simon, an old Herzlian and a disciple of Achad Ha'am respectively, representing the English Zionist Federation; Dr. David M. Eder, a well-known psychologist, delegated by Israel Zangwill's 'Jewish Territorial Organization' but soon to become a passionate Zionist, and Professor Sylvain Lévi, one of the anti-Zionist leaders of the 'Alliance Israélite Universelle'. Mr. Israel Sieff acted as secretary to the Commission and Major Ormsby-Gore (the present Lord Harlech) was attached to them as liaison officer with the Military Authorities. Major James De Rothschild, looking after the interests of his father's colonies, was also loosely connected with the Commission, and finally there was in their entourage the controversial figure of Aaron Aaronson, who acted as a kind of unofficial representative of Justice Brandeis, the American Zionist leader.

After a triumphant welcome in Tel Aviv, the Commission soon confronted grim reality. The following copy of a letter (or draft of a letter) from Chaim Weizmann to A. J. Balfour, the British Foreign Secretary, dated May 30 1918, shows how many of the problems which later disturbed relations between the Mandatory Power and the Zionist Movement were germinating even then. It is preserved in the Central Zionist Archives.

Dear Mr. Balfour,

   . . . We arrived in Palestine at a very unfortunate moment. Owing to the serious events in France, the campaign here was brought to a sudden stop, and the great hopes raised by the victorious onrush of the British troops and the capture of Jerusalem have not yet been realized.

The Arabs . . . worship one thing, and one thing only—power and success. Hence while it would be wrong to say that British prestige has suffered through the military stalemate, it certainly has not increased. . . . Rumours sinister and absurd, exaggerations of all sorts, circulate very rapidly here, and an atmosphere is created very quickly. It is not exactly dissatisfaction, but it is uncertainty, a lack of firm ground—a haziness in the outlook and a sitting on the fence.

This has natuarally made the British authorities rather nervous, and . . . they have to watch carefully and constantly that nothing should happen which might give the Arabs the slightest grievance or ground of complaint. In other words, the Arabs have to be 'nursed' lest they should stab the army in the back. The Arab, quick as he is to gauge such a situation, tries to make the most of it. He screams as often as he can and blackmails as much as he can.

*

The first scream was heard when your Declaration was announced. All sorts of misinterpretations and misconceptions were put on the declaration. The English, they said, are going to hand over the poor Arabs to the wealthy Jews, who are all waiting in the wake of General Allenby's army, ready to swoop down like vultures on an easy prey and to oust everybody from the land. German agents fostered these notions, and the anti-Zionist propaganda soon turned out to be anti-British.

The British authorities here and in Egypt tried their best to allay fears and suspicions, and were quite successful in all cases where genuine and fair-minded people were concerned; but of course they were bound to fail in the majority of cases, because the majority does not wish to be convinced. It must be added also that the authorities had no very clear conception of the aims and aspirations of the Zionist movement, and very often laboured under grave misconceptions. You know that a good many non-Jews—I won't say most of them—always envisage only one type of Jew, the financier, the exploiter, the stock-broker. . . . But the British made one fundamental mistake—they did not realize that these Jews are opponents to Zionism, and so they unjustly let us suffer for the sins of our enemies.

You will therefore realize, dear Mr. Balfour, that we found ourselves in an atmosphere very unfavourable to our work.

The British viewed us with suspicion, the Arabs with hostility, the rich Jews of Egypt with indifference. At home a carefully planned attack was launched against us just at the moment when we set foot on Palestinian soil. The whole political and military situation was very unstable, the Military Authorities here were preoccupied. Meanwhile our friends in the Jewish colonies and towns were full of hopes and expectations. So on the one hand we were hailed as the precursors of the Messiah; on the other hand we were mistrusted as the vanguard of a set of capitalist exploiters. . . .

We started our work under these mixed auspices, and we should not have been able to carry it on for very long but for the goodwill and great assistance of the Commander-in-Chief and his immediate entourage, and the guidance of the Chief Political Officer, General Clayton, his assistant Colonel Deedes, and last but not least, our own pilot Major Ormsby-Gore. The time has not yet come to give a full and just appreciation of what his guidance and assistance have meant to the Jewish cause, but it is only fair to state now that it has made it possible for us to face with courage and confidence an extremely difficult and complex situation. I should be guilty of lack of taste if I were to express my appreciation of the personalities mentioned in trivial words of gratitude. I am convinced that history will register their deeds as among the best achievements of British statesmanship.

*

Having dealt with the 'imponderabilia' of the situation I may be permitted to turn to a description of the concrete realities.

One of the objects of our mission was to organize the Jewish community here, to conduct the work of relief, to help in the development of our schools, etc. . . . Our Chief object is of course to lay plans for the future, to examine exactly by what ways and means the establishment of the National Home can be effected. We have therefore had to ask ourselves whether the present state of things in the country, which may of course only be transitory, is favourable to our plans or not; and whether again this transitional stage is not likely to leave some permanent trace behind, which may determine the orientation of policy in the future.

The British Administration here is guided by one fundamental principle laid down in The Hague convention, that in Occupied Enemy Territory the *status quo* has to be preserved. It is not for me to express an opinion on the advisability of applying rigidly to Palestine a formula which has been violated by every belligerent Power during the war, and has lost all relation to reality. We have only to accept the fact and to see what we can achieve within the limits set by the *status quo*.

At the head of the Administration we see enlightened and honest English officials, but the rest of the administrative machinery is left intact; and all the offices are filled with Arab and Syrian employees who have certainly not changed their mentality with the change of master. . . . So the English are run by the Arabs.

For the Jewish present and future this state of affairs is fraught with grave dangers, for the following reasons:

(1) The administration in this form is distinctly hostile to Jews, and abuses its present artificial position to injure Jewish interests wherever it can. Of course the Jews feel this and try to defend themselves, and this leads to friction

and bitterness. . . . I can assure you, dear Mr. Balfour, that we have tried our
level best to explain the situation to our own people, and I think we have not
been unsuccessful. But you see that explanation was necessary.

(2) The second reason cuts much deeper and goes to the root of things. As I
mentioned before, the Englishman at the head of affairs is fair and just, and in
trying to regulate the relations between the two chief sections of the community
he is meticulously careful to hold the balance. But his only guide in this difficult
situation is the democratic principle which reckons with the relative numerical
strength; and the brutal numbers operate against us, for there are five Arabs to
one Jew. The influence of the Arab must in fairness be five times greater than
the Jewish; in fact in many cases it is far more than that, as the Arabs are in the
administration and Jewish participation is very limited, because Jews never
took much part in it under the old régime; they kept aloof. The result is that
the Jews are practically handed over to the Arabs. This system does not take
into account that there is a fundamental qualitative difference between Jew
and Arab. The Turk, being himself of inferior culture, saw in the Jew a superior
to himself and to the Arab, and so by virtue of intelligence and his achievements
the Jew held a position in the country perhaps out of proportion to his numerical strength. The present system tends on the contrary to level down the Jew
politically to the status of a native, and in many cases the English administrator
follows the convenient rule of looking on the Jews as so many natives.

The military administrator, in addition, knows that the Arab is for the
moment a war asset. I do not think the English here overrate the value of this
asset, but still they necessarily attach some importance to it. What they do not
always know is that we represent an asset which, although it cannot be estimated
in rifles and machine guns, is nevertheless of very great war value and of still
greater peace value. In short they do not realize that the somewhat shifty and
doubtful sympathies of the Arabs represent in the long run infinitely less than
the conscious and considered policy of the majority of the Jewish people. . . .

*

The present state of affairs would necessarily tend towards the creation of an
Arab Palestine if there were an Arab people in Palestine. It will not in fact
produce that result because the *fellah* is at least four centuries behind the times,
and the *effendi* (who, by the way, is the real gainer from the present system) is
dishonest, uneducated, and as unpatriotic as he is inefficient. But it is also difficult to imagine how under the above described circumstances effect can really
be given to the Government's declaration in favour of a Jewish National Home.
For on the one hand the maintenance of the *status quo* principle, as I have shown,
automatically militates against any progress in that direction; while on the
other hand the attitude of the Jewish world will depend upon the development
which takes place in this country between now and the Peace Conference.

This being so, I hope that you will not think me presumptuous if I say that a great deal depends upon the achievements of the Zionist Commission. We, I mean the members of the Commission and our Political Officer, realized the serious dilemma in which we are placed, and, after consultation with General Clayton and Colonel Deedes, we came to the conclusion that it was necessary to draw the attention of the Commander-in-Chief to the situation.

I saw General Allenby about a week ago, and had a very frank talk with him. I think I am fully justified in stating that the Commander-in-Chief was in full sympathy with the views which I expressed. He realized the difficulties of our position, and he is generously giving us his support. But the Commander-in-Chief's primary duty is to deal with the military aspect of the situation, and although a man of General Allenby's calibre is sufficiently far-sighted and broad-minded to see the political value of our activity, his assistance, valuable and important as it always will be, must necessarily remain limited within the bounds of the *status quo*.

As the General put it to me: 'You have my full sympathy. I shall give you all the assistance which it is in my power to give, within the limits of the manual of military law. But if you desire anything beyond that, you must approach Mr. Balfour, who should give the necessary instructions to my chief. The principle of policy is not laid down by military authorities'. Needless to say, the Commander-in-Chief's point of view is the only one that is possible for a man in his position to take. And that is why I am writing to you.

*

What, then, could the Commission solve during the period of military occupation, assuming the consent of the Home Government can be obtained? Here are two objectives:

(1) FOUNDATION OF THE UNIVERSITY. . . . It is a matter of very far-reaching importance. I need hardly labour this point as I had the honour to speak to you about it before leaving for Palestine. We hope to achieve something tangible in this direction before very long.

(2) THE LAND SCHEME. A separate memorandum on this scheme (A scheme for the cultivation by Jewish labour of about a million dunam of uncultivated or semi-cultivated land between Jaffa and Rafa), which is at present under consideration by the authorities here, is attached. The economic aspect of the scheme is simple enough. The important question is whether the Government is prepared to agree to the political departure which it involves.

The whole of southern Palestine is, with some exceptions, practically unoccupied land. It is true that when one commences work on these vast areas all sorts of claimants will appear, but enquiry would soon show the shadowy nature of these claims. Naturally all genuine claimants would have to be compensated, and nobody would be ousted from land which is properly cultivated. But the scheme cannot be carried out without some departure from the present system of tenure and cultivation (if such it can be called). And such a departure is, I submit, justified, because the present system, means (1) that large stretches of fertile land are lying fallow, or are producing much less than they could produce, while there is a shortage of food in the world in general, and in Palestine in particular, and (2) that every *fellah* has much more land than he can cultivate properly, and is consequently content to work it very badly, so that a premium is set on laziness and inefficiency.

. . . If we are allowed to carry this scheme through, we shall know, and the whole of Jewry will know, that the foundation of the National Home is being laid in earnest.

This scheme takes us into the heart of the Arab problem. What I said in my speech at Jerusalem (on 27 April 1918) about our intentions towards the Arabs was sincerely meant. We have no desire or need to exploit or displace them. There are acres enough for us to develop without any encroachment on the real rights of the Arab inhabitants of Palestine. And that is an essential fact. For the problem of our relations with the Palestinian Arab is an economic problem, not a political one. From the political point of view the Arab centre of gravity is not Palestine, but the Hedjaz, really the triangle formed by Mecca, Damascus and Baghdad.

*

I am just setting out on a visit to the son of the King of the Hedjaz. I propose to tell him that if he wants to build up a strong and prosperous Arab Kingdom, it is we Jews who will be able to help him and we only. We can give him the necessary assistance in money and in organizing power. We shall be his neighbours and we do not represent any danger to him, as we are not and never shall be a great Power. . . . With him, I hope to be able to establish a real political entente. But with the Arabs of Palestine—in whom, so far as I can gather, the Sharif is little interested—only proper economic relations are necessary; and these will develop in the natural order of things, because they will be essential in our interests as well as in those of the Palestinian Arabs.

It will be clear to you from what I have said that the question now at issue, as we see it, is what the British occupation of Palestine is going to mean. Is its significance going to be measured geographically or historically? In the first case, you have so many square miles of territory captured from the enemy—a brilliant military feat, but nothing more than that. In the second case, you have in the British occupation a pivot on which centuries of history will turn.

In conclusion, allow me to point out the importance for the Peace Conference of what is going to happen in Palestine between now and the end of the war. It is my intention to go to America in the near future, to report there on what we are doing and going to do, and to rally American Jewish, and I am sure also non-Jewish, opinion behind us. Then I contemplate a Congress of representative Jews in Palestine to give authoritative expression to Jewish demands. The voice of such a Congress, I venture to think, will not pass unheard at the Peace Conference. . . .

... In order to carry this programme to a successful issue, it is of the utmost importance that Major Gore co-operates with us all the time. His knowledge of the situation, his sympathetic understanding of it, renders him eminently qualified to guide the work. In fact, we consider him absolutely indispensable. I therefore respectfully submit that Major Gore should be allowed to go to America with me and to return afterwards with me to Palestine, where we hope to bring the work of our Commission to a successful end for the benefit of Great Britain and of the Jewish people.

I trust that the importance of the matters at stake will be sufficient apology for troubling you with this letter at so critical a time.

With kind regards,
I am, dear Mr. Balfour,

Yours very sincerely,

(Signed) Ch. Weizmann

APPENDIX C

Letter from Dr. Weizmann, 15 November 1924, to Professor W. E. Rappard, Secretary of the Permanent Mandates Commission, League of Nations.

Private and Personal

My dear Professor Rappard,

It is after a great deal of hesitation that I decided to write to you personally and informally on the subject of the Report which is to be issued by the Permanent Mandates Commission. The immediate reason for this letter is a note, which has just reached me from Sir Frederick Lugard, in which he asks me to send on to you direct the copy of the sentence in the Report which deals with Immigration into Palestine. I beg to enclose copy of a report which appeared in the Jewish press a few days ago, and which purports to be a draft—or an extract of a draft—of the Report of the Permanent Mandates Commission.*
It is very likely that the final draft may contain some verbal alterations, which might possibly make it slightly more agreeable reading to us, but there seems to be very little doubt that the general tone of the document will remain unaltered. The passage on immigration is marked in red on page 2 of the enclosed copy. I have also marked some other points which appear to me most unfortunate—assuming that they occur in the final draft.

A word about the general tone of the document. The unbiased reader—and most certainly the interested parties, such as our Arab and other antagonists—could not help feeling on reading this document that the Permanent Mandates Commission was extremely uneasy, that it really meant to criticize the whole policy, as this Policy appeared to the Commission to be unjust and impracticable, but as it was tied by its terms of reference it had to abstain from expressing its real opinion. The document starts by stating that it is not the business of the Permanent Mandates Commission to compare and contrast the dual policy of the Mandate, but nevertheless it proceeds to do so, and finally points to the 'inevitable clash' between Zionism and the Arab majority.

I know that there are opinions current that the Balfour Declaration was made in a hurry as a war-measure, and therefore cannot be considered a serious act of well-thought-out statesmanship. This is, of course, a travesty of the truth. The Allied and Associated Powers considered this step very carefully, and the responsibilities and implications which it involved. The Balfour Declaration

* This has been sent yesterday. Ch. W.

279

was discussed in all the Chancelleries of Europe and America. The British Cabinet took great care in issuing this Declaration, and did so only after lengthy discussions in the Cabinet itself, and after securing the consent of America, France and Italy.

It was my privilege to discuss the Balfour Declaration and the Mandate with the late President Wilson, the author and spiritual father of the Covenant. It was my duty and privilege to call his attention, in very definite terms, to a *formal contradiction* which might in the future be construed by some people between the Balfour Declaration and the Covenant. I submitted to President Wilson that, if the Balfour Declaration were given to the Jewish Minority in Palestine, it would be a meaningless Document; whereas if, on the other hand, it were addressed to the Jewish People, then, of course, it would serve as a Charter for this People to re-enter Palestine. I need hardly say that President Wilson agreed with this point of view; he approved of the text of the Mandate, and consistently supported Zionism.

But whatever may be said about the Balfour Declaration, as to its 'hurried' issue, surely this cannot be said about the Mandate, which was discussed for *years* by everybody concerned. All the points which the Permanent Mandates Commission raised were carefully considered. The League approved, and adopted, the Mandate; the policy has become *chose jugée*. What useful purpose can be served by raking up the whole discussion once more? This re-opening of the discussion can only have the effect of encouraging political strife in Palestine, of unsettling the minds of the people there, just at the moment when there is every sign that the country is entering a phase of quiet and peaceful development.

Neither the League nor the Permanent Mandates Commission has really any reason to complain that Palestine is causing a great deal of trouble. Of all the countries in the Middle East, Palestine is the only one where constructive work on a large scale is being carried on. There is less friction in Palestine than in Egypt, Trans-Jordania, Iraq, to say nothing of India, or even Italy. A vociferous group of Arab propagandists, supported by forces which have very little to do either with Arab interests or with the spirit of justice which animates the League, have flooded the offices in Geneva with 'protests' and 'memoranda' full of misstatements, painting the black devil still blacker, giving impressionist pictures of the terrible state of affairs in Palestine, where the poor innocent Arabs are being bled by the 'Jews'. There is not an atom of truth in all this. The country is quiet and prospering. Arabs of Akko, of Gaza, have come to me with reproaches for ignoring their districts, saying how sorry they are that Jews don't come there.

Nobody can point to a single case of an injustice done to an Arab peasant. These poor wretches have been bled white by the *Effendis*, the very agitators who write protests to the League. The peasants have been transformed into brutes by oppression, usury and barbarism of every kind at the hands of the

Effendis. The latter are constantly offering their land to us, while in their press they admonish the people to boycott the Jews. To speak after all this of the 'inevitable clash' with the Arab majority is, to say the least, not in accordance with the actual facts. We have no quarrel with the peasant, who is more likely to receive fair treatment at our hands than from the tender care of the *Effendi*-politician.

The Commission considers it necessary to pay attention to our extremists, who have designs for supplanting the Arabs. The Permanent Mandates Commission knows, however, that the policy of the Zionist Organization is conducted in strict accordance with the Mandate and the White Paper. The responsibile authorities of the Zionist Organization have never given the Mandatory Power, or the Administration of Palestine, any reason for complaining in this respect. We have repeatedly preached care and moderation, and have encouraged—not without a measure of success—the establishment of good relations between our Arab neighbours and ourselves. I can point to a great many of my own speeches, made all over the world, and to solemn declarations made by our Congress, and by the National Assembly of the Jews in Palestine. With the exception of Israel Zangwill, who severed his connection with the Zionist Organization years ago, and of the *Jewish Chronicle*, which is not a Zionist organ, it would be difficult to point to a single offensive remark against Arab national aspirations. We, however, have been—and are still being —abused by the Arab Press. The Arabs have, in the past, exercised violence against us, but the Commission finds nothing to say about that.

That the Zionists as a whole, and our young pioneers in particular, have high hopes of building their National Home as something great and beautiful is quite true, and could not be otherwise. Does the League wish us to suppress an age-long tradition of hope, belief and yearning? Our ancestors went to the stake for this belief and hope, which is—and will remain—the fundamental tenet of our religion, and has entered the consciousness of every Jew; it has been driven into him by the inquisitions and persecutions to which he has been subjected; indeed, by untold martyrdom throughout the ages. Can, or should, a White Paper destroy this? We have no sinister designs. We say openly and candidly that we hope, by virtue of our work, once more to regenerate Palestine, and regenerate our People for the good of the People and of Humanity. We hope, for the glory of God, to redress a wrong which is crying out to Heaven. This, and this alone, is the spirit in which we enter Palestine, work for it, live for it and die for it. In signing the White Paper, we have not signed away our hopes and aspirations, or our religious beliefs, and nobody can predict what social and political forms of life are to be established in the future in Palestine.

If the White Paper were quoted by the Commission, why was not the fundamental statement of the White Paper also quoted, namely, that the Jews are in Palestine *of right and not on sufferance*. If the League were willing to grant the fundamental principle of the White Paper, it could have saved itself all the trouble of enlarging upon a long and somewhat academic discussion, and—I venture to submit—the only task—a great and noble task—that it could usefully perform, would have been to make it clear to Jew and Arab alike that it is watching that this difficult Mandate be carried out with the least possible friction, injustice or unfairness to both sides.

We are fully alive to the fact that it is difficult. It is always difficult to try to right a wrong which has continued for centuries. But this bold attempt is being made under the auspices of the Highest Tribunal in the World, and we Jews look to this Tribunal with reverence and ardent hope that it will help us in our sacred endeavour to save an old race from untold sufferings and humiliations.

I was therefore shocked and deeply outraged when I read the passage of the Report dealing with our Immigration. We presented to the League a report on our work in Palestine, on which my colleagues and I were congratulated in Geneva. I came to Geneva, not in order to be heard officially, not in order to register complaints and grievances, but to give information and to present facts. I came direct from Palestine. I have no official standing with the League, but I am the Head of the Jewish Agency, responsible for practically all the Jewish work going on in Palestine. With the exception of yourself, and Sir Frederick, none of the Commissioners took the trouble to question me. They limited themselves to a few banal, polite remarks. Yet they found it possible, and compatible with the high sense of justice characteristic of the League, to pass judgment on our immigration, and report on it as a stream of people unprepared by tradition for manual labour. It is the worst thing which could have been said because it discloses only half the truth.

We admit that Jews as a whole consist mainly of town-dwellers and that our immigrants are naturally recruited from these masses, but what we have achieved in Palestine—and we are proud of it—is the conversion of these masses of untrained people into real workers. These people have built roads and houses, drained marshes, taken under the plough tens of thousands of acres of land: fought the dunes, sands, deserts and rocks of Palestine as successfully as the Californian, Dutch or even Swiss peasants; all this in spite of their lack of tradition, and in spite of innumerable difficulties and handicaps. It is natural enough that zeal, ardour and religious devotion to a Cause, have enabled us to master these difficulties. The result is that almost everything which has been done in Palestine in the past six years—and it is not negligible by any means— has been done by these 'untrained' men. The Report of the Permanent Mandates Commission, however, is silent on this point, and under the high authority of the League, the mere, bare statement is given out to the world, that we have inundated Palestine with unproductive elements. The Arabs will now be justified in throwing this constantly into our faces, and in clamouring for new restrictions on immigration. They will have won the victory for which their agitators, in conjunction with the enemies of the Jewish People, have been craving.

Not a word, not a syllable is said about our Report, about our achievements, about the training which we are giving to our immigrants—we simply don't exist in the Report of the Permanent Mandates Commission except as an unmitigated, troublesome nuisance.

The Report will be a great shock to the Jewish Communities all over the world. Thousands and thousands have been in Palestine, have seen what we are doing there; many of our opponents have been converted to Zionism by what they have seen in Palestine, and they will stand aghast before the one-sided picture painted by the Permanent Mandates Commission.

American Jewry, which has poured millions of dollars into Palestine, and which—in America—is the most potent factor working for the League and believing in it, will be sadly disappointed on reading a Report which ignores entirely the Jewish effort in Palestine, and which limits itself to a sweeping statement detrimental to such an effort.

Forgive me, please, for this very long letter, but I am still under the first impression of the Report. I don't cherish any hopes that the tone will be altered, but I still believe that the facts may be corrected, and on the subject of Immigration we are addressing the League officially. These lines I have written simply, *ad memoriam*, to you, as one who has taken such a benevolent interest in our endeavours. I am grateful to you for all the kindness which I have received at your hands, and this emboldened me to write this very long letter. Please forgive me.

With best regards, and great respect,
believe me,
Yours very sincerely,
CH. WEIZMANN.

P.S. I also enclose a copy of the *Nation* with an article by Graham Wallas who, as you know, is neither a Jew nor a Zionist. It happened to appear this week.

APPENDIX D

Letter from Dr. Weizmann to Mr. Tom Williams, M.P., written from Rehovoth, 26 April 1939.

My dear Williams,

I arrived here just three weeks ago after an absence of nearly a year and I should like to write you of some first impressions of the effect of the London discussions on the situation.

I have come to Palestine on many occasions during the past 20 years, in times of growth and stagnation, of trouble and of prosperity. Never before, however, have I been made so intensely aware of the transformation which has been wrought here in the character of the Jew. This is no longer a colony or a settlement. It is a people in the integral sense of the term. These three years of disturbances with their daily sacrifices of precious lives, their night watches and constant risks have produced an awareness of realities, a sense of national cohesion and a doughty determination such as I had never met here before. The iron has entered the soul of this people. I have met during these three weeks people from every stratum of this complex society and from every interview the impression left is that of a fixed resolution, whatever the sacrifice demanded, to oppose to the utmost the imposition of any policy aiming at the strangulation of the National Home. Last week the Jewish Labour Party had a memorable conference of which a full report will no doubt reach you in time. It was the consensus of opinion that no sacrifice would be too heavy, if thereby the paralysis of Jewish immigration, the closing of any part of the country to Jewish settlement, and the subjection of the National Home to Arab domination could be prevented. In a resolution which had the austere moral ring of the great historical declarations of the 16th and 17th centuries, it was affirmed that by abandoning its obligation to promote the development of the Jewish National Home, for which essentially the Mandate was entrusted to the British Government, the latter would divest itself of the moral and legal title by which it governs this country and reduce itself to a mere agency of coercion. You know well what the aftermath of such declarations has been in the past. In the present case it would be fraught with supreme tragedy.

I have conveyed all this in a telegram to the Prime Minister and warned him, in as restrained language as I could use in such circumstances, of what was here at stake. I told him that the Jews of Palestine regarded the proposed establishment of an independent Palestine State, coupled with the reduction of the Jewish people to one-third of the total and with the contemplated restriction of the area of Jewish settlement to a small sector of the country, as tantamount to the reduction of the National Home to a ghetto and the virtual handing over of Jewish Palestine to the Mufti. I made it clear to him that the Jews were determined to make the supreme sacrifice rather than submit to an Arab régime. I urged that the adoption and announcement of the contemplated policy would defeat the Government's object to pacify the country, that it would compel them to use force against the Jews, would engender further bitterness between the two sections of the population and would drive the Jews, who had nothing to lose anywhere, to counsels of despair. I appealed to him in the name of justice and of the peace of the Holy Land not to disregard the advice offered to him with the full knowledge of facts and out of a deep anxiety for the welfare of all parties concerned.

I do not know what result this last minute appeal will have. The air is full of reports that conversations with the Arab leaders are being continued in Cairo and other places and that even further concessions are about to be made to them. I can only say this, that if the Government really adopts the policy outlined to us in London and endeavours to carry it into effect in Palestine it will bite on granite. At a time when millions of Jews are undergoing a sadistic persecution such as the world has not known since the darkest ages, the Jews of Palestine will not put up with the land in which a National Home was solemnly promised to them by the civilized world being closed to their harassed brethren. You will no doubt have learned about the ghastly scenes enacted here during the last few days in connection with the capture and subsequent expulsion of shiploads of what are called illegal immigrants, and of the deep resentment that these scenes have aroused among the Jews here. Untold tragedies are being enacted along these coasts. Boats, overloaded with refugees from German concentration camps, are floating about for weeks on end in the Mediterranean, their passengers starved and afflicted with the diseases of hunger and exhaustion, among them women and children of tender age. Some of these boats were recently seized by British patrol vessels, and dragged to Haifa and then pushed out again to the open sea with their human cargo, although it was known that they were not seaworthy and that their provisions would not enable them to hold out for more than a few days. Can you visualize the feelings of the Jews of this country when they witness these harrowing scenes being enacted, knowing all the time that these people could be productively absorbed in Palestine without any harm being done to the Arabs? You would pick up and care for a wounded dog when it seeks a refuge in your garden. France has taken in 400,000 refugees from Spain although it is under no legal obligation to do so. Syria has offered an asylum to the Mufti and his associates although they have been all the time abusing it for organizing murder in Palestine. But when desperate Jews are fleeing in leaky boats to the land of their supposed National Home no dictate of humanity, no doctrine of political asylum ensures them admission. Can you understand our revolt?

Talk about illegality. I wonder whom an enlightened judge would charge with illegal behaviour—the unfortunate Jews who are fleeing from the hell which is Central Europe, to the country where a National Home was promised to them, where according to a famous declaration of the British Government, they were to be admitted 'as of right and not on sufferance'—or the Government which, despite its solemn pledges and international obligations, is imposing arbitrary restrictions on Jewish immigration and is driving the wretched victims of its policy into the open seas. We have just taken the bold step of demanding that the Government should obtain the opinion of The Hague Court on the validity of political maximum restrictions on Jewish immigration, having regard to the Mandate. We did it on the precedent of the suggestion made by Lord Hailsham and Sir John Simon in 1930 in regard to the Passfield White Paper, when they urged that a violation of the Mandate would lay Great Britain open 'to a grave charge of breach of faith and disregard to its international obligations' and pleaded that the issue be submitted to The Hague Court. It will be interesting to see whether the Government will accept our suggestion.

What makes the policy of the Government so utterly amazing is the complete ignorance which it betrays of the realities of the situation in this part of the world. Every day the Arab press of the neighbouring countries reveals the fear of war that is shaking the Arab world. Their only hope is that the Western democratic powers may protect them against the onslaught of the totalitarian régimes. Never before has the British army been so popular in Egypt as it is these days. In Syria the French meet with a sympathy from the nationalist extremists such as would have been inconceivable a year ago. I am enclosing herewith a few characteristic extracts from the Egyptian and Syrian press. And at this moment when the Arabs are so evidently dependent on British help and are so conscious of it, the British Government embarks on a policy which can only be explained, if at all, by their fear that the Arabs would turn against them in case of war. For this policy the Government is prepared to sacrifice the Jews who could be of real help to them in an international conflict and whose loyalty is beyond any shadow of doubt. As the ancient Latin has it, it is sometimes 'difficult not to write a satire'.

Here in Palestine the absurdity of the proposed 'solution' strikes you at every angle. Wherever you go you see Jewish supernumerary policemen guarding essential services, Government offices and even police stations against Arab terrorists. And then you contemplate that what His Majesty's Government proposes to do in order to re-establish law and order is to hand over these Jews to the tender mercies of those against whom they today stand on guard on behalf of the Government. It simply defies reason.

I am sorry to trouble you with all this, but I am sure you will understand my feelings. Perhaps our friends in London may find it possible to convey some of this to the Government either through a deputation or in some other way, and to prevail upon them to desist from a course which, I am convinced, can end only in disaster. But it would have to be done most speedily and with more than ordinary emphasis.

With kind regards,

Yours sincerely,

(Signed) CH. WEIZMANN

Tom Williams, Esq., M.P.,
House of Commons,
London.

APPENDIX E

1. Letter from Sir Archibald Sinclair, Secretary of State for Air.

February 13th 1942.

Dear Chaim,

I am deeply distressed to hear this news of Michael. All we know at present is that his Whitley, which took off on patrol at 5.36 p.m. the day before yesterday, failed to return. Any more news which comes in will of course be sent on to you at once.

He will be a great loss to the R.A.F. Only a week or ten days ago Joubert was telling me about some good work he had been doing with his Whitley in the Bay of Biscay. Everyone liked him; everyone respected him. He brought unusual gifts to the service of his country and did his duty with courage and zeal.

You will know how truly and deeply I feel for you in the loss of your brave son.

Yours ever,

ARCHIE SINCLAIR.

2. Letter from Air Chief Marshal Sir Philip Joubert.

Headquarters,
COASTAL COMMAND.
February 20th 1942.

Dear Dr. Weizmann,

I am writing to tell you how much we feel the loss of your gallant son.

I had not met him personally, but he was known to me by his work as being outstanding for intelligence and scientific ability. I regretted very much when, by the lapse of time, it became necessary for me to remove him from my Development Unit and return him to active operations. He had done sterling work in the Development Unit and I was looking forward to the possibility of using him once again in the rôle for which he was so eminently fitted.

Your great loss is shared by us, since we feel that if your son had been spared he might have done so much to improve our methods of operations against the enemy.

Yours very truly,

P. B. JOUBERT.

APPENDIX F

Letter from Mrs. Weizmann, 9 January 1956, to Prime Minister David Ben-Gurion.

His Excellency,
The Prime Minister.

Fully realizing and deeply sympathizing with the difficult position of your situation for which as Prime Minister you are the most responsible person on whom falls the main burden, may I venture a suggestion which may prove helpful?

In your admirable speech in the Knesset you expressed in most unmistakable terms your ardent desire to meet the Prime Minister of Egypt and frankly but friendly to settle the Armistice condition of 1949. If that could be possible, such a meeting may bring us nearer to peace and end the disastrous situation which is neither peace nor war. Your peace utterances have been always left either unheard or refused by the Arab States. I believe that at this juncture direct interview between two Prime Ministers—you and Colonel Nasser—may have a good result. Don't you think that if this suggestion is made neither in the Knesset nor at a public meeting nor in the Press but directly in writing to Colonel Nasser, offering a private meeting without intermediary, it may prove helpful? He will either not answer your generous offer or refuse it; but a miracle may happen and he may accept the offer.

I think in History that pride, however important it is in view of your position, must be put aside for the benefit which it may bring. Should he agree, you will win the point and I don't need to dwell on it. Should he, however, either not answer or refuse, you can publish your letter in the Press so as to inform the big three or four Powers and acquaint the World with your goodwill and so gain the sympathy of the general public who are not anxious to lose their sons and husbands in World War III. The same will be applicable to his refusal which can be published together with your appeal.

With best regards and wishes for 1956.

NOTES

1. Weizmann, Chaim, *Trial and Error*, Hamish Hamilton, London, 1949, pp. 78-79; *Jewish Encyclopaedia*, vol. 12, p. 276.

2. Weizmann, Chaim, op. cit., p. 95.

3. A full edition of the letters of Dr. Chaim Weizmann is being prepared under the auspices of the Yad Weizmann. The Consulting Editor is Leonard Stein.

4. Weizmann, Chaim, op. cit., p. 115.

5. Dr. Moses Gaster, head of the British Sephardic Communities, one of Herzl's earliest supporters.

6. Major Sir William Eden Evans-Gordon, Bt. (1857-1913), M.P. for Stepney, Tower Hamlets, 1901-07, 'the father of the Aliens Act, 1905'. He was a member of a Royal Commission on Immigration which reported in favour of some restriction on the admission of Russian and Polish Jews and led to the passing of the Act of 1905.

7. Weizmann, Chaim, op. cit., pp. 142-145.

8. Dugdale, Blanche E. C., *Arthur James Balfour, A Biography*, Hutchinson, London, 1936, vol. 1, pp. 324-326.

9. Weizmann, Chaim, op. cit., p. 146.

10. Weizmann, Chaim, op. cit., pp. 177 et seq.

11. Weizmann, Chaim, op. cit., pp. 182 et seq.

12. Weizmann, Chaim, op. cit., pp. 192 et seq.

13. Weizmann, Chaim, op. cit., pp. 220 et seq.

14. Weizmann, Chaim, op. cit., pp. 196-197, 206.

15 Stein, Leonard: Sixth Chaim Weizmann Memorial Lecture, 15 October 1961. Reprinted by Arieli Press, Tel Aviv, 1964, pp. 26-27.

16. Stein, Leonard, op. cit., p. 26.

17. Weizmann, Chaim, op. cit., p. 217.

18. *See* Fyvel, R. T., in *Chaim Weizmann, A Biography by Several Hands*, Weidenfeld & Nicolson, London, 1962, p. 159.

19. A year later, on 22 March 1917, Balfour (who had become Secretary of State for Foreign Affairs in Lloyd George's government) said to Weizmann that if no Franco-British agreement could be reached 'we should try to interest America, and work for an Anglo-American protectorate over Palestine'. *See* Weizmann, Chaim, op. cit., p. 241.

20. Weizmann, Chaim, op. cit., pp. 235 et seq.

21. Weizmann, Chaim, op. cit., p. 227.

22. Weizmann, Chaim, op. cit., p. 202.

23. Christopher Sykes, second son of Sir Mark Sykes, a BBC producer and a

frequent visitor to Israel, visited Rehovoth with David Tutaev to prepare a radio programme, 'A Portrait of Dr. Weizmann', subsequently broadcast in the Third Programme.

24. The February Revolution of 1917 had given Russia a democratic constitution. It was superseded by the 'October' (Bolshevik) Revolution which took place on 7 November 1917 (N.S.), five days after the Balfour Declaration.

25. *See* Weizmann, Chaim, op. cit., pp. 247 et seq.

26 The wording of the proposed declaration is discussed, Weizmann, Chaim, op. cit., pp. 260-261.

27. Quoted from Weizmann, Chaim, op. cit., p. 262.

28. Weizmann, Chaim, op. cit., p. 273.

29. Weizmann, Chaim, op. cit , pp. 290 et seq.

30. Weizmann, Chaim, op. cit., pp. 294-295.

31. Weizmann, Chaim, op. cit., p. 298.

32. Weizmann, Chaim, op. cit., pp. 191-192.

33. Weizmann, Chaim, op. cit., pp 304 et seq.

34. Weizmann, Chaim, op. cit., p. 396.

35. Weizmann, Chaim, op. cit., p. 400.

36. Weizmann, Chaim, op. cit., p. 316.

37. Weizmann, Chaim, op. cit., p. 319.

38. *Anglo-Palestine Yearbook*, 1947-1948, p. 52.

39. Weizmann, Chaim, op. cit., p. 366.

40. Weizmann, Chaim, op. cit., p. 405.

41. Weizmann, Chaim, op. cit., p. 411.

42. Dugdale, Blanche, op. cit., Vol. II pp. 409-410.

43. Meinertzhagen, Colonel R., *Middle East Diary, 1917-1956*, Cresset Press, London, 1959, p. 143.

44. On the eve of the Jewish fast commemorating the destruction of the Temple, some young men and women belonging to Jabotinsky's 'Revisionist' party marched to the Wailing Wall to hold a demonstration, 'with loud demands for the ownership of the Wall and the taking of an oath to defend it at all costs'. Hyamson, Albert M., *Palestine under the Mandate*, Methuen, London, 1950, p. 120.

45. *Anglo-Palestine Yearbook*, 1947-1948, p. 52.

46. Hyamson, Albert M., op. cit., pp. 132-133.

47. Weizmann, Chaim, op. cit., p. 471.

48. e.g. Sykes, Christopher, *Cross Roads to Israel*, Collins, 1965, pp. 190-191.

49. Weizmann, Chaim, op. cit., p. 474.

50. Meinertzhagen, R., op. cit., p. 169.

51. Sykes, Christopher, op. cit., pp. 229 et seq.

52. Weizmann, Chaim, op. cit., p. 493.

53. Weizmann, Chaim, op. cit., p. 461.

54. Weizmann, Chaim, op. cit., p. 499.

55. Weizmann, Chaim, op. cit., p. 519.

56. Weizmann, Chaim, op. cit., pp. 521-522.

57. Weizmann, Chaim, op. cit., p. 519.

58. This was confirmed in Nazi documents captured after the war. *See* also *A Biography by Several Hands*, op. cit., p. 258.

59. Weizmann, Chaim, op. cit., p. 522. *See* also Sykes, Christopher, op. cit., p. 254; 'In spite of all Mr. Churchill's skill in political manoeuvre, the opponents of his Zionist policy out-manoeuvred him almost until the end'.

60. Weizmann, Chaim, op. cit., pp. 527 et seq.

61. In a 'Radio Portrait' of Dr. Weizmann which Lord Boothby gave on the BBC Third Programme on 19 December 1963, he paid Vera Weizmann this tribute: 'I do not think I have known anybody in public life who was more dependent upon his wife than was Chaim upon that very remarkable lady. . . . But she was a terrific support and help to him in the worst moments, never daunted, never. I saw them together quite often and you could see how much he leaned upon her. It was very remarkable'.

62. Dr. Bergmann was for some time head of Israel's Atomic Energy Commission.

63. Weizmann, Chaim, op. cit., pp. 520, 527-529.

64. Sykes, Christopher, op. cit., pp. 281 et seq.

65. *Anglo-Palestine Yearbook*, 1947-1948, p. 52.

66. Sykes, Christopher, op. cit., pp. 268-270. Sykes gives a figure of 240 refugees and 'about a dozen policemen were killed by the explosion or by drowning'.

67. Crossman, Richard, *A Nation Reborn*, Hamish Hamilton, London, 1960, p. 54.

68. Crossman, Richard, op. cit., p. 69.

69. Sykes, Christopher, op. cit., p. 352.

70. There were more than a hundred casualties, British, Jews, and Arabs among them. The explosion had been engineered by the Irgun Tsva'i Leumi (national military organization) which derived from Jabotinsky's Revisionists. 'The evidence of later events strongly indicates that this horrible atrocity sincerely shocked the Jewish Agency as a whole': Sykes, Christopher, op. cit., p. 358.

71. *A Biography by Several Hands*, op. cit., pp. 286-287.

72. *Ibid.*, pp. 288-289.

73. *Anglo-Palestine Yearbook*, 1947-1948, p. 38.

74. *Ibid.*, p. 43.

75. Weizmann, Chaim, op. cit., p. 543.

76. For details of the 'Bevin Scheme', *see* Zasloff, Joseph J., *Great Britain and Palestine, A Study of the Problem before the United Nations*, Munich, 1952, pp. 43 et seq. Verlagshaus der Amerikanischen Hochkommission.

77. The Irgun, in retaliation for the death sentence passed on Gruner, kidnapped a British judge and civilian. These hostages were released pending an appeal against Gruner's sentence which was being considered in London. 'For the sake of preserving the calmer mood brought about by Mr. Creech Jones's appeasement policy, it would obviously have been better to have commuted Dov Gruner's sentence at least, but the kidnapping action of Irgun had made this impolitic as it would now appear as a surrender of law to violence. Dov Gruner and his associates became popular heroes and the episode led to another bout of mutual reprisal and atrocity': Sykes, Christopher, op. cit., p. 368.

78. Weizmann, Chaim, op. cit., p. 556.

79. Sykes, Christopher, op. cit., pp. 370-371.

80. Announcement by the Secretary of State for the Colonies, Mr. Arthur Creech Jones, on 26 September 1947, confirmed by him in the House of Commons on 11 December: see Sykes, Christopher, op. cit., pp. 385 and 339.

81. Truman, Harry S., *Years of Trial and Hope*, 1946-1953, Hodder & Stoughton, London, 1956, pp. 167-169 (Doubleday, New York.)

82. Russian support at the United Nations for partition and the Jewish State provoked the most ridiculous rumours. According to Crossman, Richard, op. cit., p. 70, Bevin, the British Secretary of State for Foreign Affairs, told him in all seriousness that 'The Russians have massed an army of Jews at Odessa, ready for the attack'!

83. The British United Nations representative, Sir Alexander Cadogan, stated that the British Government would 'agree to the Commission's arrival in Palestine [only] shortly before the Mandate is terminated, in order that there may be an overlap of, say, a fortnight during which the Commission can take up its responsibilities': United Nations Palestine Commission, 1st Monthly Report to the Security Council, 19 January 1948, quoted by Zasloff, Joseph J., op. cit., p. 95.

84. 'The most serious Jewish disadvantage remained shortage of equipment, and it was galling to the Zionists that British official policy seemed designed to correct any want of balance in favour of the Arab invaders': Sykes, Christopher, op. cit., p. 402. *See* also Zasloff, Joseph J., op. cit., p. 95.

85. *See* Sykes, Christopher, op. cit., pp. 390-391, 407.

86. *See* Zasloff, Joseph, J., op. cit., p. 103, where part of Mr. Sharett's speech is quoted.

87. 'But there is no evidence of a long-standing and agreed Jewish policy to evict the settled population; on the contrary in the first half of 1948 there is considerable evidence that the Jews tried to prevent the flight': Sykes, Christopher, op. cit., p. 419.

88. Truman, Harry S., op. cit., pp. 171-172.

89. Weizmann, Chaim, op. cit., p. 577.

90. This account is given in Daniels, Jonathan, *The Man of Independence*, Gollancz, London, 1950, p. 318.

91. Weizmann, Chaim, op. cit., p. 579.

92. At a dinner party given by the United States delegation for South American delegates: see Zasloff, Joseph J., op. cit., p. 119.

93. Weizmann, Chaim, op. cit., p. 579.

94. According to Sykes, Christopher, op. cit., p. 427, 'It was kept a close secret by Dr. Weizmann and his immediate circle and was not divulged till 1962, ten years after his death'.

95. Quoted in Weizmann, Chaim, op. cit., p. 585; Dr. Weizmann's reply, *ibid.*, p. 586.

96. For Dr. Weizmann's reply, see Weizmann, Chaim, op. cit., p. 587.

97. 'Dr. Chaim Weizmann was the first totally free Jew of the modern world, and the state of Israel was constructed, whether or not it knows it, in his image. No man has ever had a comparable monument built to him in his own lifetime': Berlin, Isaiah, *Chaim Weizmann*, Weidenfeld & Nicolson, London, 1958. (The second Herbert Samuel Lecture delivered on 19 November 1957 under the auspices of the British Friends of the Hebrew University of Jerusalem.)

98. Ezer Weizmann was appointed commander-officer of the Israeli Air Force at the age of thirty-two. He later became Chief of the General Staff Branch.

99. Later, as Golda Meir, Israeli Foreign Minister.

100. For a full account of the meeting between Mrs. Meyerson and Abdullah, see Sharef, Zeev, *Three Days*, W. H. Allen, London, 1962; also Sykes, Christopher, op. cit., pp. 428-429, on Abdullah's motives in making this proposal. Arab 'unity' has remained a fiction to this day.

101. On 15 December 1957 I wrote to the Home Office asking for copies of my husband's letters, including his letter renouncing British citizenship, which were wanted for the Weizmann Archives at Rehovoth. I received a reply from a private secretary that the Home Office had no trace of my husband's letters! (Note by V.W.)

102. For a fair assessment, see Richard Crossman's essay, 'The Prisoner of Rehovoth', in *A Biography by Several Hands*, op. cit., p. 333.

103. After the Israeli victory in the Negev, and as Israeli troops began to cross the Egyptian border, the British Secretary of State for Foreign Affairs threatened to invoke 'the Anglo-Egyptian Treaty of 1936 of which the Egyptians were then struggling to obtain the annulment': see Sykes, Christopher, op. cit., p. 437. On Truman's advice, Israeli forces did not continue their pursuit into Egyptian territory.

104. *A Biography by Several Hands*, op. cit., p. 334.

105. For a description of Dr. Weizmann's scientific work, see *A Biography by Several Hands*, op. cit., pp. 348-349.

106. Entered into 24 February 1949; it still persists in 1966.

107. The Huleh was a marsh which has been drained and converted into arable land by Israel except for a small portion kept as a bird sanctuary.

ACKNOWLEDGMENTS

The authors wish to express their indebtedness to the following sources:

Weizmann, Chaim, *Trial and Error,* Harper & Row, 1949

Dugdale, Blanche E. C., *Arthur James Balfour: A Biography,* Putnam, 1937

Stein, Leonard, *Sixth Chaim Weizmann Memorial Lecture,* reprinted by the Arieli Press, 1964

Weisgal, Meyer (Editor), *A Biography by Several Hands,* Atheneum, 1963

HMSO, *Anglo-Palestine Yearbook,* 1947–1948

Sykes, Christopher, *Cross Roads to Israel,* World, 1965

Meinertzhagen, Colonel R., *Middle East Diary, 1917–1956,* Cresset Press, 1959

Hyamson, Albert M., *Palestine under the Mandate,* British Book Centre, 1951

Crossman, Richard, *A Nation Reborn,* Atheneum, 1960

Zasloff, Joseph J., *Great Britain and Palestine: A Study of the Problem before the United Nations,* Verlagshaus der Amerikanischen Hochkommission

Truman, Harry S., *Years of Trial and Hope, 1946–1953,* Doubleday, 1956

The Yad Weizmann, for permission to quote from Dr. Chaim Weizmann's letters

The *Jerusalem Post*

INDEX

Note

'C.W.' *refers to* Chaim Weizmann; 'V.W.' *refers to* Vera Weizmann.

D